THE LIFE AND ILLUSTRIOUS MARTYRDOM OF SIR

THOMAS MORE, *Formerly Lord Chancellor of England (Part III of " Tres Thomae," printed at Douai, 1588). By* THOMAS STAPLETON, S.T.D. *Translated, for the first time, into English by* PHILIP E. HALLETT, *Rector of St John's Seminary, Wonersh, and Vice-Postulator for the Cause of Canonisation of Blessed John Fisher and Blessed Thomas More*

\

New York, Cinncinati, Chicago

BENZIGER BROTHERS

PRINTERS TO THE HOLY APOSTOLIC SEE

DECLARATION

CONFORMABLY to the Decree of Pope Urban VIII, the translator declares that in the following pages the words "saint," "miracle," are employed in a purely human sense, and all intention of anticipating the judgement of the Church is utterly disclaimed.

NIHIL OBSTAT :

THOMAS MCLAUGHLIN, D.D.,

Censor deputatus.

IMPRIMATUR :

EDM. CAN. SURMONT,

Vicarius generalis.

WESTMONASTERII
Die 23ª Maii, 1928

First printed in 1928

Made and Printed in Great Britain

CONTENTS

CONTENTS

(The titles to the Chapters are Stapleton's; the subordinate
headings are inserted by the translator.)

TRANSLATOR'S PREFACE

THOMAS STAPLETON was born at Henfield, in Sussex, in July, 1535—the same month in which Blessed Thomas More was beheaded, "as if," says Fuller in his quaint way, " divine providence had purposely dropped from heaven an acorn in place of the oak that was felled."[1]

This circumstance, Stapleton tells us, as well as the similarity of their Christian names, together with the great veneration in which he held the memory of the martyred Chancellor and the exceptional opportunities he had of gaining information about him, moved him to write the Life of Sir Thomas More. Writing first the Lives of St Thomas the Apostle, and St Thomas à Becket, Archbishop of Canterbury, the " blissful martyr " of Chaucer's Prologue, he added his Life of More, far exceeding in length the two other Lives, and called the whole *Tres Thomae*. This association of More with earlier saints, and Stapleton's witness that English boys of his generation looked on him as their hero and their model, will prepare the reader to find that Stapleton conceives himself to be writing the Life of a saint. He is, indeed, a valuable link in the chain of witnesses to the common estimation of Blessed Thomas More as a saint and a martyr. Though his historical facts are for the most part remarkably accurate, yet his primary object was not to write a history, but rather a devotional work for the edification of his readers.

Stapleton left England soon after the accession of Elizabeth, and during the forty years of his exile won a great reputation as a controversial writer. The facts of his life need not be repeated here : they are to be found in readily accessible works of reference. The *Catholic Encyclopedia* has an adequate notice, and a still fuller one is to be found

[1] Fuller's *Worthies* (Sussex), ii, 398 (Edit. 1811).

ix

in the *Dictionary of National Biography*. The *Tres Thomae* was written at Douai and first published there in 1588.

In his preface Stapleton gives us his reasons for undertaking the work and the sources of his information. Almost certainly he had Roper's MS. notes before him, and he makes abundant use of More's own works—not so much the Latin Works, which, as he avers, were in everyone's hands, but chiefly the English Works, which could not be expected to be so familiar to foreign Catholics. But his Life has great and independent value in that it enshrines the personal recollections of those of More's household who were fellow-exiles for the Faith with Stapleton in the Low Countries. Still more important was the collection of letters he received from the widow of John Harris, More's secretary. They were in a decayed condition when Stapleton used them, and doubtless have long since perished, so that all we know of their contents is what he has preserved.

Father Bridgett calls Stapleton's work " by far the best Life of More,"[1] whilst Professor R. W. Chambers writes : " Stapleton's forty years' labour has been strangely neglected by his countrymen, and this neglect extends to his Latin Life of More. This most important Life was printed in Douay, Paris, Cologne, Frankfort, Leipzig, Graz, and in more recent times has been published in French and Spanish translations : it has never been either printed in England or translated into English."[2]

The numerous biographers of More have, of course, freely drawn upon Stapleton's Life and translated many extracts from it, but yet there seems room for a complete English translation. Interest in the noble-hearted Chancellor, never extinct, seems now more active than ever. A new edition of his English Works, long overdue, has now been commenced under the editorship of Mr. W. E. Campbell ;[3] whilst the Early English Text Society is printing critical editions of the early Tudor biographies of More. The Latin Life, though it has been printed so many times,

[1] *Life of Blessed Thomas More*, p. ix.
[2] *The Saga and the Myth of Sir Thomas More* (Oxford University Press, 1927), p. 11.
[3] *The Dialogue of Sir Thomas More concerning Tyndale* (Eyre and Spottiswoode, 1927).

is scarce, and many Englishmen whose Latin has become rusty will be glad of an English version.

I have used for my work a copy of the Cologne edition of 1612, kindly placed at my disposal by the Father Rector of Heythrop College. Constant reference has, however, been made to the first edition (Douai, 1588); but with the exception of one misprint, never have any divergencies been noted. Passages which Stapleton translated from More's English Works I have naturally given in the original,[1] modernising the spelling, although occasionally this has involved the expansion of passages where Stapleton has shortened or summarised More's words. Sometimes, especially for several of the letters in Chapters X and XI, I have adopted Father Bridgett's translations, to whose *Life of Blessed Thomas More*[2] I wish once and for all to express my greatest indebtedness. Extracts from the *Utopia* I have given in Ralph Robinson's translation (1556).[3] Occasionally I have adopted well-known phrases from Roper's Life, but sometimes the Latin diverges too much to justify this. Thus Blessed Thomas More will be found speaking, sometimes in Tudor English, sometimes in the language of the twentieth century. This is in the circumstances unavoidable, and the reader will not be misled if he will remember that only in quotations from the English Works can he be sure that he is reading the *ipsissima verba* of Sir Thomas More.

Stapleton makes considerable use of the correspondence of Erasmus, which he quotes from the Basle edition of 1538. As Allen's magnificent edition is not yet complete, I have thought it best to give the references to the Leyden edition of 1703 as being less inaccessible to readers.[4] The letter (S.) denotes that Stapleton's references are given as they stand.

At the time when *Tres Thomae* was written, the art of biography was in its infancy. Harpsfield's English Life of More, written in Queen Mary's reign, is considered by

[1] Rastell's Edition of 1557, quoted as E.W.
[2] Burns Oates and Washbourne. I have used the fourth edition, 1913.
[3] Printed, together with Roper's Life, in the Scott Library.
[4] The numbers quoted are of the letters, not of the pages.

Professor Chambers to be the first formal biography in our language.[1] Stapleton even claims it as a merit that he has divided his work into chapters ! The reader, therefore, must not expect to find chronological sequence : the arrangement of the matter is under various headings which overlap very considerably in time. Occasionally Stapleton places dates in the margin, but I have omitted these, and for the greater convenience of the reader have reprinted, with the kind permission of the Clarendon Press, a very valuable chronological table of More's life.

Few characters in English history have drawn to themselves such admiration and even love as Sir Thomas More. Men of all classes, non-Catholics as well as Catholics, respect and venerate him as one of the noblest, if not the noblest, Englishmen who ever lived. True it is that in the minds of some of our fellow-countrymen his fair fame has been tarnished by accusations of harshness and even cruelty towards the heretics, but the labours of Father Bridgett have not been in vain,[2] and only last year Professor Chambers, in his British Academy Lectures, dealt what it is to be hoped will prove the death-blow to these oft-repeated slanders.[3]

The news that steps are being taken to promote the speedy canonisation of Blessed Thomas More, together with his lifelong friend and fellow-martyr Blessed John Fisher, has been the occasion of a renewed outburst of devotion to these noble servants of God, and has aroused sympathetic interest even outside Catholic circles. If this book should further that cause in any degree the labours of the translator will have been abundantly rewarded. Any profits that may arise from the sale of the book will be devoted to the expenses of the process of canonisation.

[1] *op. cit.*, p. 9.   [2] *op. cit.*, Chapter XIV.   [3] *op. cit.*, p. 14.

STAPLETON'S PREFACE

FOR a long time many men of the highest renown for learning and virtue have greatly desired to have a description of the life, the character, and the most noble martyrdom for the orthodox Catholic, Apostolic and Roman Faith, of Thomas More, whose reputation for piety, learning, and wit is so widely known. Several have actually attempted to write such a book, but have been prevented from doing so either by death or by the pressure of other business. For the glory of God and for the edification of the reader, and, I will add, for the singular pleasure it gives me, I now begin my task, relying on the divine assistance and with a special trust in the prayers and intercession of More himself. It is not that I imagine that any words of mine can add to his praise. His glory in heaven is far beyond the powers of human language or human imagination : his fame upon earth is such that, far from praising his virtues as they deserve, I shall have the greatest difficulty in doing them bare justice.

Various motives have led me to write : first, the glory of God and my love for the Catholic Church, for his loyalty to which More laid down his life ; next, pity for my country in its present deep affliction and distress (More, in his lifetime, was its chief glory and proudest boast) ; then also the consolation my work will give to right-minded men and the just confusion it will cause to the wicked. For when the greatness of Thomas More is displayed before them, his high excellence in all virtue and knowledge, then those of our nation who are good and pious will rejoice, and they will imitate one of whom they are so proud : the wicked, however, the heretics and the apostates, will blush for shame and be covered with disgrace for ever on account of his unjust death. I have been moved, too, by the strong desire expressed by many learned and

virtuous men, with whom I have been on terms of familiar
intercourse during my long exile, to have a thoroughly
authentic account of Thomas More's life, and the true
cause, the manner, and the circumstances of his martyrdom.
It was for this same reason that, more than twenty years
ago, Louis Paceus, a learned and eloquent Spanish
Dominican, devoted much toil to preparing for publication
a Life of Thomas More, but death hindered the completion
of his work. I will not deny, moreover, that I have long
had a special attraction to my task. Similarity of name
has made him dearer to me, and therefore after writing a
Life of St Thomas the Apostle, and of St Thomas, Archbishop of Canterbury and Martyr, it is fitting that I should
add an account of Thomas More. Moreover, I first saw
the light of this world in the same month and year in which
More, through the gate of martyrdom, entered into eternal
light.

Finally, I write of the life of Thomas More with all
the greater pleasure and confidence because I have had
access to abundant authentic information. Many particulars I have committed to memory, but, lest they should
die with me (and old age warns me that death may not be
far distant), I have wished now to commit them to writing
for the benefit of posterity. Others, perhaps, may know
many details of the life of this holy and great man of which
I am ignorant. But meanwhile I have thought it better
to publish now the information I have gathered, and not
to wait, perhaps in vain, for the appearance of such fuller
information, for in that case both what I have collected
and what—possibly—they may know will be finally lost.
But now, when this work of mine sees the light, if they
have information of which I was not in possession, they
will have the choice either of adding to my work or of
writing an entirely new Life of Thomas More, fuller and
better than mine. For my account of his life I have
drawn from his Latin and his English writings (the latter
far exceed the former in number and length), and from the
personal reminiscences of those who for many years lived
either in the same house with him or otherwise on terms of
intimacy, and afterwards, on account of the ravages of
that soul-destroying schism, were fellow-exiles with me for

the Faith, either here in Belgium or in other parts of the world. From these I have learned in great abundance of the wise sayings and virtuous actions of Thomas More.

For example, there was John Clements, a doctor of medicine, of whom when he was yet a child More in his *Utopia* uses these words : " For John Clements my boy, who as you know was there present with us, whom I suffer to be away from no talk, wherein may be any profit or goodness (for out of this young bladed and new shot-up corn, which hath already begun to spring up both in Latin and Greek learning, I look for plentiful increase at length of goodly ripe grain)—he, I say, hath brought me into a great doubt."[1]

Also there was Dr. Clements' wife Margaret, whom More brought up with his own daughters and treated as his own child, as appears from the last letter he wrote before receiving the crown of martyrdom, in which he bade farewell to her in these words : " I send now my good daughter Clements her algorism stone, and I send her and my godson and all hers God's blessing and mine."[2]

In addition there was John Harris with his wife Dorothy Colley—she is still living in Douai—of whom the one was Thomas More's private secretary, the other the maid of Margaret Roper, More's eldest daughter. Also John Heywood, for many years a close friend of More's; and lastly William Rastell, More's nephew by his sister Elizabeth, a man of irreproachable life and one of the supreme Judges of England in the reign of Her Royal Highness Queen Mary, a man who at the close of More's life was on most intimate terms with him, as his (More's) letter to Thomas Cromwell shows.[3]

In the familiar intercourse which existed between us some years ago, owing to our common exile, from time to time I gathered from all of them many particulars of the sayings and deeds of Thomas More, which I now reproduce exactly as they are in my memory. The John Harris whom I have mentioned was a man of great industry, well versed in literature and a first-rate Patristic scholar. In this respect he was of the greatest assistance

---

[1] Introductory letter to the *Utopia*.   [2] E.W., p. 1457.
[3] E.W., p. 1422.

to Jacobus Pamelius in elucidating many passages of Cyprian and Tertullian. Nothing has helped me more than Harris's manuscript collections, including many of More's letters written in the martyr's own hand, all of which Mr. Harris's widow has handed over to me. In fine, I have searched diligently all contemporary writers who may have written something about Thomas More, Erasmus in particular and his voluminous correspondence, and other letters of More printed separately by Episcopius at Basle in 1563, Reginald Pole in his controversy with Henry VIII, John Cochlaeus writing against Sampson, Paul Jovius' *Illustrious Men*, William Paradinus in his memoirs on English affairs, the letters finally of scholars like William Budé, Beatus Rhenanus, Jerome Busleyden, Peter Giles, Simon Grinaeus and others. In the last place I mention what has been written upon the subject by Polydore Vergil, by Roverus Pontanus in his Index of memorable events, by John Fontanus in his French history of our times, by Onuphrius in his Paul III, and by Lawrence Surius in his commentaries.

Fully equipped, then, with help from all these sources, I trust that I may be able to write of the life and illustrious martyrdom of Thomas More, not merely a brief compendium but a complete and even a worthy history. I have thought it best, both to help the reader's memory and to ensure order and method in the development of the narrative, to divide up my matter into chapters.

LIFE OF SIR THOMAS MORE

CHAPTER I

HIS BIRTH, EDUCATION, AND STUDIES

HIS father was Sir John More, Knight, of whom in the epitaph which he wrote for himself after his resignation of his office of Lord Chancellor, and after Sir John's death, he speaks in the following terms : " John More, Knight and a Judge of the King's Bench, of unimpeachable character, gentle, kind and merciful, of robust health in spite of his great age, after he had lived to see his son Lord Chancellor of England thought he had lived in the world long enough, and joyfully left it to go to heaven." The name of More's mother is unknown, for she died while he was yet a child.[1] He had no brothers, but two sisters, one of whom, Jane, was married to Richard Stafferton, and the other, Elizabeth, to John Rastell, both men of good family.

PRODIGIES.

His mother, on the first night of her marriage (John Clements used to hear Thomas More recount the story on his father's authority), had a dream in which she saw depicted upon her wedding ring the faces of all the children she was destined to bear. The features of one were hardly discernible (one of her children afterwards was not born alive); another, however, shone with a splendour far beyond the rest.

[1] Family records, discovered in 1868, show that Sir John More married Agnes Graunger, and by her had three sons and three daughters. The second child, Thomas, the future Chancellor, was born on February 7, 1478. Stapleton makes him five or six years younger than he really was. (See Bridgett's *Life of Blessed Thomas More*, p. 2.)

Another prodigy is recorded of him. Once when his nurse was crossing a river by a ford, she was nearly carried away by the current, and, in her confusion, to save the child, threw him over a hedge which was along the river's bank. Afterwards when she came to look for him she was astonished to find him safe and sound, quite unhurt and smiling at her. Such portents indicated that this child would one day become great and famous.

A similar story is told of St Morontus, noble both by rank and by virtue. As to rank, he was the grandson of Erconwald, who was Major-domo in France in the reign of Sigebert.[1] A proof of his goodness is that he founded and endowed at his own expense, now nearly a thousand years ago, the well-known college of priests which still exists in Douai. Once St Riquier, who was his godfather, went to visit St Richtrude, the mother of St Morontus and the founder of the monastery of Marchiennes. As he was seated on his horse and bidding farewell, the mother bade him take her child into his arms to bless it. As he was doing so, the horse suddenly took fright and bolted, throwing the child to the ground. The little one, however, was in no way hurt by his fall, and was smiling sweetly as his mother rushed to pick him up.[2] It was fitting that a similar portent should fall to the lot of More and Morontus : both were of high rank, both officers of the Court : one was Chancellor to Henry VIII, the other held the Great Seal under Theodoric : both were saints.

EDUCATION.

As soon as More was old enough, he was sent to learn Latin in a school in London under the patronage of the King, where the well-known Nicholas Holt was the master. When he had greedily devoured the first elements of grammar, as he was clearly a boy of the very highest promise he was sent to the famous University of Oxford, for the study of philosophy and Greek.[3] It was not long

[1] Bede's *Ecclesiastical History*, Bk. III, ch. 19.
[2] In the archives of the Collegiate Church of St Amatus, Douai (S.).
[3] His reception into the household of Cardinal Morton, of which Stapleton speaks later in this chapter, must be placed between his schooling under Nicholas Holt and his entry into the University.

since Grocyn had come from Italy and introduced into England the study of Greek, lecturing publicly upon the subject in Oxford. It was from his colleague Thomas Linacre that More learnt Greek at Oxford. He says in his letter to Dorpius that he studied the Greek works of Aristotle with Linacre as the lecturer and interpreter.

His father, whilst he wished his son to be thoroughly well educated, wished him from the very first to learn frugality and abstemiousness, so that nothing should interfere with his love of study and literature. For this reason it was that, although supplied with what was necessary, More was not allowed to have even a farthing at his own disposal. This rule was so strict that he had no money even to get his boots mended unless he asked his father for it. More in later life used often to speak of his father's mode of acting, and to give it very high praise. "Thus it came to pass," he would say, "that I indulged in no vice or vain pleasure, that I did not spend my time in dangerous or idle pastimes, that I did not even know the meaning of extravagance and luxury, that I did not learn to put money to evil uses, that, in fine, I had no love, or even thought, of anything beyond my studies."

MORE'S REVERENCE FOR HIS FATHER.

He was, in truth, throughout his whole life most reverent to his father : never did he in any way give offence to him nor take offence at any word or deed of his. Even when he was Lord Chancellor of the realm he did not hesitate to go down upon his knees before his father in the public law-courts in the Palace of Westminster to beg his blessing, as is the excellent custom in our country. For amongst us every day, morning and evening, children kneel down before each of their parents to beg their blessing. If only this custom were to be observed amongst other nations, parents would have more docile sons, the State more law-abiding subjects, the Church more obedient children. For a vase which is once impregnated with perfume when it is new, will retain the scent long. And although, even among us, when children have reached man's estate and are married or hold high position in Church or State, especially when they belong to the nobility, they no longer give this token of respect to their parents, or at any rate very rarely, yet Thomas More, because of the lowly love and reverence that had been his from his earliest years, even when he held the Great Seal of England and was the first in the realm after the King, did not disdain to give his aged father this mark of honour. He kept his father in his old age in his own house, and, high in rank as he was, carried out, at his father's death, the last duties of filial piety. Such, in a word, was More's love and obedience towards his father, such, in return, the father's pride in and love for his son, that it is difficult to say whether the son was more worthy of such a father or the father of such a son. Great, certainly, was the happiness of the father in having so dutiful a son.

ENTERS CARDINAL MORTON'S HOUSEHOLD.

It happened very fortunately for the early education of Thomas More that Cardinal Morton, Archbishop of Canterbury, Primate of England not only in rank but also in virtue and learning, was struck by the talents of the boy and the quick progress he had made, and took him into his household. After keeping him there some time he sent him to Oxford, continuing there to support him. The character and greatness of Morton is described by More, who was ever grateful to his Maecenas, in the following passage from the *Utopia*. Raphael is the speaker:

" In the mean season I was much bound and beholding to the right reverend father, John Morton, Archbishop and Cardinal of Canterbury, and at that time also Lord Chancellor of England : a man, Master Peter (for Master More knoweth already that I will say), not more honourable for his authority, than for his prudence and virtue. He was of a mean stature, and though stricken in age, yet bare he his body upright. In his face did shine such an amiable reverence, as was pleasant to behold, gentle in communication, yet earnest, and sage. He had great delight many times with rough speech to his suitors, to prove, but without harm, what prompt wit and what bold spirit were in every man. In the which, as in a virtue much agreeing with his nature, so that therewith were not joined impudence, he took great delectation. And the same person, as apt and meet to have an administration in the weal public, he did lovingly embrace. In his speech he was fine, eloquent, and pithy. In the law he had profound knowledge, in wit he was incomparable, and in memory wonderful excellent. These qualities, which in him were by nature singular, he by learning and use had made perfect. The King put much trust in his counsel, the weal public also in a manner leaned unto him when I was there. For even in the chief of his youth he was taken from school into the Court and there passed all his time in much trouble and business, being continually tumbled and tossed in the waves of divers misfortunes and adversities. And so by many and great dangers he learned the experience of the world."[1]

I have copied this passage from the *Utopia* so that the reader may appreciate the greatness of the man by whom the youthful More was formed in piety and wisdom. He amused himself while still a boy by making epigrams in English which afford evidence of his piety as well as his wit. They are printed at the beginning of the large volume of his English Works. He also wrote some elegant English verses on a hanging of painted cloth in his father's house describing the vanity of human life. To them he added the following in Latin :

> Whatever man these pictures fair delight,
> Who finds in them an art that cheats his sight,
> And shows false forms as real and true as life ;
> As he has fed his eyes on symbols vain
> So let him turn to truth, his soul to gain,
> Then shall he see how frail is earthly fame
> That comes and goes but never may remain.

He scoffed at Fortune in many other verses written at the same early period of his life. Certainly, if we are to believe Erasmus, More was only a boy when he wrote the *Progymnasmata*, or verses translated into Latin from the Greek by Thomas More and William Lilly, which are prefixed to his other epigrams. For in a letter to More

[1] p. 85 (Scott Library Edition).

written in 1520 Erasmus says that most of his epigrams were composed twenty years ago, at which time More had only reached his seventeenth year.[1] From such early trifles it was easy to conjecture how extraordinary would be the intellectual power, the diligence, and the piety of the man in maturity.

[1] In 1500 More was in reality twenty-two.

CHAPTER II

HIS YOUTH

MORE'S EPIGRAMS.

THOMAS MORE, as he grew up from boyhood to man's estate, with his increase in age gave ever more striking proofs of his learning and his piety. Letters he ever loved ardently, and to his progress in them bear witness various epigrams he composed at this time, some of them translations from the Greek into Latin, others original. Their elegance and aptness is remarkable, and never do they become scurrilous or vulgar. But perhaps it will be more satisfactory to the reader to know what have been the judgements upon them of others besides myself. This is what Beatus Rhenanus writes of More's epigrams in his letter to Bilibald Pirckheimerus:[1] "Thomas More is in every way admirable. His compositions are most elegant, his translations most happy. How sweetly and easily flow his verses. Nothing is forced, harsh, awkward or obscure. He writes the purest and most limpid Latin. Moreover everything is welded together with so happy a wit that I never read anything with greater pleasure. The Muses must have showered upon this man all their gifts of humour, elegance and wit. Never, however, are his sallies mordant, but easy, pleasant, good-humoured and anything but bitter. He jokes, but never with malice : he laughs, but always without offence." This is the testimony of Rhenanus. Similar was the judgement of the learned poet, Léger Duchesne,[2] Regius Professor of Literature in Paris. For, in a collection of epigrams which he selected with great critical acumen from various writers, he inserted a larger number of More's compositions than of any other writer,

---

[1] In a letter prefixed to More's Epigrams (in volume of Latin Works, Louvain, 1566).
[2] *i.e.*, Leodegarius à Quercu.

in spite of the fact that very few of More's have survived in comparison with the very large numbers that have been published by others.

It was out of envy for the brilliance of More's wit that Germanus Brixius wrote his *Antimorus*. The elegant style of this work, however, won the admiration of Erasmus, who by letter pleaded very earnestly for his friend Brixius, begging More not to crush him with the answer he deserved. The following are the terms in which he writes of Brixius and his foolish *Antimorus* : " Since Brixius published his *Antimorus* the comments of many scholars have come to my ears. They pain me, but far greater would be my pain were such things said about you. So although I know how hard it must be for you, when you are so bitterly attacked, to soften down your answer and forbid an outlet to your wounded feelings, yet I really do think that your best course would be to treat the whole thing with the silent contempt which it deserves. You know, my dearest friend, that I would not give you such advice if there were anything in *Antimorus* that cast any stain on your reputation that it would be worth your while to trouble to remove."[1]   But before receiving Erasmus' letter, More had already drawn up a reply to the *Antimorus* on the advice of some of his most valued friends. It had been published and a few copies had gone forth, but at the appeal of Erasmus, More consented to suppress the book.

TRANSLATIONS FROM LUCIAN.

At an early age More had translated passages of Lucian into Latin : these translations he calls the first-fruits of his studies in Greek literature.[2]   Later on he translated Lucian's apology for the tyrannicide, and then, as an exercise of wit, composed a reply to it which in skill and eloquence was in no way inferior to Lucian's work.

LECTURES ON " DE CIVITATE DEI."

At the same period of his life he lectured publicly in London, in the Church of St Lawrence, on St Augustine's

---

[1] Erasmus, 503.
[2] In the letter of dedication to Thomas Ruthall (in volume of Latin Works).

De Civitate Dei. He did not treat this great work from the theological point of view, but from the standpoint of history and philosophy ; and indeed the earlier books of St Augustine's work deal with these two subjects almost exclusively. More's lectures were so well attended and highly esteemed that even Grocyn, whose supremacy in letters had hitherto been undisputed, found his audience leaving him for More. So did More, while still a youth, gain the highest distinction in poetry, oratory, philosophy, and history. John Colet, a man of keen discernment, under whose guidance More as a young man placed himself, used often to say in conversation that England had but one genius, meaning More, though at the time the island was rich in men of first-rate talents. This saying of Colet is mentioned by Erasmus in his letter to von Hutten.[1]

HIS STRUGGLES AFTER PERFECTION.

But now we must speak of the piety that distinguished him from his youth. Learning, however various and profound, without piety is as a golden ring in the snout of a sow. Nothing is more absurd than to fix precious jewels in a base setting. Learning is badly lodged in a corrupted breast. Did not even a pagan like Plato say that knowledge without virtue ought to be called cunning rather than true wisdom ? But Thomas More adorned his youth as much with solid virtue and remarkable piety as with his brilliant studies ; or, rather, he was far more zealous to become a saint than a scholar. For, even as a youth, he wore a hair-shirt, and slept on the ground or on bare boards with perhaps a log of wood as his pillow. At the most he took four or five hours' sleep, and he was frequent in watchings and fastings. Although he was practising such austerities, yet he hid them so carefully that no sign of them could be perceived.

He debated with himself and his friend Lilly the question of becoming a priest. For the religious state he had an ardent desire, and thought for a time of becoming a Franciscan. But as he feared, even with the help of his practices of penance, that he would not be able to conquer the

---

[1] Erasmus, 447.

temptations of the flesh that come to a man in the vigour
and ardour of his youth, he made up his mind to marry.
Of this he would often speak in after life with great sorrow
and regret, for he used to say that it was much easier to be
chaste in the single than in the married state. In this, indeed,
he was supported by the words of the Apostle : " Nevertheless, such shall have tribulation of the flesh."[1]   Perhaps
it was that the circumstances of the time were not pro-
pitious to his desire of embracing a stricter life, for our
religious communities had become lax, as the utter destruction and desolation of the monastic state, which followed
so soon afterwards, showed with sufficient clearness.   Or
perhaps it was that God, for his own greater glory, wished
him to remain a layman, to accept the honours and to meet
the difficulties of public life, and at the same time wished
to keep his servant unspotted and unharmed, and even to
lead him to the highest perfection of sanctity.   Certainly
when he came to the conclusion that it was not for him to
aspire to the more perfect state of life, he at least earnestly
resolved never to cease, throughout the whole course of his
life, to worship God with most sincere devotion.

LIFE OF PICO.

He determined, therefore, to put before his eyes the
example of some prominent layman, on which he might
model his life.   He called to mind all who at that period,
either at home or abroad, enjoyed the reputation of learning
and piety, and finally fixed upon John Pico, Earl of Mirandula, who was renowned in the highest degree throughout
the whole of Europe for his encyclopedic knowledge, and
no less esteemed for his sanctity of life.   More translated
into English a Latin Life of Pico, as well as his letters, and
a set of twelve counsels for leading a good life, which he had
composed.[2]   His purpose was not so much to bring these
to the knowledge of others, though that, too, he had in
view, as thoroughly to familiarise himself with them.

About the same time, and in order to deepen his own
spiritual life, he wrote a treatise on *The Four Last Things*
which is full of the deepest piety and learning, but un-

[1] 1 Cor. vii 28.   [2] See More's English Works.

fortunately unfinished. With the same end in view he used diligently to attend sermons, not indeed all and sundry, for he avoided those whose only merits were pleasing oratory or subtle disquisition, but those that were truly pious and spiritual, and most moving to the heart.

ESTEEM FOR DEAN COLET.

The best-known preacher at this time of the type that More admired was John Colet, Dean of St Paul's, London, a man whose piety was equal to his learning, whose life Erasmus has described in detail in one of his letters.[1] More's desire to listen to him was so eager and insatiable, that once when for some cause Colet's absence from the city was protracted, More, in his longing to hear the Word of God, could not restrain himself from writing to beg him to return. I add a copy of the letter because up to now it has not been printed, and it is an eloquent testimony to More's piety as a young man.

" Thomas More to his dear John Colet, greeting. As I was walking in the law-courts the other day, occupied with business of various kinds, I met your servant. I was delighted to see him, both because I have always been fond of him, and especially because I thought he would not be here without you. But when I heard from him not only that you had not returned, but that you would not return for a long time yet, my joyful expectation was changed to unutterable grief. No annoyance that I could suffer is to be compared with the loss of your companionship which is so dear to me. It has been my custom to rely upon your prudent advice, to find my recreation in your pleasant company, to be stirred up by your powerful sermons, to be edified by your life and example, to be guided, in fine, by even the slightest indications of your opinions. When I had the advantage of all these helps I used to feel strengthened, now that I am deprived of them I seem to languish and grow feeble. By following your footsteps I had escaped from almost the very gates of hell, and now, driven by some secret but irresistible force, I am falling back again into the

[1] Erasmus, 435.

gruesome darkness. I am like Eurydice, except that she was lost because Orpheus looked back at her, but I am sinking because you do not cast a glance of pity towards me.

" For city life helps no one to be good, but rather, when a man is straining every nerve to climb the narrow path of virtue, it tempts him with every kind of allurement and drags him down to its own level with its manifold deceits. Wherever you turn, what do you see around you ? Pretended friends, and the honied poison of smooth flatterers, fierce hatreds, quarrels, rivalries and contentions. Look again and you will see butchers, confectioners, fishmongers, carriers, cooks, and poultrymen, all occupied in serving sensuality, the world and the world's lord, the devil. Houses block out from us a large measure of the light, and our view is bounded not by the round horizon, but by the lofty roofs. I really cannot blame you if you are not yet tired of the country where you live among simple people, unversed in the deceits of the towns. Wherever you cast your eyes, the smiling face of the earth greets you, the sweet fresh air invigorates you, the sight of the heavens charms you. You see nothing but the generous gifts of nature and the traces of our primeval innocence. But yet I do not wish you to be so enamoured of these delights as to be unwilling to return to us as soon as possible. But if you are repelled by the unpleasantness of town life, then let me suggest that you should come to your country parish of Stepney. It needs your fatherly care, and you will enjoy there all the advantages of your present abode, and be able to come from time to time for a day or two into the city where so much meritorious work awaits you. For in the country, where men are for the most part innocent, or certainly not enchained in gross vice, the services of any physician, however moderate his attainments, can be usefully employed. But in the city, because of the great numbers that congregate there, and because of their long-standing habits of vice, no physician can do much good unless he be of the highest skill. Certainly there come from time to time into the pulpit at St Paul's preachers who hold out specious promises of help. But although they speak very eloquently, their life is in such sharp contrast to their words that they

do harm rather than good. For they cannot bring men
to believe that though they are themselves obviously in
direst need of the physician's help, they are yet fit to be
entrusted with the cure of other men's ailments. And thus
when men see that their diseases are being prescribed for by
physicians who are themselves covered with ulcers, they
immediately become indignant and refuse to accept their
remedies. But if, as observers of human nature assert,
he is the best physician in whom the patient has the greatest
confidence, it is beyond all doubt that you are the one who
can do most for the salvation of all in the city. Their
readiness to allow you to treat their wounds, their trust,
their obedience, has been proved to you by past experience,
and is, in any case, clear now by the incredibly strong
desire and keen expectation with which all are looking
forward to your coming. Come then, my dear friend,
for Stepney's sake which mourns your long absence as
deeply as a child his mother's, for your country's sake which
should be no less dear to you than are your parents, and
finally, though I cannot hope that this will be a powerful
motive for your return, for my sake who am entirely devoted
to you and anxiously awaiting your coming.

" Meanwhile, I pass my time with Grocyn, Linacre and
our dear friend Lilly. The first as you know is the guide
of my conduct, while you are absent, the second my master
in letters, the third my confidant and most intimate friend.
Farewell, and continue your love towards us.

" LONDON.
" *October* 23."

From this letter we can judge of the blessedness of More's
youth, for " blessed are they that hunger and thirst after
justice."[1] It was his hunger and thirst for justice, piety,
and holiness of life, that made More write the letter we
have quoted. For this reason did he long for the presence
of Colet, a man of such blameless life and so moving a
preacher. For this reason he desired so earnestly to hear
his holy discourses. It was for this reason that he described in such detail the dangers of city life. It was

[1] Matt. v 6.

for this reason, too, that during his absence he chose as his companions none but the learned and the pious.

"Colet," writes Erasmus, "used to preach in St Paul's daily—this practice was entirely new—besides sermons on special occasions which were delivered in the royal palaces or elsewhere. When he preached in St Paul's, he used not to choose his subject at random from the Gospel or the Epistles, but preached courses of sermons on subjects such as the Lord's Prayer or the Creed, dealing with his matter in an orderly and complete way. He attracted large audiences, which included most of the chief men in the city and the Court. He built a magnificent new school in St Paul's Churchyard, dedicated to the Holy Child, and placed it under the direction of two masters to whom he assigned adequate salaries so that they should charge no fees."[1] Of this school More in a letter to Colet writes as follows : "I am not surprised that your excellent school is arousing envy. For as the Greeks came forth from the Trojan horse and destroyed barbarous Troy, so scholars are seen to come forth from your school to show up and overthrow the ignorance of others." This was the kind of man More chose as a guide to his youth.

OTHER EARLY FRIENDS.

Of Grocyn, whom, in the absence of Colet, More used to consult, Erasmus writes : "Besides theology, he studied every other branch of learning with an exactness almost amounting to pedantry."[2] Thomas Linacre, whom More calls his master in letters, was so thoroughly well versed in Latin and Greek that even Erasmus called him his teacher[3] and Budé confessed that he had derived much help from his translation of Galen. William Lilly, the companion of More's youth, composed a Grammar so well arranged and reliable that all English boys have used it from that time until now.

Another friend of More in his earlier years was Cuthbert Tunstall. He was a man of profound learning, was often employed by the King in diplomatic work, and became Bishop, first of London, then of Durham. As the first-

---

[1] Erasmus, 435.   [2] ibid., 671.   [3] ibid., 105.

fruits of his studies, he had printed in Paris in 1529 four books on the Calculus, which he dedicated to More as his old fellow-student and most intimate friend. These are his words in the Preface : " When I looked round to see to whom, from among all my friends, I might dedicate this composition, you seemed to me the most fitting of all both on account of our intimacy and on account of your frankness ; for I know that you will be pleased at whatever good it may contain, warn me of whatever is imperfect, and forgive whatever is amiss." Tunstall was Bishop-elect of London when he wrote this Preface, as it informs us, whilst More was then Under-Treasurer to the King.

Early Studies.

Such men as these had More in his youth as masters and fellow-students, and from them, with all docility and eagerness, he learnt conscientiousness, uprightness of life, and many branches of literature. Amongst the philosophers he read especially Plato and his followers, delighting in their study because he considered their teaching most useful in the government of the State and the preservation of civic order. Accordingly in his own works he imitated Plato's manner of writing, for example in his *Utopia*, in his four books of *Dialogues* which he wrote in English on controverted points of religious doctrine, and in his *Comfort in Tribulation*, a very beautiful work in the vernacular in the form of a dialogue. Besides Latin and Greek, he learnt French as being useful for diplomatic work, partly by his private study, partly through meeting and talking with those who spoke that language. For although he had travelled in France to see the country, as is customary with young Englishmen of rank, yet he had not stayed there long. He was skilled in music, arithmetic, and geometry, and used, for the sake of recreation, to play on the viol. He studied with avidity all the historical works he could find. His mind was clear, ready, and keen ; but he had, too, an extraordinarily good memory, which he used to assist by various devices. Of his memory he thus writes, with his customary humility : " Would God I were somewhat in wit and learning, as I am not all of the worst and dullest memory.''[1] But we will have a further opportunity to speak of his intellectual gifts.

ADOPTS PROFESSION OF THE LAW.

As a young man he took up the study of law, partly to please his father who so keenly desired it that he deprived his son of all assistance in the study of Greek and philosophy, partly because, having resolved to marry, the legal career was the one in which he could best serve his country—and that this was his single aim, the rest of his life will show. He applied himself, therefore, to the study of municipal law—*i.e.*, to English law, which almost alone is in vogue in England, and made such progress in the study that he twice lectured on the subject during the vacation that begins on the feast of St John the Baptist and lasts until Michaelmas. This post of lecturer is in the highest honour amongst us and is given normally only to lawyers of great experience and only to the very cleverest amongst these. Those who are less capable, instead of lecturing, have to pay a large sum of money as a tax. His proficiency in the law led him, as the course of our narrative will show, to the very highest honours in the State.

Such then was the youth of More, such his studies, his mode of life, his piety.

[1] In the letter to Peter Giles prefixed to the *Utopia*.

CHAPTER III

HIS PUBLIC CAREER

MORE'S gifts of intellect, his literary attainments, his rank and family made it impossible that his light should remain hidden. As soon, therefore, as he reached manhood he began his career of public usefulness. Like others proficient in municipal law, he was called to the Bar and began to practise.

A CONSCIENTIOUS LAWYER.

To his clients he never failed to give advice that was wise and straightforward, always looking to their interests rather than to his own. In most cases he used his best endeavours to get the litigants to come to terms. If he was unsuccessful in this he would then show them how to carry on the action at least expense. He was so honourable and painstaking that he never accepted any case until he had first examined the whole matter thoroughly and satisfied himself of its justice. It was all the same whether those who came to him were his friends or strangers, as we shall later on show by examples : his first warning was ever that they should not in a single detail turn aside from the truth. Then he would say : "If your case is as you have stated it, it seems to me that you will win." But if they had not justice on their side, he would tell them so plainly, and beg them to give up the case, saying that it was not right either for him or for them to go on with it. But if they refused to hear him, he would refer them to other lawyers, himself giving them no further assistance.

UNDER-SHERIFF OF LONDON.

After such a blameless beginning, when he was about twenty-eight years of age, he was elected by the people of London to be Under-Sheriff for the Metropolis.[1]   In that city, you must know, there are three yearly magistrates, a Mayor and two Sheriffs.   But as these men are generally, indeed nearly always, without technical legal knowledge, a permanent magistrate is appointed to administer justice for these Sheriffs and to act as judge for the city.   A post of such authority and honour demands a man who is incorruptible, trustworthy, and wise.   For he has to give judgement in all civil causes and to maintain intact the privileges of the city.   In one of his letters to Erasmus, More lets us see how highly he valued this appointment, not as a means to his own advancement, but because of the opportunities it gave him to show, in a practical way, his love for his fellow-citizens.   He writes : " When I returned from the embassy to Flanders, the King appointed me a pension and one, indeed, not to be despised in point of honour and value.   But so far I have refused to accept it and I think I shall persist in my refusal ; because if I take it, either I must give up my present office in the city (which I like better than many another office of higher rank), or keep it only with the risk of offending the citizens, which is the last thing I would wish.   For if, as sometimes happens, any question should arise with the King as to their privileges, they would think me less impartial and trust-worthy, if I were bound to the King by an annual allow-ance."[2]

Enters the Service of the King.

But he did not remain very long in this position, for Henry VIII, who had learnt to value his wisdom, his integrity, and his diligence in two embassies in which he had taken part—one to France for the recovery of certain possessions, and the other to Flanders for the confirmation of a treaty—summoned him from the city to the Court, and made him a member of his Privy Council.   Not long after, when the King's experience of More's valuable qualities had increased, he made him a gilded knight and appointed him Under-Treasurer.   (It was the custom for the office of Treasurer-in-Chief of the realm to be held only by one

[1] On September 3, 1510, when he was thirty-two.
[2] Erasmus, 227.

of the highest rank, a Duke, Count, or Baron.) Of this twofold honour conferred on More, Erasmus writes in the following letter to Goclenius: "When you write to More, you must congratulate him on his new rank and increase of fortune. For whereas before he was only a member of the King's Council, now by the spontaneous gift of his loving sovereign, entirely unasked-for and un-looked-for, has come to him the honour of knighthood, and an office which is of the greatest dignity among the English, and carries a salary not to be despised, that of Treasurer." Erasmus wrote this letter to Conrad Goclenius in August, 1520.[1]

When More had completed a few years of honourable service in this office, he was appointed by the King Chan-cellor—that is, the supreme administrator—of the Duchy of Lancaster, which, through lack of members of the royal family, is held by the King in person. This position is one of the highest honour and has considerable emoluments attached to it.

HENRY'S AFFECTION FOR MORE.

In these positions of honour in the Court he spent about fourteen years, so high in the King's favour and so especially dear to him, that he was employed by him in every affair of importance both at home and abroad. Three or four times he was sent on embassies, on the last occasion going to Cambrai when in 1529 the celebrated treaty of peace was solemnly concluded between four of the most powerful sovereigns in the world—the Emperor Charles V, Ferdinand King of the Romans, Henry VIII of England, and Francis I of France.

When More could obtain leave of absence from public affairs, he would spend his time in relaxation with his family in his house at Chelsea, a village barely a mile away from London. But the King loved him so much, and took such great delight in his companionship, that without warning he would visit him at his home, sit down unceremoniously to table with his family, and spend a

[1] Erasmus, 520. As More received these honours in June, 1521, the letter is certainly dated incorrectly. (See Allen's Edition of Erasmus' Letters, vol. iv, p. 551.)

day or two in the country with his dear friend More. On his departure the King would say : " As I have kept you apart from your family, More, with me for these two days, add two more days to your holiday. For I should not like to think that my presence had in any way interfered with your domestic pleasures."

CREATED LORD CHANCELLOR.

So great was the King's affection for More, so high his opinion of his wisdom, his incorruptibility, and his loyalty, that, not content with the many high honours he had already conferred upon him, he created him finally Lord Chancellor of the realm. Hitherto this office had been held, almost without exception, by ecclesiastics, and those of the highest rank. Two Archbishops, one of them a Cardinal, were More's immediate predecessors in the office. For in England the Chancellor of the realm comes immediately after the King, and takes precedence of all others, however high their dignity or authority. When he appears in public, on his right is borne a golden sceptre surmounted by the royal crown as a sign of his supreme power under the King, on his left a book as a sign of his knowledge of the law. The royal seal, too, enclosed in a silken purse, is carried before him with great ceremony and laid before the tribunal at which he sits. The Chancellor's tribunal is supreme, and no appeal from it is allowed, not even to the King himself. He gives judgement not so much according to statute law as according to natural justice and equity. To him appeals may be made from any other tribunal.

The joy of the whole kingdom when More received this high office was quite unprecedented, and even outside the kingdom the famous scholars of the day, to whom More's virtues and learning were well known, joined in the chorus of delight. Thus Erasmus writes of him in his letter to John Faber, Bishop of Vienna : " It would be easy to convince you of the truth of what I say, if I could show you the letters of men of the highest rank congratulating the King, the kingdom, themselves and even me, overcome as I am with joy, upon More's receiving the honour of

Chancellor."[1] Even Cardinal Wolsey, although he was never very favourable to More, fearing him rather than loving him, when he saw that there was no longer any hope of his own restoration to his earlier dignity, stated emphatically that there was no one in England so fit for the honour as More. But the most striking witness to the virtues of More—and one that will stand for ever—is the judgement of the King himself. For no one had viewed more closely, or conceived a greater affection for, More's rare and almost divine virtues and powers of mind than had he. He, too, before blind lust had driven him into schism, was a man of penetrating judgement, and always, up to this time, chose his servants with the greatest prudence. Especially as " no one of his rank, no layman of the lower nobility, had ever, before him, been advanced to the position."[2]

We must not omit in this place to state in how unusual a way the King, then devoted to More, wished to honour him on his promotion to his high office, and how modestly and prudently More accepted the praise offered to him. For on the day of his installation, when he was to take his seat publicly in what is known as " the Star Chamber," the Duke of Norfolk, who was by far the greatest of the English nobles, and whose influence then was at its height, by command of the King and in his name, led More with all honour to the seat reserved for him as Chancellor and, when More had taken his place, spoke to the people by command of the King in the following words : " The King's Majesty has raised to the supreme dignity of Chancellor (and may it be a happy event for the whole realm), Thomas More, whose noble qualities are already as well known to you as they are to the King himself. His only motive in so doing was because he saw in More all those highest gifts of nature and grace which either he or his people could desire in the Chancellor. For his admirable wisdom, incorruptibility and uprightness, joined to a ready wit, have endeared him for many years back, not only to the whole English nation, but even to the King himself. Of his virtues, the King has had abundant

[1] Erasmus, Appendix, 426.
[2] Cardinal Pole, Bk. III (S.).

experience in many important affairs at home and abroad, in the various offices he has filled, in the delicate negotiations he has conducted with foreign princes, in constant and almost daily consultations. He has never found anyone more prudent in counsel, more sincere in utterance, more eloquent in language. The King, therefore, because he has of More the very highest expectations, and because of his ardent desire that his kingdom and his subjects should be governed with equity, justice, uprightness and wisdom, has made him Chancellor of the realm, in the confidence that, under such a Chancellor, his subjects will enjoy justice and peace, and glory and splendour incomparable will accrue to his kingdom.

" It may perhaps seem strange that one of his rank, a layman, married, not of the nobility, should be raised to a dignity which hitherto it has been the custom to confer only upon ecclesiastics, and those the greatest prelates, or men of the very highest rank. But whatever anyone may think is defective in these respects is more than compensated for by his admirable virtues and incomparable talents. The King has regarded not so much his station as his character, not so much his birth as his merits, not so much his rank as his virtues. Finally His Majesty has wished to show, in elevating Thomas More, that he has among the lesser nobility and among the laity subjects of the very highest merit, who are worthy of the highest offices in Church and State. If this is a rare favour from God, the King values it all the more and is confident that his subjects will be grateful. Take More, then, as your Chancellor with all joy and confidence : from a man of such character you may well expect the greatest benefits to accrue to yourselves and the whole kingdom."

The Duke said more to the same effect, although a speech of this kind was new and unusual. More was naturally much moved and perturbed at the unexpected words of the Duke and, modest as ever, was trembling with nervousness. But he pulled himself together, as the time and the place demanded, and answered in this wise: " Most noble Duke, and you, right honourable lords, all that the King's Majesty has at this time and place willed to be said of me, and Your Grace has so eloquently amplified, is, I fear, far above my deserts. It were greatly to be desired that I possessed such qualities, for this high office requires them. But although your speech has caused me greater fear than I can well express in my words, yet the incomparable favour of the King's Majesty who has deigned to think so highly of me, and to command that my meanness should be so honourably commended to you, cannot but be most gratifying to me. To Your Grace, also, I cannot but be most grateful, inasmuch as what His Majesty briefly commanded you have been so generous as to dilate upon with stately eloquence. For I can but take it that it is His Majesty's incomparable favour towards me, his mere goodness and the incredible inclination of his royal mind to me (with which he has now for many years, in spite of my demerits, continually favoured me), and no desert at all of my own, which has urged him to bestow upon me this new honour and these high praises. For who am I, or what is the house of my father, that the King's Majesty should continually be heaping so many great honours upon me ? I am less than all his benefits, of this office in particular I feel I am altogether unworthy, and even, I fear, unfitted. Into the Court and the royal service, as the King himself often states, I was drawn against my will. With the greatest possible reluctance did I accept this new dignity. But such is His Majesty's goodness and benignity that he appreciates highly even the mean services of his subjects and rewards munificently not only those who deserve well of him, but even those who desire to deserve well, and even if I could not do the one I have at least done the other. Wherefore you can all understand how heavily I feel the burden of obligation weighing upon me to show myself, by my diligence and zeal, grateful to the incredible goodness of the King, and equal to the honourable expectations he has formed of me. The praises to which I have listened have been painful to me, inasmuch as, in order not to appear unworthy of them, I must undertake heavier burdens and yet have fewer helps thereto. It is not that the honour is equal to my merits : it is rather that my shoulders are unequal to the burden. It is not glory that comes to me but care, an increase of anxiety rather than an increase in honour. I must bear the burden as bravely as I may : to the business before me all my strength and all my skill must be devoted. But for this the most powerful incentive will be the earnest and zealous desire, which indeed has ever in my whole life been predominant in me, but of which now especially I desire to make open acknowledgement, to make the fittest possible return to the King's Majesty for his munificent goodness to me. This I trust will be all the easier for me in that all of you have so graciously welcomed the King's munificence in my regard and have so freely conformed yourselves to his will, that I look for a continuance of your good dispositions towards me. For my earnest desire of carrying out well my duties, coupled with your indulgent kindness to me, will certainly produce the best possible results ; and these, even though small in themselves, will seem to you great and praiseworthy. For what we do with pleasure is generally done with success, and when in addition it is accepted with indulgence, then the success seems magnified. In return, then, for the high hopes you place in me, I promise that I will do, if not perfectly, at any rate as well as I can."

When More had said these and other words to the same effect, he turned his face to the high judgement seat of the Chancery and proceeded as follows : "But when I look upon this seat, and consider what great men have before me occupied it, when in particular I call to mind who he was who occupied it last of all,[1] his incomparable prudence, his skill and experience in affairs, the prosperity and the splendid fortune he so long enjoyed, his unhappy fall and inglorious end, I have in the example of my predecessor, enough to make this office difficult, and this honour none too grateful and pleasant. For following after a man of such power of intellect, such prudence, influence and splendour, I will not easily give contentment nor equal his achievements, but will be as a torch compared to the sun. Moreover, the sudden and unlooked-for fall of so great a man is a fearful warning to me not to delight too much in my new honour nor to let its empty splendour dazzle my eyes. In taking this seat, then, I assume an office full of toil and danger, void of all real and lasting honour.

1 Wolsey, for whom see Polydore Vergil (Last Book) (S.).

The higher it is, the greater is the fall that I must guard against. This is in the nature of things and has lately been fearfully exemplified.

" As I ponder over all this, I might easily at my very first entry among you lose courage and fall into despair, if I were not strengthened and refreshed by the incredible inclination of the King's Majesty towards me, and by the good-will and kind welcome that I read in your faces. But for this, my position would be no happier than was that of Damocles when seated in the chair of state of King Diony-sius, and rich in honours and delights, he saw a sword suspended above his head by only a thread. This then I shall ever have before my eyes and in my mind, that this office will be honourable and glorious to me, this dignity new and splendid, if I perform my duties with uninter-mitting care, vigilance, fidelity and prudence, and if I am convinced that my enjoyment of office may be but brief and uncertain. The one my own efforts can effect : the other my predecessor's example can teach me. Conse-quently you will understand with what great pleasure I accept this honourable office, the noble Duke's generous words of praise and the King's incomparable favour to me."

These and many other things did More say at that time and place to the great admiration of all.

MEMBER OF PARLIAMENT.

Besides other offices of State, there is another which he filled, of which we should have spoken earlier. He was a member of Parliament and was chosen as Speaker of the House of Commons : that is to say, he guided the debates in the Lower House where sit the representatives of the people and the lower nobility. It was his duty to consider all questions and motions proposed in the House, and, stating fully his reasons, to admit or to reject them. For so impor-tant a position no one is chosen unless he be a ready speaker, versed in law and familiar with the procedure of the House, and a man of great strength of character.

His Impartiality and Incorruptibility.

We will now give a few examples, which have come to our knowledge, of the integrity and prudence which characterised his public life. When he acted as a judge, he used to say that friend and foe were both alike to him. This was the experience of Giles Heron, his son-in-law, who had married his third daughter, Cecily. When he brought an action before his father-in-law, the latter warned him to cease litigation as his cause was not just. When he refused to do so, More forthwith gave sentence against him. On another occasion when dealing with the case of one who was a declared enemy of his, he was strictly impartial, and, if possible, even more so than usual. When asked why he acted thus he replied : " However bitter an enemy to me a man may be, or however much he may have injured me, I will not allow this to prejudice his case in court, where justice must be administered impartially to all."

But although he was so strictly conscientious and incorruptible, yet his rivals eagerly sought out matter for accusation against him. A certain man named Parnell, either to please these rivals of More or to indulge his own spite, told one of the chief men at the Court that More, after giving sentence in favour of one Mrs. Vaughan, a widow with whom he had had a suit at law, had accepted from her the gift of a golden cup.[1] The courtier saw to it that the story reached the King's ears, who sent a summons to the widow. At the appointed time, when she, More, and many of the great nobles were present, the King asked the Chancellor whether he had accepted a golden cup from the widow. More admitted it. The King was evidently displeased, but More begged him to ask the widow what he had done with the cup. She answered that the Chancellor had indeed accepted the cup joyfully, and had been profuse in his expressions of thanks, and, calling together his household, had spoken of the gift in words of high praise—all this went to support the accusation—but then, calling for wine, he had merrily pledged her health and at once returned the

[1] According to Roper, this incident occurred after More had resigned the Great Seal.

cup to her. The King was angry that such idle gossip should have been brought to him and that More should be subject to such annoyance ; he left the calumniator at More's disposal, read a lecture to the courtier, and praised his Chancellor's discretion.

But of More's industry in his high but difficult position as Chancellor, the following is a proof, evident and worthy of perpetual memory. That tribunal is so overburdened with law-suits that it scarcely ever happens but there are numberless cases waiting for decision. Indeed when More took office some cases were still pending which had been introduced twenty years before. But so efficiently and successfully did he carry out his duties that on one occasion —it never happened before or after—having taken his seat and settled a case, he called for the next, to be met with the answer that there was no case outstanding. " Thanks be to God," said More, " that for once this busy tribunal is at rest." Rising with joy, he ordered the fact to be inscribed in the registers of the Chancery, where it may yet be read.

But of his justice and incorruptibility in his high office, the proof which is public, best known, and unassailable is the testimony of Henry VIII himself after More had obtained permission from him to resign, as we shall relate in its place. For our present purpose it will be enough to cite his own words in a letter to Erasmus, in which as an answer to the calumnies of his enemies, he relates the King's judgement upon his conduct. " I have waited now till the meeting of Parliament," he writes, " since I exercised and resigned my office. No one yet has come forward to complain of my conduct. If I have not acted honourably, I suppose I have been clever enough to conceal my iniquities. If my rivals will not grant the one, they must at least grant me the credit of the other. But the King himself has borne witness in my favour many times, often privately and twice publicly. When my successor, a most excellent man, was installed, the King bade the Duke of Norfolk, the Lord High Treasurer of England, to speak of me in a way modesty forbids me to repeat and to bear witness that it was only with the greatest reluctance that he accepted my resignation. And not content with that, the King, in his singular goodness towards me, had the same statement repeated on a later occasion, when in his royal presence, and in the presence of many of the nobility and others of his subjects, my successor made, as is customary, his first speech in the Senate, or Parliament as we call it."[1]

More also wrote to the King himself, after his resignation, recalling to his mind the words he (the King) had used towards him at the time. " It pleased Your Highness," he wrote, " then to say unto me, that for the service which I before had done you (which it then liked your goodness far above my deserving to commend) that in any suit that I should after have to Your Grace, that either should concern mine honour or that should pertain unto my profit, I should find Your Highness a good and gracious lord unto me."[2] Certainly the praise of the King at such a moment, coupled with the promise that accompanied it, was an irrefragable proof of the integrity with which he had exercised his office.

This will be sufficient for the present on the subject of More's public life and his conduct therein, although we may have occasion later on to add a few details.

Resistance to Exactions of Henry VII.

But even when he was still a youth and a student of the law, in the reign of Henry VII, he gave a remarkable example of the honesty that was to characterise him through life. The King was endeavouring to force upon the people, through Parliament, certain unjust exactions and taxes. Although in Parliament all may say freely what they think, on this occasion others kept silence through cowardice, and it was left to More to speak openly and powerfully in opposition to the King's demands. The King was exceedingly angry, and the flame was fanned by Dudley and Empson, the authors of the exactions. More was advised by many, a Bishop among them, to acknowledge his fault to the King, to beg for pardon, and thus to placate the King. He utterly refused, saying very wisely that he was not conscious of having committed any fault, and that it was not advisable to acknowledge a fault where there was no certainty of pardon. Seven or eight years later

[1] Erasmus, Appendix, 466.   [2] E.W., p. 1423.

Henry VII was dead, and Dudley, for the evil counsel he had given to that monarch, was condemned to death. As he was being led out to his execution, More went up to him and said, " Well, Mr. Dudley, in that matter of the exactions was I not right ?" " Oh, Mr. More," he replied, " it was by God's guidance that you did not acknowledge your fault to the King, for if you had done so you would most certainly have lost your head." Thus, then, he did his duty by the State and at the same time took the best course for his personal safety.

" TROUBLESOME " TO HERETICS.

He was indeed, as we have said, a most impartial judge, but to evil-doers he was strict and severe, or, as he expressed it in the epitaph he composed for himself, " he was troublesome to thieves, murderers, and heretics " —and especially to heretics, of whom he writes thus to Erasmus : " As to my professing myself in my epitaph troublesome to heretics, I did it with the fullest deliberation. For I detest the whole tribe of them so much that there is no one to whom I wish to be more hostile than to them, unless they renounce their errors. For day by day my experience of them increases my fear of the tremendous harm they may do to the world."[1] But he was not so " troublesome " to heretics that any one of them suffered capital punishment while he was Chancellor. This is distinctly asserted by Erasmus in the letter from which we have already quoted,[2] and our annals witness to it. And if Sleidanus means to assert the opposite when, in speaking of More's action against those suspected of Lutheranism, he makes use of a phrase which in legal usage denotes capital punishment, he is, as usual, a downright liar.

[1] Erasmus, Appendix, 466.
[2] Erasmus, Appendix, 426. During the last six months, when " More, though still in office, was no longer in power," there were three heretics burnt at Smithfield. More himself refers to the cases (E.W., pp. 348 and 889). For the whole question see *The Saga and the Myth of Sir Thomas More*, by Prof. R. W. Chambers (British Academy Lecture, 1927).

CHAPTER IV

HIS WIDE LEARNING AND LITERARY LABOURS

W E have now laid before our readers the information we have been able to gather about More's public life and his irreproachable conduct therein. Now we shall try to speak of him as a literary man, of his attainments, his studies, his love of books, his labours, and his successes. In our earlier chapters we have already spoken of the studies of his boyhood and his youth. We have seen how he diligently exercised himself in writing and speaking, and gained fame as a poet, an orator, and a philosopher. Before he entered upon his public career it is not surprising that a man of such talents, having time upon his hands, could not bear to be idle. But in such a constant pressure of business as the appointments he held involved—and added to this he was married and had the care of a family—who could have expected that he would have been able to do any literary work of importance ? For the Muses love leisure and have the greatest abhorrence for the clamour of the tribunals and the bustle of the Court. Such is our sluggishness that they demand almost undivided allegiance. More's natural bent was entirely to a literary life, and often did he bewail the multitude of business he had to attend to, and the constant interruptions to which he was subject. Thus he writes, after finishing the *Utopia*, to his friend, Peter Giles of Antwerp:

" Whiles I do daily bestow my time about law matters : some to plead, some to hear, some as an arbitrator with mine award to determine, some as an umpire or a judge, with my sentence to discuss. Whiles I go one way to see and visit my friend : another way about mine own private affairs. Whiles I spend almost all the day abroad among others, and the residue at home among mine own ; I leave to myself, I mean to my book, no time. For when

I am come home, I must commune with my wife, chat with my children, and talk with my servants. All the which things I reckon and account among business, forasmuch as they must of necessity be done : and done must they needs be, unless a man will be stranger in his own house. And in any wise a man must so fashion and order his conditions, and so appoint and dispose himself, that he be merry, jocund, and pleasant among them, whom either nature hath provided, or chance hath made, or he himself hath chosen to be the fellows and companions of his life : so that with too much gentle behaviour and familiarity, he do not mar them, and by too much sufferance of his servants maketh them his masters. Among these things now rehearsed, stealeth away the day, the month, the year. When do I write then ? And all this while I have spoken no word of sleep, neither yet of meat, which among a great number doth waste no less time than doth sleep, wherein almost half the lifetime of man creepeth away."

MORE'S DILIGENCE.

This being so, what time remained for study ? He answers immediately :

" I therefore do win and get only that time which I steal from sleep and meat. Which time because it is very little, and yet somewhat it is, therefore have I once at the last, though it be long first, finished *Utopia* ; and have sent it to you, friend Peter."[1]

Ordinarily, indeed, More did not give more than four or five hours to sleep. He used to rise at two and devote himself to study and prayer until seven. The rest of the day he gave to business. Thus he was able to write, besides what we have already mentioned, very many works, Latin and more especially English. He wrote the *Utopia*, if we may believe John Paludanus, while yet a youth, but it would be more correct to call him a young man at the time. For he wrote it on his return from an embassy to Flanders, as he states in the Preface. But it is clear he had not yet been summoned by the King to the Court, from the fact of the King's offering him a pension at the close of the

[1] The letter prefixed to *Utopia*.

embassy, as we have related in the last chapter.   In fact, he wrote the *Utopia* in 1516 when he was thirty-three.[1] (When he suffered in 1535 he was fifty-two[2] years of age.)

The " Utopia."

Of the excellence of this work it is not necessary for me to speak, for it is in everyone's hands and has been translated into French, Italian, and Flemish ; but I will transcribe the opinions of some famous scholars.   William Budé in a letter to Thomas Lupset thus writes : " We owe the knowledge of Utopia to Thomas More, who has made known to the world in this our age the pattern of a happy life and a perfect rule of good behaviour.   Our age and future ages will have this history as a precious source of noble and useful laws which each one may take and adapt to the use of his own State."

John Paludanus of Cassel in a letter to Peter Giles writes as follows : " You may see in Utopia, as in a mirror, all that pertains to a perfect commonwealth.   England certainly has many excellent learned men.   For what may we conjecture of the rest if More alone has performed so much, being, first, but a young man, and, then, so fully occupied with public and domestic business, and, lastly, practising a profession quite other than literature ?"

Peter Giles in a letter to Jerome Busleyden, Provost of Aire, thus speaks of the *Utopia* : " So many miracles meet here together that I am in doubt which I should most admire, the extraordinary fidelity of his memory which could record almost verbatim so many matters heard but once " (for Giles had to give his support to the fiction), " or his wisdom in pointing out the sources—utterly unknown for the most part—of actual evils and potential benefits for the State, or the force and ease of his style which, with such pure Latinity and such eloquence, has treated of so many matters, although he is so much distracted both with public and domestic affairs."

I will add now the weighty judgement of Jerome Busleyden, a member of the Council of the Emperor.   After reading the *Utopia* he wrote to More thus : " In the happy

---

[1] In reality thirty-eight.   [2] In reality fifty-seven.

description of the Utopian commonwealth there is nothing lacking which might show most excellent learning and the highest skill in human affairs. For so varied is your learning, so wide and accurate your knowledge of affairs, that whatever you write is the fruit of valuable experience, and whatever you wish to convey is expressed most eloquently : a marvellous and rare happiness, indeed, all the rarer in that, to the envy of the many, it is possessed but by the few. Few indeed they are who have the sincerity, the learning, the integrity, and the influence needed to enable them to contribute so dutifully, so honourably, and so prudently to the common good as you have succeeded in doing. You have willed to benefit, not only yourself, but all nations of the world : you have made all men your debtors. You could have bestowed no more worthy or useful gift upon mankind than by depicting, as you have done, the perfect state, with ideal customs and laws. The world has never seen wiser, more perfect, or more desirable institutions. In their excellence they leave far behind them the famous and much-lauded states of Sparta, Athens, and Rome." Further on he makes a very wise observation, and praises the fact that " the State of Utopia as depicted by More labours not so much in making laws as in forming the most upright magistrates so that, according to their pattern, their evident integrity, their exemplary manners, and the clear mirror of their justice, the whole state and true government of every perfect commonwealth may be framed."

Paul Jovius also speaks of this renowned book in the following terms : " The fame that More has won by his *Utopia* will never die. For he describes most eloquently how in the land of that happy nation the State is governed by most wholesome laws and enjoys a rich peace. Since he loathed the corrupt manners of this wicked age, his purpose was to show by a pleasant fiction the right path to a blessed and most happy life."[1]

Certainly no one who reads this masterpiece, the *Utopia*, can fail to agree with Budé, Erasmus, Cochlaeus, Rhenanus, Busleyden, Tunstall, Cardinal Reginald Pole, Paludanus, Hutten, Vives, Grapheus, Zasius, and all other readers of

[1] *Elogia Doctorum Virorum*, tit. 89 (S.).

the work in their verdict that More had an incomparable and almost superhuman wit. In invention no work could be more happy, apt, and clever ; in expression none more worthy, rich, and elegant ; in its teaching of life and manners none more sound, earnest, and wise. The reader never tires of the book, and cannot finish it without the greatest profit to himself if he reads it with attention and a desire to learn.

HISTORY OF RICHARD III.

Almost at the same time he wrote in Latin the history of Richard III, King of England. He wrote it only to practise his pen ; he never finished it or revised it ; but yet it lacks neither polish nor elegance of style. He had written it in English at an earlier date, with greater fulness of detail, and with yet more eloquence.

REPLY TO LUTHER.

In 1523 the foul-mouthed Luther issued a foul book against Henry VIII's book on the Sacraments. More published a reply to Luther's abuse, and thought it best to answer his rudeness and scurrility in the same style. Luther should be overwhelmed with filth like that with which he had covered the King, so that finding his intemperate language used against himself he might lose the pleasure which no doubt he had found in uttering it. But as at that time More was a knight and a member of the King's Council he was conscious that rudeness and vulgarity were unbefitting his position : consequently he allowed the book to go out, not in his own name, but in that of William Ross. As a man of that name about this very time went on a pilgrimage to Rome and died in Italy, even the English themselves were quite ready to believe him to be the author. The book is a serious and solid defence of the true faith against the impudent attacks of Luther, besides being extraordinarily clever and witty. As to his answering abuse with abuse, in the last lines of the book he explains that he did it with great reluctance, but was forced to it. " Although Luther has given himself wholly over to the powers of evil and has become hardened in his schism, yet he should determine with himself to take at least some account of good manners, so that he may claim the authority of a dogmatiser rather than a low buffoon of a heretic. For if he is willing to enter upon a serious discussion, if he will withdraw his lies and false accusations, if he will have no more to do with folly, rage, and the Furies who hitherto have been his all-too-familiar spirits, if he will cleanse the filth with which he has so vilely befouled his tongue and his pen, then there will not be wanting disputants who will treat with him as seriously as the matter demands. But if he goes on with his scurrility and madness as he has begun, with his calumnious attacks, his inept folly, his stupid rage and his vulgar buffoonery, if he will use no language but that of the sewer . . . then, let others do what they will, we will decide, from this time forth, either to drag out the madman from his stronghold and show him in his true colours, or to leave our raving friend with all his Furies . . . covered with his own filth."

These are his last words to Luther, and in them he smears Luther's lips with dainties fit for such a rogue and gives him a sweet morsel suited to his palate. Certainly this book, as Cochlaeus says, " with great cleverness and play of wit, and with violent diatribe, was a most complete refutation of Luther's book. It cast back in his teeth all his infamous lies, so that he dared to utter no further word." Whereas generally Luther was very busy with his pen and ready to reply to any who attacked him, after he had read Ross, he became more dumb than a fish.

More wrote, also, against John Pomeranus a letter of admirable clarity, which has been printed separately.

These are almost all the Latin works, at any rate among those that have survived, that he wrote while still at liberty. For when he was in prison, he wrote a long treatise on the Passion of our Lord, of which the latter part is in Latin and printed among his Latin works, although the earlier and by far the larger part is in English. But of this, more hereafter.

ENGLISH WORKS.

Now I will mention what he wrote in English either in controversy with heretics or on subjects of devotion. I have already spoken of his Life of Pico of Mirandula and of

his English translation of some minor works of Pico.
He wrote his Life of Richard III while practising as a
lawyer in London.   When he was summoned to the Court
and to the Council of the King, although he had an extraordinarily busy life, yet he found time to write very many
works.   When he was knighted, in the King's Council,
and Sub-Treasurer of the realm, he wrote a treatise of
remarkable piety and learning on the Four Last Things,
but the greater part has perished.   Later on the heretics
began to come into England from Belgium, as More notes
in a letter to Erasmus. " All the heresies," he writes,
" found shelter in Belgium, and thence their books were
sent into England."[1]   Although More at the time was a
much-occupied man, as a member of the King's Council
and Chancellor of the Duchy of Lancaster, yet he found
time to write four books of dialogues on the subjects then
in controversy.   The work is lengthy, detailed, and learned :
it treats fully of the Invocation of the Saints, Pilgrimages,
Relics, etc.: it proves by many arguments which is the true
Church and that the Church is infallible.

After he had finished the Dialogues he dealt with an
heretical pamphlet which had appeared under the title of
The Supplication of Beggars, and which advised the King
that the best, and indeed the only, means for the relief
of the poor and for provision for the other needs of the State
was to confiscate at least three-quarters of all ecclesiastical
and monastic property. Against this pamphlet, which
was not a supplication but a libel, More wrote, the year
after the Dialogues, a complete reply, entitled *The Supplication of Souls*. In this book he speaks in the person of
the souls in purgatory, for whose relief, by prayers and
masses, ecclesiastical and monastic revenues were, in large
part, founded : he defends the Church's teaching on
Purgatory and prayers for the dead ; and he proves that
if monasteries were destroyed and the property of the
Church confiscated, the King's power would be lessened
and the number of beggars increased, as experience, the
teacher of fools, afterwards proved.

When, later on, Tyndall, that heresiarch who afterwards
suffered at Vilvorde in Brabant the just penalty of his

[1] Erasmus, 1223.

impiety, attacked More's Dialogues, the latter, although
then Lord Chancellor, wrote a long work to refute him.
Of the nine books into which this refutation is divided,
three were written while he was Chancellor, six after he
had resigned. In the single year which intervened between
his resignation and his imprisonment[1] he wrote also,
against the Sacramentarian John Frith, a book on the
True Presence of the Body and Blood of Christ, then
an *Apology* and a defence of that *Apology* under the
title of *The Debellation of Salem and Bizance*. Finally he
wrote in five books *An Answer to the . . . Book which a
Nameless Heretic hath named : The Supper of the Lord.* In
prison he wrote *A Dialogue of Comfort against Tribulation,*
in three books—a work of great beauty, full of piety and
learning, which hardly has an equal amongst works of the
kind. There, too, he wrote *A Treatise Historical containing
the Bitter Passion of our Saviour Christ,* according to the four
Evangelists, beginning at the text " The feast of un-
leavened bread was at hand "[2] and continuing as far as
the words "They laid hands upon Jesus."[3] At that point
hands were laid upon him, by the increased strictness of
his confinement, so that all further opportunity of writing
was denied him. This lengthy treatise is written with
careful detail and is full of the deepest piety.

MORE'S KNOWLEDGE OF DIVINITY.

All the English works of More were published in one
large volume in the reign of Queen Mary. When I read
the greater portion of this volume thirty years ago, I found
More to have been a most diligent student of the Holy
Scriptures, and to have had a considerable acquaintance
with the Fathers and even with the disputes of the Schools.
His quotations, even if not very numerous, are always
forthcoming where needful and always to the point.
They are drawn from Augustine, Jerome, Chrysostom,
Cyril, Hilary, Bernard, and Gerson. We know that after-

[1] In reality nearly two years, for he resigned the Great Seal on
May 16, 1532, and was imprisoned on April 13, 1534.
[2] Luke xxii 1.
[3] Matt. xxvi 50.

wards, when difficulties arose with the King, in self-defence
he alleged that he had spent seven years[1] in the study of
the Fathers in order to get to know their view of the Pope's
Primacy. Of the result of this study, more will be said
hereafter. For the present it is enough to remark what
a store of patristic learning a man of his attainments
and extraordinary memory could thus obtain. For even
though he was reading with one special object in view,
who can doubt that he would have noted, by the way,
many passages that bore on modern heresies. I have
come to the conclusion, in reading through his works, that
he paid special attention to the study of dogmatic theology.
For when he speaks of grace, free will, merit, faith, charity
and other virtues, original sin and even predestination, he
is so guarded and exact in his statements that a professional
theologian could scarcely speak more accurately. That
he had carefully read St Thomas is proved by a story
told by John Harris, his secretary. Once a pamphlet
recently printed by a heretic was brought to More's notice
while he was travelling by water from his home at Chelsea
to London. When he had read a little he pointed out with
his finger some passages to Harris. " The arguments,"
said he, " which this villain has set forth are the objections
which St Thomas puts to himself in such and such a
question and article of the Secunda Secundae, but the
rogue keeps back the good Doctor's solutions." I myself
once heard him arguing with Father Alphonsus, of the
Friars Minor, who had been confessor to Queen Catharine,
the first wife of Henry VIII. He was defending the opinion
of Scotus on attrition and contrition as safer and more
probable than the opinion of Occam. It might well
appear astonishing that a man whose whole life was filled
with the affairs of public life and the Court, who was, too,
well versed in general literature, should not only have
dipped into scholastic theology, but have been thoroughly
familiar with it.

[1] So in E.W., p. 1426, but the original MS. has " ten."

Influence of More's Writings.

More's English controversial works did great good at the time and were read and reread three or four times by many serious scholars, some of whom drew up " tables " of the work as an aid to memory, as he himself had occasion to note.[1] Afterwards they were reprinted in the reign of Queen Mary and were of the greatest use during the restoration of Catholicism that then took place. For during that bright interval, which by the great mercy of God was granted to us between the two periods of schism, nothing more powerfully strengthened and promoted the Catholic cause than the numerous works of More in English, edited with great care and labour by William Rastell, as we have said in the Preface. Many other works of More, however, both Latin and English, perished in the bitter persecution which befell his household after he was taken away from it, as shall be afterwards related : those that we have were, so to say, snatched from the flames and preserved by the special care of his friends. For immediately after his death, More's large and valuable library, together with the rest of his furniture, was sacked by Thomas Cromwell, the Keeper of the King's Seal, and a fit tool for a tyrant. More's untiring energy is shown by the fact that all that he composed for publication during his whole life, English and Latin works alike, was written by his own hand, as he was unwilling to rely on the industry of another.

More's Admiration for Erasmus.

As to his love of letters, in the early enthusiasm of his youth it was not only devout but, we might even say, superstitious. No one loved Erasmus more than he, and it was a literary friendship. In turn Erasmus loved him, and deservedly. More's friendship for Erasmus, however, honoured Erasmus more than it benefited More. But as that Protestant heresy increased, for which Erasmus had so widely sown the accursed seed, More's love towards him decreased and grew cool. More had blamed Tyndall for rendering the word " ecclesia " by " congregation "

[1] E.W., p. 845.

and " presbyter " by " elder." Tyndall answered that
More's darling Erasmus had done the same and therefore
was also to be blamed.   More's answer was : " Had I found
with Erasmus, my darling, the cunning intent and purpose
that I found with Tyndall, Erasmus, my darling, should
be no more ' my darling.' "[1]   That is to say, as he could
not excuse the fact, at least, for friendship's sake, he excused
the intention.   Towards the end of his life More realised
that many points in the writings of Erasmus needed correction, and tried hard to persuade him to follow the
example of St Augustine by revising all his works and
issuing a book of " Retractations."   John Fisher, Bishop
of Rochester, wrote to the same effect, as is clear from
Erasmus' answer.[2]   But Erasmus, who was as unlike
St Augustine in humility as he was in doctrine, refused and
destroyed More's letter so that it should not be inserted
in his collected correspondence.

DEFENCE OF CLASSICAL LEARNING.

By his zeal for letters More merited to share with Richard
Pace—a man of high rank, learned and prudent, who had
undertaken important embassies for Henry VIII—the title
of " Patron of Literature in England."   Thus from the
Court he wrote to the University of Oxford a powerful
discourse to confute certain foolish preachers who from
the pulpit attacked the study of Latin and Greek.   So also
once when a preacher had attempted to take the same line

[1] E.W., p. 422.

[2] Stapleton's marginal reference (Bk. XXII, p. 852) takes us to a letter
to John Gacchus (Appendix, 345) in which Erasmus defends himself
from the charge of favouring Luther's opinions.   Possibly it is a misprint or possibly it is quoted in support of the following statement that
Erasmus had not the humility of St Augustine.

Amongst the letters to Bishop Fisher I cannot find justification for
Stapleton's inference, although sometimes Erasmus hints at disagree-
ments in opinion—e.g., Letters, 389, and Appendix, 306.   In the former
he writes : " You will not offend me even if you disagree with the books
I have brought out."

As to More, Father Bridgett (Life, p. 83 n.) suggests that Stapleton
may be mistaken, for in another letter More expresses complete satisfaction with all that Erasmus had written.   But there was plenty of
time after the date of this letter (1519) for More, in the light of later
experience of heresy, to revise his opinion.

in the presence of the King, at More's instance he was
forced after the sermon to beg pardon and to acknowledge
his rashness. To Martin Dorpius, too, who for a time
showed himself hostile to the study of letters and especially
of Greek, More wrote a long and most learned letter on the
necessity for the knowledge of Greek, which was printed
at Basle by Episcopius in 1563. Thus, then, he was united
in the closest bonds of friendship with all those, both at
home and abroad, who at that period enjoyed a reputation
for eloquence and learning, as will appear in the following
chapter.

The following passage is taken from the letter to the
University of Oxford which we have just mentioned.
" Although no one denies that a man may be saved without
a knowledge of Latin and Greek or of any literature at all,
yet learning, yea, even worldly learning, as he calls it "
(More is referring to a certain preacher whose impudence
was more evident than his culture), " prepares the mind
for virtue. Everyone knows that the attainment of this
learning is almost the only reason why students flock to
Oxford. But as for rude and unlettered virtue, every
honest woman can teach it to her children quite well at
home. Moreover, it must be remembered that not all who
come to you, come for the study of theology. The State
needs men learned in the law. A knowledge of human
affairs, too, must be acquired, which is so useful even to
a theologian, that without it he may perhaps sing pleasantly
to himself, but will certainly not sing agreeably to the people.
And this knowledge can nowhere be drawn so abundantly
as from the poets, orators and historians. There are even
some who make the knowledge of things natural a road to
heavenly contemplation, and so pass from philosophy and
the natural arts—which this man condemns under the
general name of worldly literature—to theology, despoiling
the women of Egypt to adorn the queen. And as regards
theology itself, which alone he seems to approve, if indeed
he approves even that, I do not see how he can attain it
without the knowledge of languages, either Hebrew, Greek
or Latin ; unless, indeed, the easy-going fellow thinks
that sufficient books on the subject have been written in
English. Or perhaps he thinks that the whole of theology

is comprised within the limits of those questions on which
such as he are always disputing, for the knowledge of which
I confess that little enough Latin is wanted.   But to confine
theology, the august queen of heaven, within such narrow
limits would be not only iniquitous but impious.   For does
not theology also dwell in the Sacred Scriptures, and did
it not thence make its way to the cells of all the ancient
holy Fathers, Augustine, I mean, Jerome, Ambrose,
Cyprian, Chrysostom, Cyril, Gregory and others of the
same class, with whom the study of theology made its
abode for more than a thousand years after the Passion of
Christ before those trivial questions arose ?   And if any
ignorant man boasts that he understands the works of
these Fathers without a thorough knowledge of the language
in which each wrote, he will have to boast a long time before
scholars will believe him."   I have quoted these passages,
which form but a small part of a lengthy address, so that the
reader may to some extent be able to judge how earnest
was More in his advocacy and defence of letters.

Moreover, his very long letter to Martin Dorpius on the
necessity of the study of Greek, printed at Basle in 1563
by Episcopius (the printer has prefixed to it an erroneous
title " Apology for the Moria of Erasmus," whereas, in fact,
this point is only touched upon incidentally), is a most
evident proof of his wide acquaintance with both sacred
and profane literature, and of his advocacy of both the one
and the other in opposition to the barbarous tastes of the
age.

Thus, then, I have dealt with his varied and wide learning
and with his literary labours, so far as I have been able to
do so from the particulars which have come to my knowledge.

CHAPTER V

THE MANY FAMOUS SCHOLARS WHO WERE HIS FRIENDS

WHAT we have tried to say about the wide and varied learning of Sir Thomas More will be more convincing to the reader if we treat briefly of the literary men of that age, both at home and abroad, with whom he was on terms of mutual friendship and esteem. For one of skill and renown in literature has a special power to draw to himself the goodwill of many whom he has not met in person, especially of other famous scholars whom the common fellowship of letters in every age and circumstance binds together.

It is no small proof of erudition to gain the praise of the greatest scholars ; and to enjoy the friendship of men of renown is no small happiness. Alexander of Macedonia, seeing in the Troad the statue which Patroclus had erected to his friend Achilles, exclaimed : " Happy Achilles, to have such a friend !" Certainly if a similarity of disposition is the basis of friendship, if like consorts with like, then the number of men renowned for learning whom More counted among his friends is a most evident sign of his deep learning.

ENGLISH FRIENDS.

We will begin with our own countrymen, and afterwards go on to foreigners. It is true to say that there was no scholar of repute in England during More's lifetime (and the multitude of scholars there might well be compared to the bursting forth of the fresh foliage in spring) with whom he was not on terms of close friendship. In his early years, as we have already said, his intimate friends were John Colet, John Grocyn, and Thomas Linacre, men of deep learning and refined tastes, whom he looked on as his teachers. As companions in his studies he had William

Lilly, whom we have mentioned above, William Mountjoy, to whom several of the letters contained in the collected correspondence of Erasmus were directed, and William Latimer. This man, a Catholic, must not be confused with Hugh Latimer, the heretic of Edward VI's reign. In a letter to Erasmus William Latimer speaks of More in the following terms : "You know yourself how keen More is, how powerful in intellect, how energetic in all that he undertakes ; in a word, how like he is to you."[1]

More had other friends and companions in the pursuit of polite literature. One was Thomas Lupset, to whom were addressed several still-extant letters of Erasmus, which bear witness both to his profound scholarship and to his intimate friendship with More. In one of More's letters to Erasmus occur the following words : "Our friend Lupset lectures on Greek and Latin literature to a large audience at Oxford with very great praise to himself and no less benefit to his scholars. He has taken the place of my John Clements." Another was Thomas Eliot, a well-known English writer, whose wife also gave herself to the study of literature in Sir Thomas More's school, of which we shall speak hereafter. There was also John Croke,[2] who was the first teacher of Greek at Leipzig, and was Greek tutor to King Henry himself. A letter of More's to him is still extant in manuscript, and from it I transcribe the following long passage:

"Whoever has led you, my dear Croke, to believe that my love for you is lessened because for so long you have neglected to write to me, either is himself deceived or has cunningly deceived you. Although I certainly take the greatest pleasure in your letters, yet I am not so proud as to claim as a right that you should pay me the tribute of daily salutation, nor am I so sensitive and querulous as to be offended at some trivial neglect of duty, even if such a duty existed. Indeed I should feel that I were acting very unjustly were I to exact letters from others when I am only too conscious of my own negligence in this regard. Therefore be reassured on this head, for my affection to

[1] Erasmus, 301.
[2] Richard Croke is the person here meant; *cf.* Gillow, *Bibliographical Dictionary of the English Catholics*," s.v.

you has not grown so cold as to need to be fanned into flame again by continual letters. I shall be delighted if you will write when you have the opportunity, but I would certainly never desire you to interrupt those useful labours to which so constantly you devote yourself to the advantage both of yourself and of your scholars, or to waste the time that should be given to your lectures in writing compliment-ary letters to your friends. The other part of your excuse I will have nothing to do with, for there is no reason why you, my dear Croke, should fear my nose like the trunk of an elephant. For your letters are not so poor that they need fear to approach any living man, nor am I so long-nosed that I would have any man fear my censure. As for the place which you ask me to procure you, both Pace, who loves you dearly, and I have spoken to the King," etc.

This letter of More's throws a clear light upon his friend-ship for Croke and upon his sincere goodwill towards all his friends and towards scholars in general.

CARDINAL POLE.

Amongst More's friends also was Reginald Pole, at that time a young man, but afterwards a Cardinal of great renown. Of his intimate friendship with More and the Bishop of Rochester, he was most proud, as the following words testify: " But if you think that the reason for my great grief was that they who were put to death were my friends, I do indeed acknowledge and loudly proclaim that they were to me of all friends most dear. For why should I seek to hide that of which I am as proud as I would be did I enjoy the friendship of all the Kings and Princes in the world ?"[1] Of the friendship between More and Pole, although there was a great difference in their ages, I have discovered evident proofs from some letters of More written with his own hand. One is a letter written from the Court to Reginald Pole and John Clements jointly, who were then students at Oxford. " I thank you, my dear Clements," he writes, " for being so keenly solicitous about the health of my family and myself that although absent you are careful to warn us what food to avoid. I thank

[1] *De Unitate Ecclesiae,* Bk. III (S.).

you, my dear Pole, doubly for deigning to procure for me
the advice of so skilful a physician, and no less for obtaining
from your mother—noblest and best of women, and fully
worthy of such a son " (she was Countess of Salisbury and
of royal blood)—" the remedy prescribed and for getting
it made up. Not only do you willingly procure us advice,
but equally evident is your willingness to obtain for us the
remedy itself. I love and praise both of you for your
bounty and fidelity."

In a letter written to Margaret, his daughter, More also
makes mention of Pole, writing as follows : " I cannot put
down on paper, indeed I can hardly express in my own
mind, the deep pleasure that I received from your most
charming letter, my dearest Margaret. As I read it there
was with me a young man of the noblest rank and of the
widest attainments in literature, one, too, who is as conspicuous for his piety as he is for his learning. He thought
your letter nothing short of miraculous, even before he
understood how you were pressed for time and distracted
by ill-health, whilst you managed to write so long a letter.
I could scarce make him believe that you had not been
helped by a master until I told him in all good faith that
there was no master at our house, and that it would not be
possible to find a man who would not need your help in
composing letters rather than be able to give any assistance
to you."

From these two letters it is clear that there existed no
ordinary friendship between Sir Thomas More and Reginald
Pole, between the Martyr and the noble Confessor for the
faith.

Archbishop Lee.

Nor should I omit to mention among the learned friends
of More Edward Lee, a man of high literary attainments,
and afterwards Archbishop of York. This Lee was a
powerful opponent of Erasmus, and wrote with vigour
and with deep learning against his *Annotations upon the New
Testament*. But More, although he loved Erasmus, dis-
liked controversy and distrusted Lee's judgement, nevertheless did not allow his close friendship with the latter
to be broken. Of this the following letter is a witness :

" You ask me, my dear Lee, not to lessen my affection for you in any way. Trust me, good Lee, I shall not. Although in this case my sympathies are with the party which you are attacking, yet I trust that you will withdraw your troops from the siege with perfect safety. I shall ever love you, and I am proud to find that my love is so highly valued by you. If ever occasion requires it, my zeal on your behalf shall be no less fervent than it is now on the other side. So that if ever you bring out a book of your own (and I doubt not that you will bring out many), and Erasmus, casting a critical eye upon it, should write a pamphlet in an attempt to refute it (although it would be much more seemly that he should not retaliate), I, although my talents are poor, will yet stand by you to defend you with all the energy of which I am capable. Farewell, my most dear friend."

BISHOP FISHER.

Two other most learned men, England's shining lights, were also intimate friends of More—viz., John Fisher, Bishop of Rochester, and Cuthbert Tunstall, Bishop first of London and afterwards of Durham. The former, as he was his companion in martyrdom, so he had been his very intimate friend for many years previously. When More was called to the Court and made a member of the King's Council, Fisher wrote to him in the following terms to commend to him his Cambridge scholars : " I beg that, through your good offices with our Most Gracious King, we at Cambridge may have some hope that our young men may receive encouragement to learning from the bounty of so noble a Prince. We have very few friends at Court who have the will and the power to commend our interests to the King's Majesty, and among them we reckon you the chief ; for hitherto, even when you were of lower rank, you have always shown the greatest favour to us. We rejoice that now you are raised to the dignity of Knighthood and become so intimate with the King, and we offer you our heartiest congratulations, for we know that you will continue to show us the same favour. Please now give your help to this young man, who is well versed in theology and a zealous preacher to the people. He puts his hopes in your influence with our noble King and in your willingness to accept my recommendation."

To this letter of Fisher's, More's reply, which follows, will show how intimate was the friendship of the two men. " As to this priest, Reverend Father, of whom you write that he will soon obtain a prebend if he can obtain a powerful advocate with the King, I think I have so wrought that our Prince will raise no obstacle. Whatever influence I have with the King—it is very little, but such as it is— is as freely at your disposal, for yourself or your scholar, as a house is to its owner. I owe your students constant gratitude for the heart-felt affection of which their letters to me are the token. Farewell, best and most courteous of Bishops, and continue your affection for me."

Again, in another letter to the same he writes : " I cannot express in words my delight, both for your own sake and for the sake of our country, that your Lordship writes in a style that might well pass for Erasmus'. As for the subject-matter, ten Erasmuses could not be more convincing." And he concludes : " Farewell, my Lord Bishop, most highly esteemed for virtue and learning."

BISHOP TUNSTALL.

But More's most intimate friendship was with Tunstall. Him More could never extol highly enough : of his company he was never tired : in his letters, his wit, his judgement, his virtues, his piety, he took inexpressible delight. In the epitaph which More composed for himself he speaks thus of Tunstall : " In the whole world could scarcely be found one more learned, more wise, more virtuous than he." And in the beginning of his *Utopia* he writes thus :

" The King's Majesty sent me ambassador into Flanders, joined in commission with Cuthbert Tunstall, a man doubtless out of comparison, and whom the King's Majesty of late, to the great rejoicing of all men, did prefer to the office of Master of the Rolls. But of this man's praises I will say nothing, not because I do fear that small credence shall be given to the testimony that cometh out of a friend's mouth : but because his virtue and learning be greater, and of more excellence, than that I am able to praise them : and also in all places so famous and so perfectly well known, that they need not, nor ought not of me to be praised, unless I would seem to show and set forth the brightness of the sun with a candle, as the proverb saith."

And again in one of his letters to Erasmus : " Several matters in that embassy gave me great delight. First the constant company of Tunstall for so long a time, than whom no one is more widely versed in literature, no one stricter in life and conduct, no one more pleasant to live with."[1]

I have seen several manuscript letters of More to Tunstall which afford obvious proof of their mutual friendship and of More's high opinion of his friend's judgement. I will give a few extracts. One is as follows : " Although all the letters I receive from you, my honoured friend, are pleasing to me, yet the one you last wrote is the most pleasing of all ; for besides its eloquence and its expressions of friendship—merits which are shared by all your letters and render them highly agreeable to me—it gave me especial satisfaction by its praise of my Commonwealth (would that it were as true as it is flattering). I asked our friend Erasmus to describe to you in conversation my views on that subject, but forbade him to urge you to read the book. Not that I did not wish you to read it—nothing would have pleased me more—but I was mindful of your wise resolution not to take into your hands any modern authors until you had finished with the ancients—a task which, measured by the profit you have derived from them, is fully accomplished, but, measured by the love you bear them, can never come to an end. I feared that when the learned works of so many other authors could not engage your attention, you would never willingly descend to my trifles. Nor would you have done so, unless you had been moved rather by your love of me than by the subject of the book. Wherefore, for having so carefully read through the *Utopia*, for having undertaken so heavy a labour for friendship's sake, I owe you the deepest gratitude ; and my gratitude is no less deep for your having found pleasure in the work. For this, too, I attribute to your friendship which has obviously influenced your judgement more

[1] Erasmus, 227.

than strict rules of criticism. However that may be, I cannot express my delight that your judgement is so favourable. For I have almost succeeded in convincing myself that you say what you think, for I know that all deceit is hateful to you, whilst you can gain no advantage by flattering me, and you love me too much to play a trick upon me. So that if you have seen the truth without any distortion, I am overjoyed at your verdict ; or if in reading you were blinded by your affection for me, I am no less delighted with your love, for vehement indeed must that love be if it can deprive a Tunstall of his judgement."

Like all More's other letters, this one testifies not only to his wit and literary style, but also to his humility and sincerity.

In another letter to Tunstall he writes as follows : " That in your letter you thank me so carefully for my services on behalf of your friends, is a mark of your great courtesy. What I did was quite trifling : it is only your goodness that exaggerates it. But you scarcely do justice to our friendship, for you seem to think that what I may do puts you under an obligation, whereas you should rather claim it as due to you and yours by right, etc. . . . The amber which you sent me—a rich and noble tomb for flies— was most acceptable on many grounds. As for the material, in colour and brightness it can challenge comparison with any precious stone, and as for the form, it is all the more excellent in that it represents a heart—a symbol of your love for me. For thus do I interpret your meaning. As the fly, winged like Cupid and as fickle as he, is so shut up and enclosed in the substance of the amber that it cannot fly away, so embalmed in the aromatic juice that it cannot perish, so your love will always remain constant and un- changed. That I have nothing to give you in return does not greatly trouble me. For I know you do not look for gifts in exchange, and moreover, I am willing to remain under an obligation to you. But yet I am somewhat dis- tressed that my capabilities are so poor, for do what I will, I must ever seem unworthy of such proofs of your friend- ship. Wherefore, since I cannot hope to win the approval of others, I must be content that you know, as well as I do myself, the depth of my affection for you."

Tunstall was the author of a very learned book upon the Real Presence of the Body and Blood of our Lord in the Eucharist. Although in the first religious troubles in England he temporised and yielded to the King's will—as, indeed, all the Bishops did at that time with the sole exception of the Bishop of Rochester—yet in every other way he constantly held and taught the orthodox Catholic faith. He lived on until the time of Elizabeth, who now reigns, and when he saw that she wanted to introduce heresy again into England, he spontaneously undertook the long journey from Durham to London, although he was an old man more than ninety years of age.[1] He had been her godfather in baptism, and now he admonished her seriously and earnestly to make no change in religion, warning her that if she dared to do so, she would forfeit God's blessing and his own. She paid no heed to his words, but placed him in confinement, where he ended his life with a noble confession of his faith, thus washing out the stain of sinful schism he had before contracted.

Foreign Friends : William Budé.

These, then, were More's literary friends in England. On the Continent there was Erasmus, whom More, in the deep sincerity of his soul, loved more than he deserved (though at that time the labours of Erasmus in the cause of literature were, indeed, highly meritorious), and besides him many other friends of the highest renown for learning. Budé was one of the chief, to whom More writes in the following terms: " I doubt, my dear Budé, whether it is advisable ever to possess what we dearly love unless we can retain possession of it. For I used to think that I would be perfectly happy if it should once be my lot to see Budé face to face, of whom by reading I had created a beautiful image in my mind. When at last my wish was fulfilled, I was happier than happiness itself. But, alas ! our duties prevented us from meeting often enough to satisfy my desire of conversing with you, and within a few days, as our kings were obliged by affairs of state to

---

[1] As Tunstall was born in 1474, he was several years short of ninety at Elizabeth's accession (see *Dictionary of National Biography*).

separate, our intercourse was broken off when it had
scarce begun ; and as each of us had to follow his own
prince, we were torn apart, perhaps never to see each other
again. My sorrow at having to leave you can only be
compared to my joy at meeting you. Yet you can assuage
my grief a little, if you will deign from time to time by letter
to make yourself present to me. This favour, however,
I would not dare to ask, if an overwhelming desire did not
urge me thereto.''

Again, in another letter to the same correspondent he
writes : '' I never skim any of your works, but study them
seriously as works of the first importance. To your treatise,
however, on Roman Measures[1] I gave a very special
attention such as I have given to no ancient author. You
have made it necessary for your readers to give a sustained
attention by your careful choice of words, your well-
balanced sentences, the studied gravity of your diction, and
not least by the serious and difficult nature of the matters
you treat of—matters almost lost in antiquity, and requiring
the deepest research. But yet if any one will turn his eyes
to what you have written and give it careful and continued
attention, he will find that the light you have thrown upon
your subject brings the dead past to life again. Whilst
he ponders your words, he will live in imagination through
all the past ages, and will be able to gaze upon, to count
and almost to take into his hands, the hoarded wealth of
all kings, all tyrants and all nations, which is more than
any misers have been able to do. I can hardly enumerate
the multitude of reasons for which I am attached to you,
my dear Budé. You are so exceedingly good to me :
whomsoever I may love, you, by good fortune, love also :
you possess so many excellent virtues : you are, as I judge,
to some extent at least, fond of me : you have earned the
gratitude of all men for your useful literary labours : though
a married man you have happily acquired a degree of
learning that was once the exclusive possession of the clergy.
Indeed I am hardly content to call you a layman when by
your many splendid gifts you are so highly raised beyond
the level of the laity.''

Budé's own opinion of More is clearly indicated in the

[1] *De Asse et Partibus ejus.*

letter we have above quoted. It contains the following sentence : " More, whose *Utopia* you have given me, is extraordinarily keen of intellect, witty and mature in his judgements upon human affairs."

MARTIN DORPIUS.

Martin Dorpius, a man of remarkable learning and piety, was another very dear friend of More. The latter writes of him to Erasmus as follows : " I cannot omit to send my greetings to Martin Dorpius, who is dear to me for his singular erudition and on many other grounds, not the least that by his criticisms on your *Moria* he gave you the occasion of writing your *Apology*."

To this Dorpius More wrote a long, learned letter on the necessity of the study of Greek, which was printed at Basle in 1563 by Episcopius (junior), together with the rest of More's minor works. Dorpius was convinced by this letter and changed his views, for he was as sincere as he was intelligent, and noted for his piety as much as for his learning. The study of Greek literature, which before he had attacked, he now publicly defended and approved. More wrote to him a second letter, giving him very high praise. This letter is somewhat long and has never yet been printed, but I will quote the eloquent words in which More couches his praise of Dorpius. " It was not difficult for me to foresee that you would one day think otherwise than then you thought. But that you would not only become wiser, but even in a most eloquent address proclaim that you had changed, openly, sincerely and straightforwardly, this indeed went far beyond my expectation, and indeed almost beyond the hopes and desires of all, for it seemed vain to look for such transparent honesty and want of affectation. Nothing indeed is more sad than that men should form varying judgements about identical problems ; but nothing is more rare than that after they have published their views, argued strongly for them and defended them against attack, they then, acknowledging the truth, should change their course, and, as if their voyage had been in vain, sail back into the port from which they came. Believe me, my dear Dorpius, what you have done with such great humility, it is almost impossible to demand even from those whom the world nowadays considers as most humble. Men are commonly so wrong-headed in their folly that they prefer to proclaim aloud that they still are fools rather than own that they ever were. How much more virtuously have you not acted, my dear Dorpius. Although you are so keen-witted, so learned and so eloquent that whatever be the thesis you may desire to defend, improbable as it may be, or even purely paradoxical, you are able to win the agreement of your readers, yet in your love of truth rather than shams you have preferred publicly to acknowledge that once you were deceived, rather than go on deceiving.

" But what am I to say of a further act of modesty which throws into the shade even that singular modesty which I have been praising ? Although it was due to the clearness and sincerity of your mind that you saw the truth, yet you chose to ascribe it to the admonitions of others, and even to mine. Thus although the first rank in wisdom is yours by right, and is given to you by common consent, yet you deliberately put yourself in the second rank. It is certainly the duty of the learned to raise you again to your rightful position. For that letter of mine was wordy rather than convincing ; and when I compare it with your address, so eloquent, so full of cogent arguments, I feel quite ashamed, my dear Dorpius, to see what little power my words could have had to win your assent, although your modesty or your courtesy leads you now to ascribe such power to them. But the praise that you seek to avoid is yours all the more surely. So, my dear Dorpius, you must understand that this act of yours, of such rare virtue, has procured for you glory of the noblest kind, which will never die."

Hence it appears that Dorpius had at first been an enemy to Greek studies, that More had composed a very careful letter to him and had shown by the strongest and clearest proofs that a knowledge of Greek was necessary to every scholar, but especially to a theologian or a philosopher, and that he had thoroughly convinced his opponent —a thing which Erasmus, who employed against the same Dorpius the weapon of sarcasm rather than solid reason, was never able to do. Yet we see in this letter how studiously More disclaims the praise that Dorpius freely accords him, and how these two men strive with each other in holy humility. The whole episode proves the zeal of Sir Thomas More in promoting both at home and abroad the study of literature and eloquence, and especially of Greek. Thus, as it had come to his knowledge that the authorities at Louvain had deprived Dorpius of his professorship because he had acknowledged the change in his views, More writes of them in the same letter in the following terms: " If they go on boldly in the path they have chosen, attempting to suppress polite literature and to drive it from the schools, in a very short time I expect to see a marvellous change. Learned men will arise everywhere. Those teachers in the public academies who now look on the study of literature with indifference will themselves be accounted but indifferently learned. It pains me, my dear Dorpius, to think of these things, because, I cannot help feeling a certain pity for those who by the action of a few bigoted partisans are undeservedly compromised. But the praise that will be your portion is a far more agreeable thought to me than the confusion that will overwhelm them."

But now let us turn to other learned friends of More. In a letter to Budé he sends greetings to John Lascaris and Philip Beroaldus. These are his words : " Please greet for me that good and learned man Lascaris. I have no doubt that you have already given my best wishes to Beroaldus, without my reminding you ; you know how dear he is to me—and deservedly so, for I have hardly ever met a more learned man or a more pleasant companion."

Of Jerome Busleyden, who founded at Louvain the College of the Three Languages and wrote to More the letter—so excellent both in form and in substance—which is prefixed to the *Utopia* in the edition of his works, More speaks thus in one of his letters to Erasmus : " Several matters in that embassy gave me great delight. First the constant company of Tunstall," etc. (we have quoted this passage earlier in the chapter). " Then I acquired the friendship of Busleyden, who received me with a magnificence worthy of his high rank " (he was at the time Ambassador and Councillor to the Emperor, and Provost of Aire), " and a courtesy in harmony with his goodness of heart. He showed me his house, so marvellously built and so splendidly furnished, a large number of antiquities in which you know I take great delight, lastly his well-filled library and the treasures of his mind, more richly stocked than any library, so that I was overwhelmed with amazement."

PETER GILES.

In the same letter he goes on to speak of another intimate friend, the learned Peter Giles, citizen and pensioner of Antwerp. " But in all my wanderings nothing was more to my wishes than my intercourse with Peter Giles of Antwerp, a man so learned, witty, modest and lovable that I declare I would willingly purchase my intimacy with him at the cost of a great part of my fortune." Of this Peter Giles he speaks thus in the beginning of the *Utopia* :

"Whiles I was abiding at Antwerp oftentimes among other, but which to me was more welcome than any other, did visit me one Peter Giles, a citizen of Antwerp, a man there in his country of honest reputation, and also preferred to high promotions, worthy truly of the highest. For it is hard to say whether the young man be in learning, or in honesty more excellent. For he is both of wonderful virtuous conditions, and also singularly well learned, and towards all sorts of people exceeding gentle : but towards his friends so kind-hearted, so loving, so faithful, so trusty, and of so earnest affection, that it were very hard in any place to find a man, that with him in all points of friendship may be compared. No man can be more lowly or courteous. No man useth less simulation or dissimulation, in no man is more prudent simplicity. Besides this, he is in his talk and communication so merry and pleasant, yea and that without harm, that through his gentle entertainment, and his sweet and delectable communication, in me was greatly abated and diminished the fervent desire, that I had to see my native country, my wife and my children, whom then I did much long and covet to see."

Such were the friends like to himself, whom More loved. Another one of his friends was Beatus Rhenanus, a most learned man, who wrote to Bilibald Pirckheimerus a letter in praise of More which is prefixed to the latter's Epigrams in his collected Latin Works. Of him More wrote in a letter to Erasmus (it is not in the latter's collected correspondence) : " I have a great affection for Rhenanus and I owe him much gratitude for his extremely kind preface. I should long ago have sent him a letter of thanks had not that fatal disease of laziness held me captive."

JOHN COCHLAEUS.

To these men must be added John Cochlaeus, the renowned adversary of Luther, who from Germany frequently interchanged letters with More. The following extract is from one of More's letters to him : " I cannot say, honoured sir, how great is my debt to you for being so kind as to keep me well informed in all that occurs in your country. For Germany now daily brings forth monsters more numerous and grotesque than Africa was wont to do. For what can be more monstrous than the Anabaptists, and how many plagues of this kind have arisen now for years together ? Indeed, my dear Cochlaeus, when I see things daily going thus from bad to worse, I expect that some one will soon stand forth and teach that we must utterly deny Christ. For such is the popular folly that no rogue, however absurd, will ever lack a following." This was no idle fancy, for soon after a Dutchman named David George announced himself to be the Christ, and had a number of followers in Basle. In Poland and Transylvania the Trinitarians spread their teaching, renewing the errors of the Arians and the Sabellians.

Again, in another letter to Cochlaeus, he writes : " I beg you, my dearest Cochlaeus, by our mutual love to believe that none of my friends' letters for many years has been so acceptable to me as that lately received from you. Of the many reasons for this I will mention the two most important ones. First, then, because I perceive in your letter your deep affection for me. It was not indeed unknown to me, but now it is more clear than ever before, and gives me the most exquisite delight. To say nothing of your deserts, who would not be proud to have gained the friendship of so renowned a man ? Second, because in your letter you have kept me informed of the doings of Princes, etc."

These letters, or rather extracts from these and other letters of More to Cochlaeus, were published by the latter at Leipzig in 1536.

FRANCIS CRANEFELD.

Amongst More's learned and famous friends, one of the most eminent was Francis Cranefeld.   He was a brilliant Latin and Greek scholar, and made excellent translations, which have survived, from the Greek into Latin of Procopius' work *On the Buildings of Justinian,* and of some writings of St Basil.   Because of his first-rate legal abilities, his wisdom, and his integrity, he was first a Pensioner of Bruges and afterwards a Councillor of the Emperor.   It was Erasmus who had introduced Cranefeld to More, and for this service Cranefeld expresses his deep gratitude in a letter to Erasmus, which is to be found in the latter's collected correspondence.[1]   It runs thus: "I cannot refrain from thanking you, most learned Sir, although my powers of expression are but poor, for the benefit you have lately conferred upon me, which will be ever remembered amongst us.   So highly do I value it that I would not exchange it for all the wealth of Croesus.   ' What benefit ?' you ask.   For introducing me to More, your most dear friend, or, as I may now call him, our friend.   At his invitation I visited him often after your departure, not to enjoy so much his more than Sybaritic banquets as his learning, his urbanity and his generosity.   Wherefore I acknowledge that I am deeply in your debt, and I hope to give you evidence of my gratitude."   And a little further on: " More has sent for my wife a gold ring on which is written in English : ' Good will gives value to all things.'   To me he has given ancient coins, one of gold and one of silver, the one having the effigy of Tiberius, the other of Augustus. I wanted to tell you this, for I will ever acknowledge that to you also I owe gratitude for all these benefits."

Such were the terms in which Cranefeld described to Erasmus his friendship with More and More's courtesy. Erasmus replied as follows : " This exemplifies the old proverb, ' One daughter has brought me two sons-in-law.' You thank me because by my help you have obtained so

[1] Erasmus, 532.

lovable a friend; and More on his side thanks me because I have helped him to know Cranefeld. I knew that with such similarity in character and taste friendship would at once be established between you if only you could get to know each other. To have such friends is a privilege as inestimable as it is rare."

Of this close and intimate friendship of Cranefeld with More Erasmus writes in a letter to More himself in which at the same time he recommends to him a new friend, Conrad Goclenius. "My dear More," he writes, "most heartily do I approve your noble sentiment that rather than in anything else you desire to grow rich in trusty and sincere friends. In this you consider life's chiefest joys to consist. Many there are whose chief care it is to avoid being deceived by false gems. But such things you despise and think yourself passing rich if another true friend is added to your treasure. Others may take their pleasure in dicing, chess, hunting or music, but to you no pleasure is comparable to a quiet conversation with a friend who is both scholarly and ingenuous. Although, then, you have so rich a store of friends, yet since an avaricious man is never satisfied, I am giving you another—as I have often done before with happy result—whom you can love wholly and unreservedly. It is Conrad Goclenius, a Westphalian, who, in the College of the Three Languages which has lately, as you know, been founded at Louvain, lectures on Latin literature, gaining praise from all and conferring inestimable benefits on the whole Academy." And again, at the end of the letter : " As soon as you know Goclenius more intimately I hope that you will both be grateful to me, as happened lately in the case of Francis Cranefeld, who has taken possession of you so fully that I am almost envious."[1]

I will add here one or two letters of More to Cranefeld which testify abundantly to the friendship that existed between them. They are extant in More's own handwriting and were most kindly lent to me by Cranefeld's son, a man of great distinction in literature, and a Licentiate in Canon and Civil Law, who is still living in Louvain. Two friends kindly procured them for me, one John Camerinus, a Doctor

[1] Erasmus, 556.

of Canon and Civil Law, president of the Donatian College
at Louvain, and a man of great authority, the other Maxi-
milian Vignacurtius, a noble of Arras, a learned youth of
blameless life.

In one of these he writes thus :

" My dear Cranefeld, I realise and acknowledge my debt
to you. You continue to do what is to me more pleasant
than anything else—*i.e.*, writing to me of your affairs and
your friends. For what to Thomas More ought to be or
could be more consoling in sorrow or joyful in prosperity
than to receive letters from Cranefeld, the most beloved
of all men, unless it were possible to enjoy his actual
presence and conversation ? Although, indeed, as often
as I read what you have written, I seem to myself to be
conversing with you face to face. Thus my greatest grief
is that your letters are not longer, although even for this
I have found some sort of a remedy. For I read them very
often and very slowly, so that rapid reading may not too
soon deprive me of my pleasure. So much for that.

" As to what you write about our friend Vives—I refer
to the discussion about ill-tempered wives—I am so far of
your opinion that I do not think it possible to live, even with
the best of wives, without some discomfort. ' If any one
is married he will not be free from care,' says Metellus
Numidicus, and rightly in my opinion. This I would say
with all the more confidence were it not that generally
we make our wives worse by our own fault. But Vives
is of such wit and prudence, and has such an excellent wife,
that he can not only escape all the troubles of married life
so far as that is possible, but even find great enjoyment
therein. But the minds of all are so fully occupied with
public affairs, now that war begins everywhere to rage so
fiercely, that no one has leisure to attend to domestic cares.
If hitherto a man has had family troubles, they are now
quite forgotten in the general calamity. But enough of
this.

" My thoughts come back to you, for as often as I call
to mind your courtesy and love towards me, as I do very
often, all my griefs vanish. I thank you for the pamphlet
which you sent me. I offer you my hearty congratulations

on the increase in your family, not only for your own sake, but also for the sake of your country, to which it is a matter of the greatest concern that parents by large families should increase the population. None but children of highest excellence can spring from such a father as you. Farewell, and give to your good wife my affectionate regards. Tell her I offer my heart-felt prayers for her health and prosperity. My wife and children send you their best wishes, for, from what I have told them, they have become as well acquainted with you and as fond of you as I am myself. Once more, good-bye.

" LONDON,
    "*August* 10, 1524."

That this friendship lasted long without interruption will be seen from another letter written four years later which I will here add. More writes thus :

" As God loves me, my dear Cranefeld, I am filled with shame when I think of your unbounded goodness to me, for so often, with so much love and care, do you send me your greetings, whilst so rarely do I salute you in return. Certainly you might excuse yourself on the score of the cares of business no less easily, and indeed no less truthfully, than I. But so blameless and constant are you that although in your friends you are ready to excuse everything, yet you yourself continue unmoved in your resolution and do nothing that demands your friends' forgiveness. But believe me, my dear Cranefeld, if anything should ever occur to make it necessary for your friends to rally round you, you will not find me wanting. As to my lady your good wife—for I do not wish to repeat the mistake I made before in the order of my salutations—please greet her and your whole family on my behalf. My family in turn sends heart-felt good wishes. Good-bye. From my little country retreat.

    "*June* 10, 1528."

ANTONIO BONVISI.

Amongst the friends of Sir Thomas More I cannot here omit Antonio Bonvisi, an Italian of the greatest worth and prudence. In circumstances in which especially friends

are tested he proved his love and fidelity towards More,
providing him with necessaries during his imprisonment
and showing him a tender care in many various ways.
There is still extant a very beautiful Latin letter which More
wrote to him with a coal a little before his death. In it
he pours out his gratitude to his faithful friend and bids
him a tender farewell. This letter is placed at the head
of More's Latin Works,[1] otherwise I would insert it here.

More was so ready to give his friendship to good and
learned men that when he was urged by Erasmus to extend
his goodwill to Germanus Brixius, who had written
Antimorus against some of his (More's) epigrams, he
replied in the following eloquent and generous terms:
" You tell me that if I knew Brixius more intimately, I
should find that no one was more worthy of my love than
he. Believe me, my dear Erasmus, I have not so lofty an
opinion of myself as to consider anyone unworthy of my
love, however lowly his estate, provided he be not a wicked
man who does not deserve to be loved by anyone. I am
quite willing to admit that he deserves the love of greater
men than myself. For I must say that he seems to me to
have a little too much, I will not say of pride, but of a lofty
and noble spirit, to suit entirely my weakness and lowliness,
unless I were willing to be as badly matched in friendship
as two oxen of different height yoked together to the
plough." And a little later : " Although Brixius attacked
me groundlessly with such violence that clearly he would
have utterly ruined me, had he had the power; yet as you,
my dear Erasmus, hold more than half of my soul in your
possession, that fact that Brixius is your friend shall weigh
more with me than that he is my enemy."[2]

Of these learned men, then, More, himself eminent in
learning, was the intimate friend. To these, both at home
and abroad, for the sake of their virtue and their scholarship,
he was bound by the closest of bonds.

Simon Grinaeus.

But what is astonishing in so fervent a Catholic and so
zealous a defender of the Catholic faith is that he honoured

[1] In the Louvain Edition of 1566 (S.).
[2] Erasmus, 555.

men of learning so highly, solely with an eye to their literary attainments, that even to heretics eminent in literature he did not refuse his favour and his good offices. At the time when he was Chancellor, Simon Grinaeus, a well-known Lutheran, came to England and presented himself to More with a letter of introduction from Erasmus recommending him as a man of learning, skilled in Greek and of the highest eminence in polite letters. How More welcomed him, Grinaeus himself shall testify. He brought out an edition of Plato's works in Greek, with some Greek commentaries of Proclus, and dedicated it to John More, the son of Sir Thomas. In the letter of dedication he writes as follows : " Your father at that time held the highest rank, but apart from that, by his many excellent qualities, he was clearly marked out as the chief man in the realm, whilst I was obscure and unknown. Yet for the love of learning in the midst of public and private business he found time to converse much with me: he, the Chancellor of the Kingdom, made me sit at his table : going to and from the Court he took me with him and kept me ever at his side. He had no difficulty in seeing that my religious opinions were on many points different from his own, but his goodness and courtesy were unchanged. Though he differed so much from my views, yet he helped us in word and in deed and carried through my business at his own expense. He gave us a young man, of considerable literary attainments, John Harris, to accompany us on our journey, and to the authorities of the University of Oxford he sent a letter couched in such terms that at once not only were the libraries of all the Colleges thrown open to us, but the students, as if they had been touched by the rod of Mercury, showed us the greatest favour. Accordingly I searched all the libraries of the University, some twenty in number. They are all richly stocked with very ancient books, and with the permission of the authorities I took away several books of the commentaries of Proclus—as many perhaps as could be set up in print within a year or two. I returned to my country overjoyed at the treasures I had discovered, laden with your father's generous gifts and almost overwhelmed by his kindness."

Such was More's courtesy to scholars, such his esteem for

learning, such his favours and keen interest in the cause of letters.   To this kindliness of More scholars owe the Greek commentaries of Proclus and the emended text of Plato. For as his own store of learning was exceedingly large, so did he love learning in others.

But he was very far from showing any favour to the errors of Grinaeus.   At that time he was Chancellor of the realm, and in that office opposed an active resistance to heresy, as he was bound to do.   A proof of this is the long controversy with this same Grinaeus which More began at his home and afterwards continued by correspondence, in which he sought to wean him from his grievous heresies. (I have seen an account of this controversy written out in English by More, but it is imperfect.)   Moreover, under colour of courtesy and honour More kept Grinaeus all the time he was in England under guard and constant observation.   He never allowed him to leave his side or the company of John Harris so long as he was in England, and he took the greatest care, warning him most strictly, that he should never utter to anyone a single word on religion.

I will close this chapter by quoting Erasmus' description of More's amiability and sweetness of character in his letter to Ulrich von Hutten.   " He seems born and framed for friendship and is a most loyal and faithful friend.   Nor does he fear the large circle of friends of which Hesiod disapproves.   He is easy of access to all.   He is not slow to give his affection, he is studious to foster a friendship and constant in keeping it.   If he chances to get familiar with anyone whose views he cannot correct, he manages to loosen and let go the intimacy rather than break it off suddenly.   When he finds any sincere and according to his heart, he so delights in their society and conversation as to place in it the principal charm of life.   Though he is somewhat careless about his own affairs, no one could be more diligent in the affairs of others.   In a word, if anyone wishes to have a perfect model of true friendship, he cannot do better than look at More.   In society he is so polite, so sweet-mannered, that no one is of so melancholy a disposition as not to be cheered by him, and there is no misfortune that he does not alleviate." [1]

[1] Erasmus, 447.

CHAPTER VI

HIS HOLINESS OF LIFE

SO far we have described Thomas More as a good citizen and a learned man. But a Cato or a Cicero might thus be described. In order, then, that the reader may realise that More was a great man in every respect, that he was no less remarkable for his solid piety than for his learning and professional abilities, we will speak now of his virtues, his religion, his charity, his humility, his simplicity of life, and other qualities proper to a Christian, in so far as the particulars permit that hitherto have come to our knowledge, and in so far as those who were intimate with him were able to observe. For if there are some virtues whose acts must appear outwardly and therefore can hardly be hidden, there are others that cannot be observed without the greatest difficulty.

MORE'S CLEVER LITERARY FICTIONS.

More was as clever in hiding his virtues as he was in feigning the circumstances in which his books were written. His *Utopia*, for instance, is introduced so naturally and in circumstances so aptly conceived and so probable that it deceived many of the cleverest, who thought they were reading what More had actually heard, and not a work of pure imagination. To this end serve the Introduction, and the Preface of Peter Giles, who, consenting to More's fiction and taking the place assigned to him, played his part very craftily. The artifice is not too difficult to detect, but the reader is beguiled, as Paul Jovius says, " by a pleasing romance." With equal cleverness he introduces Ross as travelling in Italy and, at the instigation of his host, replying to Luther. Without Ross's knowledge, his reply is then published by his questioner. Indeed, during More's lifetime no one had any suspicion that Ross was not the author of the book. Luther was extremely annoyed at finding himself so severely castigated, without knowing whom he might attack in return. With no less skill he pretends that his book *A Dialogue of Comfort against Tribulation* was written in Hungary in the vernacular, translated into Latin, and again from the Latin into English. His references to Henry's cruelty, to the disturbances in England, to the fear and expectation of the spread of heresy there, to what comfort the good may have in view of such evils, present or to come, are all disguised cleverly and naturally in the person of a Hungarian who speaks of the cruelty of the Turkish Emperor, the unrest in Hungary, and the fear of future evils, so that you would be convinced that a Hungarian is speaking of his own land and not More of England. But as in artifices of this nature he was resourceful, and indeed a past master, so he took the greatest pains to hide, as far as possible, his virtues from public view. Although living in the gaze of the public and filling many posts in the State, yet he was not known by men for what he really was, and even from those who lived with him under the same roof he was able to hide much. But what was obvious and what his family and his friends could observe, we will relate exactly as it has come from their lips.

Love of the Mass.

First, then, as regards the service of God, he lived almost the life of a monk. Every day before all other business, except sometimes his morning studies, he heard Mass. This self-imposed daily obligation he fulfilled so strictly, that once when hearing Mass he was summoned by the King, even two or three times, but refused to leave before it was finished. To those who urged him to come away from the Mass and to attend upon the King, he replied that he must first finish his act of homage to a higher King.

Example of St Ludger.

I am hereby reminded of a similar act of piety on the part of St Ludger, the first Bishop of Münster, and I am sure my readers will pardon the digression. He was once summoned by the Emperor Charlemagne to the Court.

He arrived one evening, and very early next morning he was sent for by a chamberlain. He was at the time chanting the Canonical Hours with his followers, and replied that he would come when they were finished. His message was taken back to the Emperor, who summoned him a second and even a third time. But the Bishop, considering that the service of God was to be preferred to all things else, delayed to come until all the Psalms were ended. When at length he appeared in the Emperor's presence, he was asked why he had despised his sovereign's command. Fearless in his gaze and yet more fearless in his heart, he answered: " The obedience that I have ever given to you, Sire, is conditioned by the higher obedience I owe to God. It was not, therefore, through contempt of your Imperial Majesty, but for the sake of your salvation that I was solicitous first to complete my duty to God." Delighted with this answer the Emperor replied: "My Lord Bishop, I thank you, for I find you now such as I have always believed you to be."[1] Neither did More's devotion, all the more to be admired in a layman, in any way displease Henry, who was at that time a pious and God-fearing King.

His Devout Prayers.

But to go on, he recited each day morning and evening prayers, to which he added the Seven Penitential Psalms and the Litanies. Often, too, he said in addition the Gradual Psalms and the *Beati Immaculati*.[2] He had also certain private prayers, some in Latin and some in the vernacular, which are to be found in his collected English Works. Following the example of St Jerome and others, he selected certain Psalms of which he made, so to say, a Psalter or compendium of the Psalms. This he used constantly, and it is to be found with the prayers just mentioned. In his fervent zeal for prayer he built at his home, in a remote part of the building,[3] an oratory where he could

---

[1] Surius, *Mart.* 26, cap. 32 (S.).

[2] The 118th Psalm, by far the longest of all, consisting of 176 verses.

[3] The more natural interpretation of Stapleton's words both here and in Chapter IX is that the " New Building " adjoined the main building, but Roper's testimony is decisive that it was " a good distance from his manor house."

enjoy solitude and give himself to study, prayer and meditation. Whenever he returned from the Court he used at once to go there, and, so to say, shaking off the dust of Court affairs, give himself up to complete recollection.

A MODEL PARISHIONER.

In his parish church in the village of Chelsea he also built a chapel[1] and furnished it abundantly with all things necessary for Divine Worship and with all suitable ornament and decoration. He was ever very liberal in gifts of this nature, bestowing much gold and silver plate upon his church. He used to say : " The good give, the wicked take away." He was accustomed to put on a surplice and chant the responses with his priest in the parish church, even when he was Lord Chancellor. Once the Duke of Norfolk came upon him when he was so employed and warned him that the King would certainly be displeased at such a proceeding as too lowly, and as unbefitting the high position he held. He replied : " It cannot be displeasing to my lord the King that I pay my homage to my King's Lord." Often he used to serve Mass for the priest, taking the place of the clerk.[2] Sometimes in the parochial processions he would carry the Cross before the priest. Far from refusing or being ashamed to perform the duty of a common clerk or verger, he took the greatest delight therein, joining as it were with David as he danced before the Ark of the Lord and said : " I will make myself meaner than I have done, and I will be little in my own eyes."[3] This he did regularly except when he was Lord Chancellor. While he held that dignity he was urged by his friends, on account of his high office, to ride on a horse in the tiring processions of the Rogation Days in which often a long distance is traversed and there is much walking to be done. He answered : " I will not follow on horseback my Lord, who goes on foot." This was said with reference to the Crucifix in which he venerated his Lord.

Although for some years he was the busiest of men, yet once he had gone into church he never allowed in that

---

[1] " Sacellum," *i.e.*, the south aisle.
[2] " Idiota."   [3] 2 Kings vi 22.

sacred place any single word of worldly affairs to be uttered. As often as he entered upon any new office, or undertook any business of difficulty, he used to fortify himself with Holy Communion. Sometimes he used to go on pilgrimages to shrines distant as much as seven miles from his home, and always on foot, a thing which even the labouring classes will scarcely do.

ZEAL IN WRITING AGAINST HERETICS.

It was from his deep religious sentiment that flowed the ardent zeal which animated him for the defence and the exposition of the Catholic faith against the heretics. He, unaided, did more in this field of labour than all the English clergy of that time together. Layman though he was, and constantly busied with affairs of State, he yet made time for this work ; and although he was so high in honour, he did not disdain the ungrateful task. We have already shown[1] how numerous and valuable were his writings in defence of the faith, how learned, how convincing, how eloquent—and he has hardly a rival for eloquence amongst English writers. When the heretics found themselves so powerfully attacked by him, they basely spread about the report that he had been hired by the clergy for the purpose in return for large sums of money. What he answered will be related in its proper place.[2] A letter of his to John Cochlaeus bears witness to his heart-felt zeal. " I only wish," he writes, " that I had such a knowledge of Holy Scripture and theological matters as would enable me to write to some purpose against those pests." Of More's zeal Erasmus, too, speaks in one of his letters. " He hates the criminal doctrines," he writes, " by which the world is now miserably troubled. So attached is he to piety that he does not hesitate to say that if he had to move in one direction or another, it would be towards superstition rather than towards impiety."[3]

[1] See Chapter IV.
[2] See Chapter VIII.
[3] Letter to John Faber, Bp. of Vienna, Appendix, 426.

Conversion of William Roper.

From his love of God was derived the efficacy of his prayers. His holy prayers were very powerful with God. " For the continual prayer of a just man availeth much,"[1] prayer that is ever busily active and energising. We will now give some examples. More's son-in-law, William Roper, who married Margaret, More's eldest daughter, fell for a time into heresy. More endeavoured to reclaim him by frequent earnest expostulations. But when he saw that his words were fruitless, " Henceforth," he said, " I will not argue with you, but will pray to God for you." A few days afterwards Roper of his own accord told More that he now detested the heresies he had embraced, as by the grace of God he now saw the light of the truth and believed in it. In after years Roper was renowned for his zeal for the faith. He was a most fervent Catholic to the very end of a long life, and a constant and generous benefactor to Catholics imprisoned in England or in exile abroad. A few years ago he fell asleep peacefully in the Lord.

Recovery of his Daughter Margaret.

Margaret, More's daughter, once had a most severe attack of the sweating sickness. In such a sickness the only hope of life lies in a free flow of perspiration, but in this case, through her own carelessness or the negligence of those around her, the flow was hindered, and finally ceased altogether, so that the whole poison of the disease was retained in the body and she became delirious. Her father was in the greatest distress, for he loved her beyond all his other children. He asked the doctor whether a clyster would be of any use, and as the doctor thought it could do no harm, although the chance of its doing any good was very remote, it was tried. More, meanwhile, betook himself to prayer, and the remedy proved successful. She recovered her senses, perspiration again flowed freely, and over her whole body appeared spots[2] which in others are certain signs of

[1] Jas. v 16.

[2] Stapleton says that the spots are called " ronchae "—a word I have failed to trace elsewhere. Cresacre More says, " God's marks (an evident and undoubted token of death) plainly appeared upon her " (Life, p. 137).

approaching death or appear after death, but in her were signs of recovery. This wonderful cure was, as the doctor himself asserted, due to her father's prayers rather than to medical skill.

ELIZABETH DAUNCY'S VISION.

More's second daughter, Elizabeth, who was married to John Dauncy, during her last illness became unconscious for a considerable time before death. Coming again to herself she explained with tears and sighs that while out of the body she had suffered most grievous punishments, and if the prayers of her father had not obtained pardon for her she would have had to suffer them for ever. This happened after More's martyrdom.

STORY OF THE CITIZEN OF WINCHESTER.

The following incident is especially remarkable as showing More's sanctity and the efficacy of his prayers. A certain citizen of Winchester was for a long time so troubled by the gravest temptations to despair that prayer and the advice of his friends seemed of no avail. At length by a friend he was brought to see More, who, pitying the man's misery, gave him good and prudent counsel. It was not by his words, however, but by his prayers to God that More at length obtained for the man relief from his grievous temptation. The man remained free from his distress so long as More was at liberty and he had access to him. But when More was imprisoned the temptation returned with still greater force than before. The unhappy man, so long as More was in the Tower, spent his days in misery without hope of cure. But when he heard that More was condemned to death he went up to London in order that, at whatever risk to himself, he might speak to him as he was going out to execution. On More's way, then, from the Tower to the scaffold he burst through the guards and cried out with a loud voice: "Do you recognise me, Sir Thomas? Help me, I beg you: for that temptation has returned to me and I cannot get rid of it." More at once answered: " I recognise you perfectly. Go and pray for me, and I will pray earnestly for you." He went away, and never again in his whole life was he troubled with such temptations. Such was the power of More's intercession.

Whenever any woman, in his house or in the neighbourhood, was labouring in childbirth, he would always give himself to prayer and continue until he received tidings of a safe delivery.

More's Reverence for the Lord's Day.

His reverence for the feasts of the Church was so great that even when he was in solitary confinement he was always careful to have his best clothes brought to him on all the feast days. When wonder was expressed at his acting thus when he was alone, he replied that he did it not to be seen by men, but for the glory of God.

These are the details we have been able to gather concerning his truly Christian piety.

His Charity to the Poor.

To his charity towards his neighbour, his constant generous almsgiving bears witness. He used personally to go into dark courts and visit the families of the poor, helping them not with small gifts but with two, three, or four pieces of gold, as their need required. Afterwards, when his dignity as Chancellor forbade him to act thus, he used to send some of his household who would dispense his gifts faithfully to needy families, and especially to the sick and the aged. This task was often laid upon Margaret Gigs, the wife of John Clements, whom More had brought up with his own daughters. The chief festivals of the year were his favourite times for sending such gifts. Very often he invited his poorer neighbours to his table, receiving them graciously and familiarly. The rich were rarely invited, the nobility hardly ever. Moreover, in his parish, Chelsea, he hired a house in which he placed many who were infirm, poor, or old, providing for them at his own expense. In her father's absence, Margaret Roper took charge of these. One poor widow, named Paula, who had spent all her money in litigation, he took into his own family and supported. Whenever he undertook the causes of widows and orphans, his services were always given gratuitously.

His Love of all Men.

Christ gave a sure test of a true Christian when he said : " By this shall all men know that you are my disciples, if you have love one for another."[1] Accordingly, in order that he might exclude no one from true Christian charity, More drew up for himself a remarkable argument, clear and evident in its reasoning, which for the common good of my readers I will here transcribe. He wrote it with a coal in prison. I think it worthy to be written in letters of gold.

" Bear no malice nor evil will to no man living. For either that man is good or naught. If he be good, and I hate him, then am I naught. If he be naught, either he shall amend and die good and go to God, or abide naught and die naught, and go to the devil. And then let me remember that, if he shall be saved, he shall not fail, if I be saved too, as I trust to be, to love me very heartily, and I shall then in likewise love him. And why should I now, then, hate one for this while, which shall hereafter love me for evermore ? And why should I be now, then, enemy to him, with whom I shall in time coming be coupled in eternal friendship ? Or, on the other side, if he shall continue naught and be damned, then is there so outrageous eternal sorrow towards him,[2] that I may well think myself a deadly cruel wretch if I would not now rather pity his pain than malign his person. If one would say that we may well, with good conscience, wish an evil man harm, lest he should do harm to such other folk as are innocent and good, I will not now dispute upon that point, for that root hath more branches to be well weighed and considered, than I can now conveniently write, having none other pen than a coal. But verily thus will I say, that I will give counsel to every good friend of mine, but[3] if he be put in such room, as to punish an evil man lieth in his charge by reason of his office, else leave the desire of

---

[1] John xiii 35.   [2] *i.e.*, to come upon him.
[3] *i.e.*, unless.

punishing unto God, and unto such other folk as are so grounded in charity, and so fast cleave to God, that no secret, shrewd, cruel affection, under the cloak of a just and virtuous zeal, can creep in and undermine them. But let us that are no better than men of a mean sort ever pray for such merciful amendment in other folk, as our own conscience showeth us that we have need in our self."[1]

Words such as these testify not less to More's holiness than to his wisdom, his constant patience and humility. Remarkable, then, was More's love of God and his neighbour.

Food and Clothing.

A few words will suffice to describe the care he gave to his body. He partook only of one dish at table, generally beef, of which he was fond, although for the sake of his position and for his family other dishes were on the table. But he satisfied himself with whatever kind of food first offered itself. As a young man he abstained altogether from wine for a long time, and as an old man he took it only when diluted with water, as Erasmus remarks in his letter to Ulrich von Hutten.[2] He paid little attention to his clothing. He wore silk, indeed, when his official position demanded it : otherwise he wore the simplest garments and thought so little about the matter that he would always wear the same clothes unless his servant reminded him. For he had among his servants one, whom he called his tutor, whose duty it was to buy him boots, shoes, and other necessary things. Once it happened that he went out with badly torn boots. His secretary, Harris, remonstrated with him. "Ask my tutor to buy me a new pair," was his only reply. In short, as to what regarded the body, this man in his deep holiness wished, like a monk, to be under the authority of others and to obey their commands, either that his mind—noble and lofty as it was—might not be disturbed by such trivial details, or, as I prefer to think, that he might exercise the fundamental Christian virtue of humility. For this reason, although he was a man of the soundest judgement, in many points of business or of study he would ask the advice of

---

[1] E.W., p. 1405.　　　　[2] Erasmus, 447.

Harris, his amanuensis, and beg him to warn him of any mistake he might make. Harris was, indeed, a man of ability and sound judgement, deeply attached to More and even more faithful than an Achates.

PENITENTIAL EXERCISES.

That More was not simply a good Christian, but a deeply religious man, is shown by the fact that throughout his whole life on certain days and at certain times he wore a hair-shirt and took the discipline. These days were Fridays, the vigils of the saints, and the Ember Days. Often under his Chancellor's robes his body was clothed in a hair-shirt. The day before his death, or rather his passion, he sent to his daughter Margaret his hair-shirt and discipline, with a short letter written with a coal, which we shall give in its place.[1] The conflict now being over, he laid down his arms and sent back his weapons. It was in the little oratory of which we have spoken above that he took the discipline, for a long time, indeed, so secretly that no one, not even his wife, knew it. Afterwards, through the pious curiosity of some of his family, the thing became known, but only to a very few of those who lived with him. More than twenty years ago Margaret, the wife of Dr. Clements, showed me the holy man's hair-shirt when I was at Bergen near Antwerp on a visit to my father of pious memory, Dr. Clements himself, and other Englishmen who had taken up their abode and were bringing up their families in that town. The hair-shirt was knotty, like a net, much rougher, I should think, than are commonly the hair-shirts of religious. His discipline, through some negligence, had been lost.

We have described, then, his love of God and his neighbour, his temperance, frugality, and mortification. So did he " live soberly, justly and godly in this world."[2] So did he mortify his earthly members, " bearing about in his body the mortification of Jesus Christ."[3]

But this will be made yet more clear when we shall have to speak of some of his virtues more in detail, and when we shall show what a model father he was to his children and household.

[1] See Chapter XIX.   [2] Titus ii 2.   [3] 2 Cor. iv 10.

CHAPTER VII

HIS CONTEMPT OF HONOURS AND REPUTATION

IN order to understand still better the true piety and solid virtue of Thomas More, and the nobility of his mind, we will now consider the value he placed on what the world most admires. For certainly he had abundant opportunities to obtain what others in their folly love and desire. He was in the King's Court : his honours were many: he was a man of wide learning: he wrote many books : his achievements brought him high praise. If he did not become rich, he certainly could have done so. His intellect was keen, his memory extraordinary. Nature, good fortune, and his own diligence combined, it is difficult to decide in what proportion, to raise him to eminence. It is not only easy but it is customary for advantages of this nature to taint the soul, to coarsen it, to entice it to vanity. But, as will appear, Thomas More was so strong in spirit, so filled with divine grace, that none of these things had power to weaken him or to turn him away ever so little from a true knowledge of God and of himself. He never failed to recognise that all his gifts came from God, that he himself was no whit the better or the greater for them. Ever grounded in humility and self-contempt—the true Christian philosophy of life—he had no desire for honours and wealth, and when they came he lost none of the piety which had characterised his earlier life.

MORE's DISLIKE OF COURT LIFE.

Though not of high station, he was summoned to Court and made a member of the King's Council, and such a one that Queen Catharine, Henry's first wife, a woman of great prudence and piety, used to say often to the King that of all his councillors More alone was worthy of the position and the name. Nevertheless, he judged himself to be quite unfitted to that mode of life and, in fact, loathed the life of the Court, which so many foolish men long for so ardently. Once the Bishop of Rochester congratulated him on his position at Court, the influence he had with the King and the King's trust in him, which, indeed, was the fullest, as the succession of honours that fell to his lot shows. He answered in these words : " It was with the greatest unwillingness that I came to Court, as everyone knows, and as the King himself in joke often throws up in my face. I am as uncomfortable there as a bad rider is in the saddle. I am far from enjoying the special favour of the King, but he is so courteous and kindly to all that everyone who is in any way hopeful finds a ground for imagining that he is in the King's good graces; like the London wives who, as they pray before the image of the Virgin Mother of God which stands near the Tower, gaze upon it so fixedly that they imagine it smiles upon them. But I am not so happy as to perceive signs of favour or so hopeful as to imagine them. But the King has virtue and learning, and makes great progress in both with daily renewed zeal, so that the more I see His Majesty advance in all the qualities that befit a good monarch, the less burdensome do I feel this life of the Court."

Although, then, life at Court was not in itself attractive to More, yet he took some little pleasure in it in so far as it was a school of goodness and piety, as it certainly was during the first twenty years of Henry's reign. On this subject Erasmus, in a latter to Henry Guildford, wrote as follows : " The high reputation for virtue that the English Court continues to enjoy, possessing as it does, besides a King richly endowed with all the qualities of a perfect monarch, and a Queen worthy of him, so many men of unimpeachable character, of learning and of piety, has moved the Prince of Bergen to send his son Anthony to no other school " (A.D. 1519).[1]

---

[1] Erasmus, 475.

RESIGNATION OF THE GREAT SEAL.

But when its character began to change and lust began
to rule in place of virtue, then More left the Court, resigning
the high office he held. After he had held the post of
Lord Chancellor for two years and a half—as our annals
bear witness—he grew utterly tired of the Court and its
life. He had never loved it : he began now to hate it.
With the greatest difficulty he obtained leave from the
King to resign his high dignity and to be freed from the
servitude of the Court. When his desire was granted he
regarded it as an incomparably great benefit. We have
already spoken of his resignation, amid the praises of all,
of the office which he had held. Now we will show how
joyfully and with what purpose he gave it up, and how
convincing a testimony his resignation was to his virtue.
As to the former, he writes thus to Erasmus : " Almost
from boyhood, my darling Desiderius, up to the present
day I have ever longed to be free from public business
so that at length I might have an opportunity to live to
God and to myself. By the goodness of Almighty God
and by the favour of an indulgent Prince I have at last
obtained this boon." After some particulars as to his bad
health on account of an affection of the chest, he resumes :
" I turned all these matters over in my mind and saw that
either I would have to lay down my office or fail in the
due performance of its duties. I could not carry out
all the tasks my position imposed on me without endanger-
ing my life, and if I were to die I should have to give up
my office as well as my life. At length, I determined to
give up one rather than both. Wherefore, for the benefit
both of public business and my own health, I humbly
appealed, and not in vain, to the goodness of my noble
and excellent Prince. His exceeding great favour to me,
far above my deserts and beyond all my hopes and desires,
had honoured me with the highest dignity in the whole
kingdom (as you know), but now that I grew weary under
the burden his kindness was pleased to relieve me. I
ask the prayers of all the saints that God, who alone can
do so, will by his grace reward worthily the most indulgent
affection of my noble Sovereign towards me ; that whatever

space of time is left to me may not be passed in idle and inglorious ease, but be used profitably, and that I may as far as possible regain my bodily health."[1]

In the same sentiments he wrote at the time to John Cochlaeus : " Although my looks have not pitied me, yet my health for some months past has caused me anxiety. Even now I cannot shake off my indisposition, although I have succeeded in freeing myself from all my public offices. I could not, therefore, give due attention to my duties as Chancellor without allowing my health to become daily more impaired. Thus I was influenced by a desire to gain a restoration to health. But still more was I concerned for the public weal, for I saw there would be much inconvenience if the derangement of my health were to bring about a derangement of public business. The leisure which the kind favour of my noble Prince has graciously granted at my petition, I intend to devote to study and prayer."

Again, in the epitaph which he composed for himself after his resignation and had erected in his parish church, he uses the following words :

" He, therefore, irked and weary of worldly business, giving up his promotions, obtained at last by the incomparable benefit of his most gentle Prince, if it please God to favour his enterprise, the thing which from a child in a manner always he wished and desired : that he might have some years of his life free, in which he little and little withdrawing himself from the business of this life, might continually remember the immortality of the life to come."[2]

HIS REASONS FOR RESIGNATION.

More wrote this himself, and of course it is most true. Yet those who were at the time most intimate with him assert that these were not the sole nor the principal reasons why he resigned all his honours and begged permission to retire from Court. The King, who had already married Anne Boleyn, not only against the counsel of More, as we shall see later, but even in defiance of the Apostolic See, began to be changed into another man. For having

[1] Erasmus, 1223.　　　　[2] Rastell's translation.

once thrown off the restraints of shame and honour, he cast himself headlong into every kind of lust and evil desire. When the King despised the supreme authority of the Holy See and determined to have his own way and give play to his lust, More saw very clearly that in other matters too the King would in the future follow his own will and desires even against the advice of his whole Council or of Parliament. Far-seeing as he was, he knew that for the future he could not please the King without offending his Creator. He knew that contempt of the Apostolic See would lead to schism and heresy, and that even in his position of Chancellor he would not be able to remedy the evil under such a King. In a word, he saw that his conscience could no longer conform to the King's will. He preferred, then, to forfeit his honours rather than his honour. Lastly, he longed to have leisure for prayer, self-knowledge, and study, especially that he might launch out in full battle array against the heretics with whom he had already had many skirmishes. These were the true and the principal causes, as he explained them to his friends. For as to his health, it was not bad enough to hinder him from spending the whole year that intervened before his imprisonment in publishing the numerous lengthy works against the heretics which we have above mentioned. Nor was his age so advanced that he was unfit for further charges, for he was not yet fifty. It was a little more than two years afterwards that he suffered, and then he had not completed his fifty-second year.[1] In truth, wishing as ever to hide his virtues, he attributed to necessity what really was the free choice of his conscience. He wished to leave the Court without offending the King and without seeking for the praises of men. That the chief motive of his resignation was that he foresaw calamities for the country which he could in no wise hinder, is evident from several conversations of his that have been reported.

His Remarkable Foresight.

One day during his tenure of office his son-in-law Roper, in whom especially he used to confide, was praising the

[1] He was fifty-four in 1532 and fifty-seven at his death.

flourishing state of affairs in England. The country was wealthy: the King was beloved at home and abroad. But More was in no way deceived by the aspect of affairs, and answered that however happily things were proceeding at the moment, it was necessary to pray earnestly that the King might not be soon changed for the worse and have councillors weak enough to abet him in evil.

On another occasion when More happened to be walking with Roper along the bank of the Thames, Roper was thanking God for the purity of the faith and for the zeal of the King in upholding it, adding that scarcely ever had divine worship, devout prayer, and purity of life been held in such high honour in England as at that time. More answered : " It is now indeed as you say, my son ; but a time will soon come when you will see all this zeal for religion, together with us and others who cultivate it, brought into contempt and despised, and made of no more account than we make of these poor little ants." As he spoke he scattered with his foot an ant-hill that he happened to see by the way.

One day, returning from the Court, he found his daughters and grandchildren devoutly praying. " Pray earnestly now, my children," he said, " while prayer is sweet and easy to you, for it will very soon come to pass —and you will need the very greatest fortitude if you would stand firm—that nothing will seem more despicable than love of prayer." Every Englishman knows how exactly his words have been realised for many years past.

The marriage of Anne Boleyn took place after his resignation, and while he was living a private life, for in his official capacity he would never approve of it. A friend of his was one day telling him that she was leading a life of continual pleasure at Court, with dances day and night, and that nothing could be more gay than life now was there. More replied: " These dances of Anne Boleyn are bringing with them another game of quite a different kind. Her dances are playing with our heads like footballs, but the same game will be played with her own head."

The event very soon showed the truth of this prediction. For, as we shall hereafter more fully show, by Anne's instigation many good men were beheaded, notably John

Fisher, Bishop of Rochester, and Thomas More himself (for Henry VIII, like another Herod, was enchanted by her dancing); but Anne herself suffered a like death, though for a very different cause.

As, then, it was for such good motives that More resigned his high honours, it is clear that he was in no way puffed up by them or carried away by any vain desire for power and influence. He proved the truth of what Erasmus wrote to John More, his son, while his father was still in office. "It is due to philosophy that your father's high honours have in no wise elated him, and that the continual stress of business has not made him in any way less courteous."[1] For one whom high honours have made haughty or supercilious, or have filled with vainglory, would prefer to throw virtue to the winds rather than fall from his dignity. To resign it would never enter his mind. More, then, obtained from Henry what Cassiodorus long ago obtained from his prince, that he might renounce all titles of honour and give himself entirely to fruitful study and prayer.

More praises Warham's Resignation.

But More's heroic deed can be praised worthily only in the words of More himself, the wise, the learned, the eloquent. We will, therefore, give his words. We do not mean that he praised his own act, for what would be a greater proof of vanity than that? But he praised the resignation of another Chancellor, and afterwards, by imitating it, praised it still more. Not so long before, Warham, Archbishop of Canterbury, obtained leave from the King to resign his office as Chancellor. After him followed Wolsey, Archbishop of York, and after him More. Of Warham's act More thus writes:

"I ever judged your paternity happy in the way you exercised your office of Chancellor, but I esteem you much happier now that you have laid it down and entered on that most desirable leisure, in which you can live for yourself and for God. Such leisure, in my opinion, is not only more pleasant than the labour you have forsaken, but more

---

[1] In the letter of dedication to John More which Erasmus prefixed to his Greek edition of Aristotle. (See Chapter X.)

honourable than all your honours.   To be a judge is the lot of many, and sometimes of very bad men.   But you possessed that supreme office which, when relinquished, is as much exposed to calumny as it formerly conferred authority and independence ; and to give up this willingly is what none but a moderate-minded man would care, and none but an innocent man dare, to do.

" I do not know which to admire the most, your modesty in willingly laying down an office of such dignity and power, your unworldliness in being able to despise it, or your integrity in having no fear of resignation ; but together with many other men I give to your act my most cordial approval as certainly most excellent and wise.   Indeed I can hardly say how heartily I congratulate you on your singular good fortune and how I rejoice in it for your sake, for I see your paternity retiring far away from the affairs of the world and the bustle of the courts, raised to a rare eminence of fame both on account of the honourable manner in which you have held your office and the honourable way in which you have resigned it.   Happy in the consciousness of duty well done, you will pass your time gently and peacefully in literature and philosophy.   Whilst daily I appreciate more and more the happiness of your lot, I realise my own misery ; for although I have no business worth mentioning " (yet he was at this time a member of the Royal Council, Under-Treasurer of the realm, and often employed in legations), " yet my attention is fully occupied, for poor talents find even trivial things as much as they can manage.   I have so little free time that I can rarely visit your paternity or excuse my remissness in writing —indeed I have scarcely been able to get ready this present letter.

" Herewith I would beg your grace to accept a little book " (the *Utopia*).   " It was written in undue haste, and I fear it is lacking in wit, but a friend of mine, a citizen of Antwerp (Peter Giles) allowed his affection to outweigh his judgement, thought it worthy of publication and without my knowledge had it printed.   Although I know it is unworthy of your high rank, your wide experience and your learning, yet I venture to send it, relying on the ready kindness with which you welcome all works of fancy, and trusting to the favour I have always experienced from you. Thus I hope that even if the book pleases you but little, yet your good-will may be extended to the author.   Farewell, my Lord Archbishop."

In these words, then, did More praise the Archbishop's noble act.   But as he sincerely admired and diligently praised the virtues of others, so was he careful to imitate them.   All the praise, then, that he duly gave to Warham's act must be credited to himself.   No one but a humble man would care to act as More did, no one but a man of integrity would dare to.   It is difficult to decide which was most admirable, his modesty in laying aside his honours, his magnanimity in despising them, or his integrity in not fearing to resign.   In every way he was worthy of the highest praise.   In a word, both in his tenure of office and in his resignation he gained fame that has hardly a parallel.

More goes on Embassies.

But to pass on, he was engaged in many important embassies.   Often did he go to France to draw up treaties or to claim property.   He accompanied Henry to France when that King and Francis I of France visited each other at Ardres.[1]   It was there that More had the pleasure of meeting his friend Budé, as is mentioned in the extract from his letter to Budé, which we have given above.   Twice he went on missions to Flanders with great state, in company with Cuthbert Tunstall.   But though others might be dazzled by the splendour of these embassies, they were quite out of harmony with More's modest and humble disposition.   We quote from another letter to Erasmus : " You would hardly believe how unwilling I am to be involved in all these negotiations of princes : nothing could be more distasteful to me than this legation."   And in another letter to the same : " The work of an ambassador has never had much attraction for me."[2]   And again in an unprinted letter to Tunstall : " What possible gain is it to me to be employed in embassies, for although my

---

[1] " The Field of the Cloth of Gold," 1520.
[2] Erasmus, 540 and 227.

Prince is generously inclined towards me, yet far from seeking advancement at Court I turn away from it with loathing?"

HIS LITERARY MODESTY.

As to his *Utopia*, we have already seen what praise it deservedly won from all the learned. Yet he did not want it to be published, but only to be shown to a few friends as an amusing fiction. It was afterwards printed, but of this action he never approved. I have already mentioned what he wrote to his friend Tunstall on the subject. He ascribes it to personal affection that Tunstall should read and approve of his trifles, as he calls the *Utopia*. In another unpublished letter to a scholar who had praised the book he writes: " I cannot help feeling that the opinion you have of me arises from your affection rather than your judgement. For when love takes deep root in a soul it generally casts a shadow over men's thoughts. This I see has happened to you, especially as it is my *Utopia* that has given you such great pleasure. For my view of the book is that it is worthy only to remain as unknown as the island itself." This letter was written to a correspondent called " Anthony." No surname is given, and I will not hazard a guess, although I could. And in yet another letter to a man who held a high position at Court, but whose name is unknown, he thus writes: " I had it in mind to espouse *Utopia* my to Cardinal Wolsey alone (if my friend Peter had not, without my knowledge, as you know, tarnished the brightness of her virginity), if indeed I would have espoused her to anyone and not rather kept her always with me in single blessedness, or perhaps consecrated her to Vesta and consumed her in the goddess' sacred fires." So poorly did he think of that work which the whole world admires.

Anyone who reads his works which we have mentioned, or his letters from which we have quoted and will often quote, will certainly not deny his powers of expression and the elegance of his style. Yet with his customary modesty he constantly bewails his lack of eloquence. In the letter to Peter Giles, prefixed to the *Utopia*, he writes : " But if it were requisite or necessary that the matter should also have been written eloquently, and not alone truly, of a surety that thing could I have performed by no time nor study." And yet in truth, not only was the subject of the book clearly conceived, but also developed with the greatest eloquence.

In an unprinted letter to Budé, he writes as follows: " If it were not for the vehemence of my desires, I would not dare to ask you to lessen the pain of your absence by writing to me. For I fear that engaged as you are in the affairs of the Most Christian King, you will not enjoy much leisure, and for my part I am only too conscious of my remissness in this kind of duty, when letters ought to be answered. It is not only my lack of eloquence, my dear Budé, that keeps me from writing to you, but still more my respect for your learning. Shame would even have forbidden me to write this letter, unless another kind of shame had wrung it from me. This is the fear lest the letters that you have received from me should be published along with yours. If they should go forth to the world alone, their defects would be abundantly clear, but if they were side by side with yours their shameful poverty would be exposed as by a light of fierce and unpitying brilliance. For I remember that in our conversation mention was made of the letters that I had formerly sent you, which you had it in your mind to publish if you thought I would raise no objection. It was only a passing suggestion, and I forget what reply I gave. But now, as I think the matter over, I see that it would be safer if you would wait awhile, at least until I revise my letters. It is not only that I fear there may be passages where the Latin is faulty, but also in my remarks upon peace and war, upon morality, marriage, the clergy, the people, etc., perhaps what I have written has not always been so cautious and guarded that it would be wise to expose it to captious critics."

Notice how he rates his style far below Budé's, how he refused to publish his letters unless they were revised, how he is anxious even about the Latinity of his letters, though in this there certainly was no ground for fear. If Erasmus, if George Cassander and other sciolists had been as prudent and as humble as More, there would have been no need for that cleanser of libraries that we call the *Index Expurgatorius*, issued by the authority of Pope and King ; nor would there be in the Church such a multitude of pamphlets, useless, frivolous, scandalous, and offensive.

Again, although by common consent he was as elegant a poet as he was an eloquent orator, yet he was never so satisfied with his poems as to wish them to be given to the public. Thus in a letter to Erasmus he writes: " My epigrams have never pleased me very much, as you yourself well know, my dear Erasmus ; for if they had not won greater favour from you and from some others than they ever had from me, in all probability they would not now be in existence."[1]

More never had any greater ambition to win literary fame than he had to gain honours of State : although he showed himself in the highest degree worthy of both the one and the other, yet he deliberately despised them both. Though to tread the path of high honour is as dangerous as to walk upon the house-tops, yet he remained unharmed. Vainglory, the cause of so many grievous falls, had no power over him, for he was strong and valiant and firmly grounded in the love of God.

[1] Erasmus, 555.

CHAPTER VIII

HIS CONTEMPT OF WEALTH

NOW we will show More's contempt of riches—another snare of the world. So many were the offices he held in the State, so important, so profitable, for so long a time, so much favour and influence did he enjoy with King Henry, that, if he had desired it, he could easily have increased his fortune and have become one of the wealthiest of the English nobles. He would but have had to adopt the common practices of courtiers, not necessarily of those who now in England, where the greatest corruption is rife, in a very short time acquire for themselves wealth, property, and land, but practices which even at that time, when ordinary honesty prevailed, men of average goodness did not shrink from employing. He was of good family, the only son of his father ;[1] he was a most skilful lawyer, a successful advocate, Speaker of the House of Commons, Under-Sheriff of the City of London, member of the King's Supreme Council ; he was often employed on embassies ; he was Under-Treasurer of the kingdom, Chancellor of the Duchy of Lancaster, and finally Lord Chancellor of the realm ; he was high in the King's favour, eminent for his wisdom, wit, and learning, holding public appointments from his youth until his fiftieth year. In so rich a kingdom could he not have gathered together a very large fortune, had he wished ? But in his whole life he did not increase his income beyond £60 per annum or a little more. Yet there lives now in England a minister of foul lust who by similar appointments raised his fortune within five years to £60,000. Moreover, there would seem to have been ample justification for More to increase his income, for he supported in his house his four children, one son and three

---

[1] More's brothers probably died in infancy (see Chapter I, note 1).

daughters, together with the wife of the one, and the husbands of the others, and all their children, who before his imprisonment already numbered eleven, as we know from his epitaph.

The King offered him an honourable and generous pension when he returned from a successful embassy, but he utterly refused it. As we have explained already, he was afraid that he would be forced to give up his honourable post of Under-Sheriff of the City, which although less profitable to himself was more useful to the State, or else would lose the confidence of the citizens.[1]

HE REFUSES GIFTS FROM THE CLERGY.

Later on the heretics spread the report that he was hired by the body of the clergy at a great price to write diligently against them, for his cowardly opponents could manufacture no graver charge. He answered them as follows : " As for all the lands and fees that I have in all England, besides such lands and fees as I have of the King's most noble grace, is not at this day, nor shall be while my mother-in-law liveth (whose life and good health I pray God long keep and continue), worth yearly to my living the sum of full £50. And thereof have I some by my wife and some by my father (whose soul our Lord assoil), and some have I also purchased myself, and some fees have I of some temporal men. And then may every man well guess, that I have no very great part of my living by the clergy to make me very partial to them.

" And over that, this shall I truly say, that of all the yearly living that I have of the King's gracious gift, I have not one groat by the means of any spiritual man, but far above my deserving have had it only by his own singular bounty and goodness and special favour towards me.

" And verily of any such yearly fees as I have to my living at this time of any other, I have not had one groat granted me since I first wrote, or went about to write my dialogue, and that was, ye wot well, the first work that I wrote in these matters.

---

[1] Erasmus, 227, quoted in Chapter III above. Later on he seems to have accepted the pension (Bridgett, op. cit., p. 76).

" But then say the brethren, as their holy father writeth and telleth also divers whom he talketh with, that I have taken great rewards in ready money of divers of the clergy for making of my books.

" In good faith I will not say nay, but that some good and honourable men of them would in reward of my good will and my labour against these heretics have given me much more than ever I did or could deserve. But I dare take God and them also to record, that all they could never feoff me with one penny thereof, but (as I plainly told them) I would rather have cast their money into the Thames than take it. For albeit they were, as indeed they were, both good men and honourable, yet look I for my thanks of God that is their better, and for whose sake I take the labour and not for theirs.

" And if any of the brethren, believing their holy fathers, think, as some of them say, that I have more advantage of these matters than I make for, and that I set not so little by money, as to refuse it when it were offered, I will not much dispute with them longer upon the matter. But let them believe as they list, yet this will I be bold to say for myself, although they should call me Pharisee for the boast and Pelagian for my labour too, that how bad soever they reckon me, I am not yet fully so virtueless, but that of mine own natural disposition, without any special help of grace thereto, I am both over-proud and over-slothful also to be hired for money to take half the labour and business in writing that I have taken in this gear since I began."[1] These words testify no less to his virtue than to his wit.

Examples from the Lives of the Saints.

Whilst I read the lines written by the noble-hearted Chancellor, I recall the great patriarch, Abraham, returning from the slaughter of the four Kings and refusing the booty offered him, and I seem to hear him say : " I lift up my hand to the Lord God the most high, the possessor of heaven and earth, that from the very woof thread unto

[1] E.W., p. 867.

the shoe latchet, I will not take of any things that are thine, lest thou say I have enriched Abraham."[1]

Another scene, too, comes to my mind. The great Spiridion, so renowned for his holiness, lays his hands upon the Emperor Constantius and restores him to health. The Emperor offers him a fabulous sum of money, but I seem to hear his reply : " It is not right, Sire, to repay my kindness with evil. I have come a long and difficult journey in obedience to your command, and you in return give me gold—the source of all evil."[2]

I recall, too, the Egyptian hermit Ephestion. Melania, a noble matron, had placed without his knowledge a sum of money in his cell. When she refused to receive it back he threw it into the river.[3]

Such was More's contempt for money : in like manner he, too, although he could easily have acquired riches, refused to do so.

It is also in point to mention here how, filling so many offices and appointments, he was absolutely innocent of all corrupt acceptance of gifts. Once when an accusation of this nature was brought against him, it was turned to ridicule, as we have related above.[4]

How little he cared about amassing wealth, how thoroughly he despised it, and how bravely he bore the loss of it is shown by his resignation of his offices and by his noble witness to the truth, which cost him not only his wealth, but also liberty and life itself.

THE BURNING OF HIS BARNS.

Especially noble was his conduct on one occasion when, for a trial of his courage and patience, Almighty God permitted his family to suffer misfortune and loss. He had just returned from a foreign embassy and was away from home with the King, when he received a letter written by his son-in-law on behalf of his distracted wife to tell him of a calamity that had occurred. Through the carelessness of a neighbour, part of his house and his barns, together

[1] Gen. xiv 22.
[2] Surius, *Life of Spiridion*, tom. 6 (S.).
[3] Surius, *Life of S. Melania*, tom. 1 (S.).
[4] See Chapter III.

with some barns standing near his property but belonging to his neighbours, had been utterly destroyed by fire. It was the month of August, and the barns were full of the newly gathered corn. We give the reply he wrote to his wife.

"Mistress Alice, in my most hearty wise I recommend me to you. And whereas I am informed by my son Heron of the loss of our barns and our neighbours' also [by fire], with all the corn that was therein ; albeit, saving God's pleasure, it is great pity of so much good corn lost, yet since it hath liked him to send us such a chance, we must and are bounden, not only to be content, but also to be glad of his visitation. He sent us all that we have lost, and since he hath by such a chance taken it away again, his pleasure be fulfilled. Let us never grieve thereat, but take it in good worth and heartily thank him as well for adversity as for prosperity. And peradventure we have more cause to thank him for our loss than for our winning. For his wisdom better seeth what is good for us than we do ourselves. Therefore, I pray you be of good cheer, and take all the household with you to church, and there thank God both for that he hath given us and for that he hath taken away from us, and for that he hath left us, which, if it please him, he can increase when he will. And if it please him to leave us less yet, at his pleasure be it.

"I pray you to make some good ensearch what my poor neighbours have lost, and bid them take no thought therefor ; for, and I should not leave myself a spoon, there shall no poor neighbour of mine bear no loss happened by any chance in my house. I pray you be with my children and your household merry in God. And devise somewhat with your friends what way were best to take for provision to be made for corn for our household, and for seed this year coming, if ye think it good that we keep the ground still in our hands. And whether ye think it good that we shall do so or not, yet I think it were not best suddenly thus to leave it all up and to put away our folk off our farm, till we have somewhat advised us thereon. Howbeit if we have more now than ye shall need, and which can get them other masters, ye may then discharge us of them. But I would not that any man were suddenly sent away he wot ne'er whither.

" At my coming hither I perceived none other but that I should tarry still with the King's grace. But now I shall, (I think) because of this chance, get leave this next week to come home and see you ; and then shall we further devise together upon all things what order shall be best to take. And thus as heartily fare you well, with all our children, as ye can wish. At Woodstock the third day of September, by the hand of your loving husband, Thomas More, Knight." [1]

How characteristic is this letter ! It shows the man of prudence, without undue solicitude for the goods of this world. It bespeaks the wise administrator, but above all the good Christian who in everything conforms himself to the will of God, and is more anxious about the losses of his neighbours than about his own. And now notice how, as to a second Job, God soon restored to him twofold as a reward for his saintlike patience and contempt of earthly goods. It was in the month of September that he received the news of this misfortune and sent the answer we have just quoted. In the October following he was appointed Chancellor of the realm, receiving thereby a position of such importance that not only was it easy for him to build up again his granaries, but even, if he wished, add new ones to those he had before.

[1] E.W., p. 1419, where the date is given as " the thirde daye of Septembre." Stapleton, however, prints " 13 Septembris."

CHAPTER IX

HOW MORE RULED HIS HOUSEHOLD

WE have spoken of Sir Thomas More as a married man, laden with honours, and master of a sufficient fortune, but we must now describe more particularly his family life, his manner of ruling his household and educating his children. As we have already found him to be a public-spirited citizen, a wise councillor, a learned and devout man, so now we shall find him, unless I am much mistaken, to be the best of fathers and a most capable ruler of a household.

DESCRIPTION BY ERASMUS.

First, as regards his family, Erasmus gives a general description from what he had himself witnessed on a long visit to England during which he was a frequent visitor to More's house. He writes as follows : " More has built for himself on the banks of the Thames not far from London a country-house which is dignified and adequate without being so magnificent as to excite envy. Here he lives happily with his family, consisting of his wife, his son and daughter-in-law, three daughters with their husbands and already eleven grandchildren. It would be difficult to find a man more fond of children than he. His wife is no longer young ; but of so accommodating a disposition is he, or rather of such virtue and prudence, that if any defect appears that cannot be corrected, he sets himself to love it as though it were the happiest thing in the world. You would say that Plato's Academy had come to life again. But I wrong More's family in comparing it to Plato's Academy, for in the latter the chief subjects of discussion were arithmetic, geometry and occasionally ethics, but the former rather deserves the name of a school for the knowledge and practice of the Christian faith.

No one of either sex there neglects literature or fruitful reading, although the first and chief care is piety. There is no quarrelling; a bitter word is never heard; no one is ever known to be idle. Moreover it is not by harshness or angry words that More maintains so happy a discipline in his house, but by kindness and gentleness. All attend to their duty ; but diligence does not exclude merriment."[1]

But we will recount some details, some of which are found in the letter of Erasmus to von Hutten, others of which we have ourselves gathered from More's relatives and friends. " He took to wife a very young girl whom he educated in literature and in every kind of music. After she had borne him four children she died. Not long afterwards he married a widow, more for the care of his children than for his own pleasure. She is now getting on in years and is of a disposition none too tractable—although she is a keen and careful housekeeper—yet he has persuaded her to learn to sing to the lyre or the lute, the monochord or the flute, and in this way to fulfil the daily task which her exacting husband imposes."[2]

MORE'S CARE FOR HIS SERVANTS.

Of the education of his children we will speak later, but now we will describe the care he exercised in regard to his servants. He would never allow them to waste their time in sloth or improper pastimes, as happens only too often in the houses of the English nobility where there is kept, according to the custom of the nation, a large crowd of idle and gossiping retainers. Some of those, therefore, whose office it was to accompany him abroad he placed in charge of his garden, which he divided into sections— for it was large—assigning to each his share. Some he made to sing, others to play the organ : he allowed no one, not even if he were of noble rank, to play at dice or cards. To ward off danger of unchastity he arranged that his men-servants and maid-servants should sleep in separate parts of the building, and should rarely meet together :

[1] Erasmus, Appendix, 426.
[2] Erasmus, 447. The passage is considerably shortened.

only in cases of necessity were the women allowed to enter the part of the house in which the men lived.

Whenever he was at home it was his custom to gather together every evening before bedtime a large part of his household for night prayers. Together all would kneel and recite the three Psalms, " Have mercy on me, O God," " To thee, O Lord, have I lifted up my soul," and " May God have mercy on us"; the " Hail, holy Queen," with its prayer; and finally the " Out of the depths " for the dead.[1] He continued this practice even when he was Lord Chancellor.

On Sundays and feast days no one was allowed to be absent from the services of the Church, and More insisted that all should be there at the very beginning of the service. On the greater feasts, Christmas and Easter, he made all rise at night and assist at the whole of the office.

When anyone committed a fault, More would administer reproof with such gentleness that afterwards the offender would love him all the more. Margaret Gigs, the wife of Doctor Clements, who, as we have several times stated, was almost from her infancy brought up with More's daughters, used to relate how sometimes she would deliberately commit some fault that she might enjoy More's sweet and loving reproof. Twice only in his life was he ever known to be angry. Every year on Good Friday he called together the whole of his family into what was called the New Building—a large edifice—and there he would have the whole of our Lord's Passion read to them, generally by John Harris. From time to time More would interrupt the reading with a few words of pious exhortation.

After he resigned the Chancellorship he dismissed all his men-servants except two, and obtained good places for them with new masters, or otherwise amply provided for them. " In truth," writes Erasmus, " this house seems to be under a lucky star, for no one who lives there ever fails to advance in fortune, and no one has ever there lost his good name."[2]

[1] Psalms l, xxiv, lxvi, and cxxix.
[2] In the letter to Ulrich von Hutten (No. 447).

MEALTIME IN MORE'S HOUSE.

At table a passage of Sacred Scripture was read with the commentaries of Nicholas of Lyra or some other ancient writer. One of his daughters would be the reader. The passage from Scripture was intoned in the ecclesiastical or monastic fashion, and was ended with the words " and do thou, O Lord, have mercy on us," as in religious houses. The reading was continued until a sign was given, and then More would ask one of the company how this or that passage should be understood. Thereupon an intimate friendly conversation would take place. But if, as often happened, some learned guest were present, a more formal discussion of the passage read would be held. Afterwards More in his inimitable way would suggest some lighter topic, and all would be highly amused. Henry Patenson, More's fool, would now join in the conversation. (Some four years before his passion, however, at the time when he became Chancellor, More removed his fool from his table and gave him to his father.) More's four children—*i.e.*, his son and his three daughters—together with Margaret Gigs used to take their turn in reading at table until the former were married, when Margaret Gigs alone read.

Lastly, as a proof of the religious spirit in which he ruled his family, we may quote from a letter he received from his daughter Margaret during his imprisonment. " Father," she wrote, " what think you hath been our comfort since your departing from us ? Surely the experience we have had of your life past, and godly conversation, and wholesome counsel, and virtuous example, and a surety not only of the continuance of that same, but also a great increase by the goodness of our Lord."[1]

This, then, is what we have to say of More as the ruler of a household.

[1] E.W., p. 1432.

CHAPTER X

THE EDUCATION OF MORE'S CHILDREN AND GRAND-CHILDREN

WE must now speak of More as a parent and describe, as well as we can, how he employed his great gifts in the education of his children. We may be sure that he ever acted as befitted a scholar and a saint. His first care was the religious training of his children : second only to this was his zeal for their advancement in learning. As to teaching them how to become rich and gain high positions in the world, it never entered into his mind. " His house," writes Erasmus with perfect truth, " was a school for the knowledge and practice of the Christian faith."[1]

As soon, then, as his children were old enough to begin their education, he taught them personally or by a tutor. We will mention the three chief men who acted in More's house as instructors to his children and grandchildren.

JOHN CLEMENTS.

The first was John Clements, afterwards famous as a Doctor of Medicine and a Greek scholar, of whom, as we have already said, More makes mention in the beginning of the *Utopia*. Later on he lectured on Greek literature at Oxford with great success. More, in an unprinted letter to Erasmus, speaks of him as follows : " Clements my son lectures at Oxford to an audience larger than has ever gathered to any other lecturer. It is astonishing how universal is the approbation and the love he gains. Even those to whom classical literature was almost anathema now show attachment to him, attend his lectures and gradually modify their opposition. Linacre, who, as you know, never praises anyone extravagantly, cannot contain his admira-

---

[1] Erasmus, Appendix, 426.

tion for his letters, so that, although I love Clements so much, I am almost tempted to envy him for the high praises heaped upon him." John Clements has translated various works from Greek into Latin—among other things many letters of Gregory Nazianzen, which are no longer extant, and the *Synaxarion* of Nicephorus Callistus, or homilies on all the saints of the Greeks, according to their calendar. I can testify that he translated these two works with the greatest accuracy and eloquence, for at his request I helped him to compare his text with the Greek original. His wife Margaret had formerly been his pupil, together with More's own daughters, but now, incredible though it may seem, she helped her husband to get the exact force of the Greek idiom in more difficult passages.

OTHER TUTORS.

Clements was succeeded as tutor in More's family by William Gunnell, a very learned man, who afterwards lived for many years at Cambridge, lecturing and holding positions of authority.

Gunnell was succeeded by Richard Hirt, who taught the grandchildren after the marriage of More's children. I find also that a certain Drew and a Nicholas were tutors of More's children or grandchildren, as will appear from the following letters.

SUBJECTS OF STUDY.

The subjects of study were not only Latin and Greek literature, but also logic and philosophy, in which subject formal disputations were arranged, and also mathematics. Sometimes, too, the writings of the Fathers were read, as I will show from More's correspondence. The pupils exercised themselves in the Latin tongue almost every day, translating English into Latin and Latin into English. More had written in Latin to the University of Oxford a sort of apology for classical learning, from which we have quoted above.[1] I have seen another Latin version of this made by one of his daughters, and an English version by

[1] See the end of Chapter IV.

another. To show the reader how zealously More trained his children in studies of this kind and his reasons for doing so, I will quote in full a letter that has never yet been printed, addressed by him to William Gunnell, one of his tutors.

THE PUPILS IN MORE'S SCHOOL.

First, however, it will be well to enumerate briefly the children and grandchildren of More who were educated in his house, so that the reader may be as well acquainted with the pupils of the school as he has already become with the tutors.   More had no children by his second wife, who was a widow when he married her, but by his first he had one son, John, and three daughters, Margaret, Elizabeth, and Cecily.   Margaret was married to William Roper and bore him two sons, Thomas and Anthony, and three daughters, Elizabeth, Mary, and Margaret.   Of these Mary, who was most like her mother, became a lady of great learning and lady-in-waiting to Queen Mary.   She translated into English that part of the treatise on our Lord's Passion that Sir Thomas More had written in Latin, and did it in so pure and eloquent a style that it can hardly be distinguished from the style of her grandfather.   She translated also the Ecclesiastical History of Eusebius from Greek into Latin, but, as Bishop Christopherson wrote a version that was more exact, she did not publish hers. Elizabeth, More's second daughter, married John Dauncy and bore him five sons, John, Thomas, Bartholomew, William, and Germain, and two daughters, Alice and Elizabeth.   Cecily, More's third daughter, became the wife of Giles Heron and had two sons, John and Thomas, and one daughter, Anne.   John More, Sir Thomas's only son, took to wife Anne Cresacre, and had of her five sons, Thomas, Augustine, Edward, Bartholomew, and another Thomas, and one daughter, Anne.   This numerous progeny recalls the verse of the Psalmist : " Thy children as olive plants, round about thy table." [1]   Of those just mentioned, More's own four children and eleven of his grandchildren were instructed in his school during his lifetime.   Of his twenty-one grandchildren ten were born after his martyr-

[1] Psalm cxxvii 3.

dom. Margaret Gigs, afterwards the wife of John Clements, was educated with his children. Now let us come to More's letter to Gunnell.

LETTERS ILLUSTRATING THE EDUCATION OF MORE'S CHILDREN.

" I have received, my dear Gunnell, your letter, elegant, as your letters always are, and full of affection. From your letter I perceive your devotion to my children ; I argue their diligence from their own. Every one of their letters pleased me, but I was particularly pleased, because I notice that Elizabeth shows a gentleness and self-command in the absence of her mother, which some children would not show in her presence. Let her understand that such conduct delights me more than all possible letters I could receive from anyone. Though I prefer learning joined with virtue to all the treasures of kings, yet renown for learning, when it is not united with a good life, is nothing else than splendid and notorious infamy : this would be specially the case in a woman. Since erudition in women is a new thing and a reproach to the sloth of men, many will gladly assail it, and impute to literature what is really the fault of nature, thinking from the vices of the learned to get their own ignorance esteemed as virtue. On the other hand, if a woman (and this I desire and hope with you as their teacher for all my daughters) to eminent virtue should add an outwork of even moderate skill in literature, I think she will have more real profit than if she had obtained the riches of Croesus and the beauty of Helen. I do not say this because of the glory which will be hers, though glory follows virtue as a shadow follows a body, but because the reward of wisdom is too solid to be lost like riches or to decay like beauty, since it depends on the intimate conscience of what is right, not on the talk of men, than which nothing is more foolish or mischievous.

" It belongs to a good man, no doubt, to avoid infamy, but to lay himself out for renown is the conduct of a man who is not only proud, but ridiculous and miserable. A soul must be without peace which is ever fluctuating between elation and disappointment from the opinions of men

Among all the benefits that learning bestows on men, there is none more excellent than this, that by the study of books we are taught in that very study to seek not praise, but utility. Such has been the teaching of the most learned men, especially of philosophers, who are the guides of human life, although some may have abused learning, like other good things, simply to court empty glory and popular renown.

" I have dwelt so much on this matter, my dear Gunnell, because of what you say in your letter, that Margaret's lofty character should not be abased. In this judgement I quite agree with you ; but to me, and, no doubt, to you also, that man would seem to abase a generous character who should accustom it to admire what is vain and low. He, on the contrary, raises the character who rises to virtue and true goods, and who looks down with contempt from the contemplation of what is sublime, on those shadows of good things which almost all mortals, through ignorance of truth, greedily snatch at as if they were true goods.

" Therefore, my dear Gunnell, since we must walk by this road, I have often begged not you only, who, out of your affection for my children, would do it of your own accord, nor my wife, who is sufficiently urged by her maternal love for them, which has been proved to me in so many ways, but all my friends, to warn my children to avoid the precipices of pride and haughtiness, and to walk in the pleasant meadows of modesty ; not to be dazzled at the sight of gold ; not to lament that they do not possess what they erroneously admire in others ; not to think more of themselves for gaudy trappings, nor less for the want of them ; neither to deform the beauty that nature has given them by neglect, nor to try to heighten it by artifice ; to put virtue in the first place, learning in the second ; and in their studies to esteem most whatever may teach them piety towards God, charity to all, and Christian humility in themselves. By such means they will receive from God the reward of an innocent life, and in the assured expectation of it, will view death without horror, and meanwhile possessing solid joy, will neither be puffed up by the empty praise of men, nor dejected by evil tongues. These I consider the genuine fruits of learning, and though I admit that all literary men do not possess them, I would maintain that those who give themselves to study with such views, will easily attain their end and become perfect.

" Nor do I think that the harvest will be much affected whether it is a man or a woman who sows the field. They both have the same human nature, which reason differentiates from that of beasts ; both, therefore, are equally suited for those studies by which reason is cultivated, and becomes fruitful like a ploughed land on which the seed of good lessons has been sown. If it be true that the soil of woman's brain be bad, and apter to bear bracken than corn, by which saying many keep women from study, I think, on the contrary, that a woman's wit is on that account all the more diligently to be cultivated, that nature's defect may be redressed by industry. This was the opinion of the ancients, of those who were most prudent as well as most holy. Not to speak of the rest, St Jerome and St Augustine not only exhorted excellent matrons and most noble virgins to study, but also, in order to assist them, diligently explained the abstruse meanings of Holy Scripture, and wrote for tender girls letters replete with so much erudition, that now-a-days old men, who call themselves professors of sacred science, can scarcely read them correctly, much less understand them. Do you, my learned Gunnell, have the kindness to see that my daughters thoroughly learn these works of those holy men. From them they will learn in particular what end they should propose to themselves in their studies and what is the fruit of their endeavours, namely the testimony of God and a good conscience. Thus peace and calm will abide in their hearts and they will be disturbed neither by fulsome flattery nor by the stupidity of those illiterate men who despise learning.

" I fancy that I hear you object that these precepts, though true, are beyond the capacity of my young children, since you will scarcely find a man, however old and advanced, whose mind is so firmly set as not to be tickled sometimes with desire of glory. But, dear Gunnell, the more I see the difficulty of getting rid of this pest of pride, the more do I see the necessity of getting to work at it from childhood. For I find no other reason why this

evil clings so to our hearts, than because almost as soon as
we are born, it is sown in the tender minds of children by
their nurses, it is cultivated by their teachers, and brought
to its full growth by their parents ; no one teaching even
what is good without, at the same time, awakening the
expectation of praise, as of the proper reward of virtue.
Thus we grow accustomed to make so much of praise, that
while we study how to please the greater number (who will
always be the worst) we grow ashamed of being good (with
the few). That this plague of vainglory may be banished
far from my children, I do desire that you, my dear Gunnell,
and their mother and all their friends, would sing this song
to them, and repeat it, and beat it into their heads, that
vainglory is a thing despicable, and to be spit upon ; and
that there is nothing more sublime than that humble
modesty so often praised by Christ ; and this your prudent
charity will so enforce as to teach virtue rather than reprove
vice, and make them love good advice instead of hating it.
To this purpose nothing will more conduce than to read
to them the lessons of the ancient Fathers, who, they know,
cannot be angry with them ; and, as they honour them for
their sanctity, they must needs be much moved by their
authority. If you will teach something of this sort, in
addition to their lesson in Sallust—to Margaret and
Elizabeth, as being more advanced than John and Cecily—
you will bind me and them still more to you. And thus
you will bring about that my children, who are dear to
me by nature, and still more dear by learning and virtue,
will become most dear by that advance in knowledge and
good conduct. Adieu.

"From the Court on the Vigil of Pentecost." [1]

This letter of More on the education of his children is
worthy of him : it shows the love of a father, the wisdom of
a philosopher, and the faith of a Christian. If the State
had many such fathers to teach their children to fly from
vainglory, to love virtue, and to be diligent in learning,
vice would not be so rampant nor accursed pride so preva-
lent. More in his wisdom avoided the error, so common

[1] Father Bridgett's translation with one passage added.

in parents, of which Augustine in his treatise on Christian Education writes as follows : " Christian parents, when they send their sons to school, say to them, ' Be diligent in learning.' ' Why ?' ' That you may become a man— *i.e.*, that you may take a prominent place amongst men.' But no one says to them, ' That you may be able to read the Gospels.' We have taken immense pains to learn what must certainly perish, and we shall perish with it." That More did not share such sentiments the single letter that we have quoted is a proof. When More was away from home, following the King and the Court as he so frequently had to do, he made it his practice often to write to his school, receiving frequent letters in return. By this interchange of courtesy he stimulated their diligence, practised their powers, and urged them to greater progress. As an illustration I will add one or two more of his letters.

" Thomas More to his whole school :

" See what a compendious salutation I have found, to save both time and paper, which would otherwise have been wasted in reciting the names of each one of you, and my labour would have been to no purpose, since, though each of you is dear to me by some special title, of which I could have omitted none in a set and formal salutation, no one is dearer to me by any title than each of you by that of scholar. Your zeal for knowledge binds me to you almost more closely than the ties of blood. I rejoice that Mr. Drew has returned safe, for I was anxious, as you know, about him. If I did not love you so much I should be really envious of your happiness in having so many and such excellent tutors. But I think you have no longer any need of Mr. Nicholas, since you have learnt whatever he had to teach you about astronomy. I hear you are so far advanced in that science that you can not only point out the polar-star or the dog-star, or any of the constellations, but are able also—which requires a skilful and profound astrologer— among all those heavenly bodies, to distinguish the sun from the moon ! Go forward then in that new and admirable science by which you ascend to the stars. But while you gaze on them assiduously, consider that this holy time of Lent warns you, and that beautiful and holy poem of

Boetius keeps singing in your ears, to raise your mind also to heaven, lest the soul look downwards to the earth, after the manner of brutes, while the body looks upwards. Farewell, my dearest.

"From Court, the 23rd March."[1]

Although he was in high office and always busily engaged in affairs of State, yet here he comes down to the level of his children's studies, jokes with them in neat and witty phrases, while each of them had, by a carefully written composition, to give a proof of his diligence. Lest it should be thought that such correspondence was rare or occasional, I will add other letters of More to his school (although they are by this time almost worn to pieces) in which he gives advice, exhortation, and precepts for letters of this nature, treating of diligence, of invention, of the right disposition of words, etc.

" Thomas More to his dearest children and to Margaret Gigs, whom he numbers amongst his own :

" The Bristol merchant brought me your letters the day after he left you, with which I was extremely delighted. Nothing can come from your workshop, however rude and unfinished, that will not give me more pleasure than the most accurate thing another can write. So much does my affection for you recommend whatever you write to me. Indeed, without any recommendation, your letters are capable of pleasing by their own merits, their wit and pure Latinity. There was not one of your letters that did not please me extremely ; but, to confess ingenuously what I feel, the letter of my son John pleased me best, both because it was longer than the others, and because he seems to have given to it more labour and study. For he not only put out his matter prettily and composed in fairly polished language, but he plays with me both pleasantly and cleverly, and turns my jokes on myself wittily enough. And this he does not only merrily, but with due moderation, showing that he does not forget that he is joking with his

[1] Father Bridgett's translation.

father, and that he is cautious not to give offence at the same time that he is eager to give delight.

"Now I expect from each of you a letter almost every day. I will not admit excuses—John makes none—such as want of time, sudden departure of the letter-carrier, or want of something to write about. No one hinders you from writing, but, on the contrary, all are urging you to do it. And that you may not keep the letter-carrier waiting, why not anticipate his coming, and have your letters written and sealed, ready for anyone to take? How can a subject be wanting when you write to me, since I am glad to hear of your studies or of your games, and you will please me most if, when there is nothing to write about, you write about that nothing at great length. Nothing can be easier for you, since you are girls, loquacious by nature, who have always a world to say about nothing at all.

"One thing, however, I admonish you, whether you write serious matters or the merest trifles, it is my wish that you write everything diligently and thoughtfully. It will be no harm, if you first write the whole in English, for then you will have much less trouble in turning it into Latin ; not having to look for the matter, your mind will be intent only on the language. That, however, I leave to your own choice, whereas I strictly enjoin you that whatever you have composed you carefully examine before writing it out clean ; and in this examination first scrutinise the whole sentence and then every part of it. Thus, if any solecisms have escaped you, you will easily detect them. Correct these, write out the whole letter again, and even then examine it once more, for sometimes, in rewriting, faults slip in again that one had expunged. By this diligence your little trifles will become serious matters ; for while there is nothing so neat and witty that will not be made insipid by silly and inconsiderate loquacity, so also there is nothing in itself so insipid, that you cannot season it with grace and wit if you give a little thought to it. Farewell, my dear children.

"From the Court, the 3rd September." [1]

[1] Father Bridgett's translation.

This letter of More shows very clearly his careful diligence and zealous solicitude that his children should be instructed and frequently exercised in literature. Not only does he exhort them as a father, but like a master he teaches them, and by his most eloquent letters points out the way to them and stimulates them by his example, himself first carrying out what so earnestly he desires them to do. So much indeed did he have this matter at heart, so carefully did he watch over the instruction of his children in religion and learning that when there seemed to be some little negligence, or at any rate not that diligence he so earnestly desired, he made up his mind to leave the Court and his public career rather than allow the education of his family to fall below the high standard he had fixed.

In this sense he wrote to Margaret, his favourite daughter.

" I was delighted to receive your letter, my dearest Margaret, informing me of Shaw's condition. I should have been still more delighted if you had told me of the studies you and your brother are engaged in, of your daily reading, your pleasant discussions, your essays, of the swift passage of the days made joyous by literary pursuits. For although everything you write gives me pleasure, yet the most exquisite delight of all comes from reading what none but you and your brother could have written." And the letter concludes: " I beg you, Margaret, tell me about the progress you are all making in your studies. For I assure you that, rather than allow my children to be idle and slothful, I would make a sacrifice of wealth, and bid adieu to other cares and business, to attend to my children and my family, amongst whom none is more dear to me than yourself, my beloved daughter."

Such letters well describe the tenderness of his fatherly love and care. How much pleasure and delight he took in the diligent labours of his children, how large a portion of earth's joys he placed in their progress, how generously he praised their success will appear from yet another letter to all his daughters, which therefore I will transcribe in full.

" Thomas More to Margaret, Elizabeth, Cecily his dearest
    daughters, and to Margaret Gigs as dear as though
    she were a daughter :

    " I cannot express, my dearest children, the very deep
pleasure your eloquent letters gave me, especially as I see
that although travelling and frequently changing your
abode you have not allowed your customary studies to be
interfered with, but have continued your exercises in logic,
rhetoric and poetry.   I am now fully convinced that you
love me as you should since I see that, although I am
absent, yet you do with the greatest eagerness what you
know gives me pleasure when I am present.   When I return
you shall see that I am not ungrateful for the delight your
loving affection has given me.   I assure you that I have no
greater solace in all the vexatious business in which I am
immersed than to read your letters.   They prove to me the
truth of the laudatory reports your kind tutor sends of your
work, for if your own handwriting did not bear witness to
your zealous study of literature, it might be suspected that
he had been influenced by his good-nature rather than by
the truth.   But now by what you write you support his
credit, so that I am ready to believe what would otherwise
be his incredible reports upon the eloquence and wit of
your essays.
    " So I am longing to return home that I may place my
pupil by your side and compare his progress with yours.
He is, I fear, a little lazy,[1] for he cannot help hoping that
you are not really quite so advanced as your teacher's
praise would imply.   Knowing how persevering you are,
I have a great hope that soon you will be able to overcome
your tutor himself, if not by force of argument, at any rate
by never confessing yourselves beaten.   Farewell, my most
dear children."

    [1] " . . . qui paulo segnior est hac in re, quia desperare non potest
quin vos inventurus sit citra praeceptoris praedicationem subsistere."
Cresacre More translates this rather difficult passage as follows :
" . . . who is slow to believe, yea out of all hope or conceit to find
you able to be answerable to your master's praises." (*Life of More*,
Hunter's Edition, p. 151.)

We learn from this letter of More what great progress
his children had made, how high a standard their literary
exercises reached, how eagerly he urged them forward and
with what great delight he heard of their advance in
learning.

For More's school, Erasmus annotated the *Nux* of Ovid,
and to it also he dedicated his work. Of this school,
too, Louis Vives makes honourable mention in the book he
wrote for Catharine of Castile,[1] Queen of England, on the
education of a princess. Finally to John More, the only
son of Sir Thomas More, Erasmus dedicated his edition of
Aristotle, and Simon Grinaeus his edition of Plato, as to
a young man deeply versed both in Greek and in philosophy. We have quoted above some portions of their
dedicatory letters, but I will add a few details, which are
more properly in place here, from the letter of Simon
Grinaeus to John More.

"To you," he writes, "who by the right of your father's
virtues are the heir to all that his good deeds have effected,
it was necessary that I should dedicate these books of
Proclus,[2] which are full of admirable teaching and have
been published by our labour indeed, but by the benefits
I have received from your family. I hope too that while
on the one hand your name will be an ornament to my
books, on the other hand they may be of considerable use
to you, conversant as I know you to be with all these serious
questions, both by your long intercourse with your father
and by the company of your highly cultured sisters.
Enthusiasm for learning has carried you and your sisters—
a prodigy in our age—to such heights of proficiency that no
difficult question of science or philosophy is now beyond
you. To minds so appreciative of all that is beautiful,
what can be more suited than this author whose skill is
unrivalled in clearness of exposition, depth of treatment
and breadth of view?"

These are the words of Grinaeus in the letter of dedication
to John More, which he prefixed to his edition of Plato.

[1] *i.e.*, Catharine of Aragon. The two provinces of Aragon and
Castile were united in 1479.
[2] *i.e.*, the well-known commentator on Plato. See Smith's *Dictionary
of Greek and Latin Biography and Mythology.*

Lastly I will place one of More's letters to his daughter Margaret, which expresses very beautifully the depth and tenderness of his paternal love.

" You ask, my dear Margaret, for money, with too much bashfulness and timidity, since you are asking from a father who is eager to give, and since you have written to me a letter such that I would not only repay each line of it with a golden philippine, as Alexander did the verses of Cherilos, but, if my means were as great as my desire, I would reward each syllable with two gold ounces.   As it is, I send only what you have asked, but would have added more, only that as I am eager to give, so am I desirous to be asked and coaxed by my daughter, especially by you, whom virtue and learning have made so dear to my soul. So the sooner you spend this money well, as you are wont to do, and the sooner you ask for more, the more you will be sure of pleasing your father.   Good-bye, my dearest child." [1]

But Margaret Roper deserves a chapter to herself.

Father Bridgett's translation.

CHAPTER XI

MARGARET ROPER

ACCORDING to Holy Scripture, "A wise son maketh his father glad,"[1] and before we conclude this portion of our work in which we describe More as a father, we must speak of one of his children who was wise indeed, and made the heart of her wise father exceeding glad. What progress she made we will show by some of her father's letters to her, which make delightful reading not only by the charm of their style, as do all More's letters, but by the novelty of their subject-matter. They will prove that in literature and other branches of study she attained a degree of excellence that would scarcely be believed in a woman. From them it will also appear how thorough and how successful was the education of the rest of his children, but of them we shall say nothing, not because nothing deserves to be said, but because insufficient details have come down to us. But of Margaret, More's eldest daughter, the wife of the excellent William Roper, some of her father's letters which I have found give us adequate knowledge.

MARGARET'S LITERARY SKILL.

More than all the rest of his children, she resembled her father, as well in stature, appearance, and voice, as in mind and in general character. She wrote very eloquently prose and verse both in Greek and Latin. Two Latin speeches, written as an exercise, which I have myself seen, are in style elegant and graceful, while in treatment they hardly yield to her father's compositions. Another speech, first written in English, was translated by both the father and the daughter separately into Latin with such great skill that one would not know which to prefer. When More

[1] Prov. x 1.

wrote his book on the Four Last Things, he gave the same subject to Margaret to treat, and when she had completed her task, he affirmed most solemnly that the treatise of his daughter was in no way inferior to his own. As St Augustine had his Adeodatus, whose admirable talents he could never sufficiently admire, so had More his Margaret.

She emends a Faulty Text of St Cyprian.

The learned John Coster in his commentaries on Vincent of Lerins[1] writes thus of her : " At one time an English Doctor of Medicine, named Clements, a man of great eminence and a first-rate Greek scholar, used very kindly to talk over literary matters with me. He spoke much of Sir Thomas More, with whom he had lived on terms of intimacy, of his gentleness, his piety, his wisdom and his learning. Often, too, he spoke of Margaret, More's daughter, whose talents and attainments he highly extolled. ' To show you,' he said, ' the truth of what I say, I will quote you a very corrupt passage from St Cyprian, which she, without any help from the text, restored most happily. This was the sentence. *Absit enim ab ecclesia Romana vigorem suum tam prophana facilitate dimittere, et nisi vos severitatis, eversa fidei majestate dissolvere.* This text was so corrupt as to be meaningless, but Margaret, by proposing *nervos* for *nisi vos*, gave to the passage an easy and obvious sense, thus : ' Far be it from the Roman Church to relax its vigour with such culpable negligence or to weaken the bonds of severity in a manner so unbefitting the dignity of the faith.' "

Jacobus Pamelius acknowledges the emendation made by Margaret in his notes upon this passage of Cyprian.[2]

A letter to her from Erasmus is to be found in the 26th Book of the latter's correspondence dated 1529.[3] He writes to her not only as to a gentlewoman, but as to an eminent scholar.

[1] On Vincent's ninth chapter (S.).
[2] Cyprian, Book II, Letter 7. According to Pamelius, Letter 31 (S.).
[3] Erasmus, 1075.

She obtains Access to the Tower.

Of all More's children Margaret alone had, by permission of the King, access to him during his imprisonment. This she obtained by a skilful ruse. She wrote to her father a letter in which she seemed to urge him to give up his own determination and conform himself to the King's will. These were far from being her real sentiments, for no one understood and sympathised with her father's mind more fully than she ; but she expected that as usual her letter would be intercepted and examined by the King's Council, and hoped that she would be allowed permission to visit him in order to induce him to follow the King's desire. Her ruse succeeded, and for a considerable time she was allowed access to him. When at length visits were forbidden, she wrote him many letters and received from him many in reply, as later on will be shown in its due place. Our task at present is to show from her father's letters how high were her literary attainments.

Letters of More to his Daughter.

We have before related how great was the praise given to one of her letters by Reginald Pole who chanced to be with More when it came. We will now add the portions of More's letter which follow the passage already quoted.[1] If we had no other evidence of her scholarship, this one letter of More would provide abundant testimony. " Meanwhile," he writes, " something I once said to you in joke came back to my mind, and I realised how true it was. It was to the effect that you were to be pitied, because the incredulity of men would rob you of the praise you so richly deserved for your laborious vigils, as they would never believe, when they read what you had written, that you had not often availed yourself of another's help : whereas of all writers you least deserved to be thus suspected. Even when a tiny child you could never endure to be decked out in another's finery. But, my sweetest Margaret, you are all the more deserving of praise on that

[1] See the earlier part of Chapter V.

account. Although you cannot hope for an adequate
reward for your labour, yet nevertheless you continue
to unite to your singular love of virtue the pursuit of
literature and art. Content with the approbation of your
conscience, in your modesty you do not seek for the praise
of the public, nor value it over much even if you receive it,
but because of the great love you bear us, you regard us—
i.e., your husband and myself—as a sufficiently large circle
of readers for all that you write.

" In your letter you speak of your approaching confinement. We pray most earnestly that all may go happily
and successfully with you. May God and our Blessed
Lady grant you happily and safely a little one like to his
mother in everything except sex. Yet let it by all means
be a girl, if only she will make up for the inferiority of her
sex by her zeal to imitate her mother's virtue and learning.
Such a girl I should prefer to three boys. Good-bye, my
dearest child."

It is abundantly clear from this letter that Margaret's
learning was of no ordinary or common kind. She had
produced works which fully deserved to be published and
read by all, although the bashfulness of her sex, or her
humility, or the almost incredible novelty of the thing (as
More hints) never allowed her to consent to publication.

Should anyone suspect that so high an opinion of the
daughter is to be ascribed to the over-indulgent love of the
father (though More was the last man to be guilty of such
distortion of judgement), then let him recall the similar
or even more favourable judgement of the learned Reginald
Pole, which we have quoted above in another connection.[1]
If even that is deemed insufficient, we will now add another
of More's letters in which we shall see the admiring judgement passed by the most learned of the English Bishops
upon Margaret's learning and literary style.

" Thomas More to his dearest daughter Margaret:

" I forbear to express the extreme pleasure your letter
gave me, my sweet child. You will be able to judge better
how much it pleased your father when you learn what

[1] See the earlier part of Chapter V.

delight it caused to a stranger. I happened this evening to be in the company of his Lordship, John, Bishop of Exeter, a man of deep learning and of a wide reputation for holiness. Whilst we were talking I took out from my desk a paper that bore on our business and by accident your letter appeared. He took it into his hand with pleasure and examined it. When he saw from the signature that it was the letter of a lady, he was induced by the novelty of the thing to read it more eagerly. When he had finished he said he would never have believed it to have been your work unless I had assured him of the fact, and he began to praise it in the highest terms (why should I hide what he said?) for its pure Latinity, its correctness, its erudition, and its expressions of tender affection. Seeing how delighted he was, I showed him your speech. He read it, as also your poems, with a pleasure so far beyond what he had hoped, that although he praised you most effusively, yet his countenance showed that his words were all too poor to express what he felt. He took out at once from his pocket a portague which you will find enclosed in this letter. I tried in every possible way to decline it, but was unable to refuse to take it to send to you as a pledge and token of his good-will towards you. This hindered me from showing him the letters of your sisters, for I feared that it would seem as though I had shown them to obtain for the others too a gift which it annoyed me to have to accept for you. But, as I have said, he is so good that it is a happiness to be able to please him. Write to thank him with the greatest care and delicacy. You will one day be glad to have given pleasure to such a man. Farewell.

"From the Court, just before mid-night, September 11th."

Margaret's eloquence, learning, and wit must indeed have been extraordinary to have earned from a man so prominent such high praise and so valuable a gift.

I have in my possession a speech of hers. It is eloquent, clever, and perfect in its use of oratorical devices. It is in imitation, or rather in rivalry, of Quintilian's speech on the destruction of the poor man's bees through the poison that had been sprinkled upon the flowers in the rich man's garden. Quintilian defends the cause of the poor man : Margaret of the rich. The more difficult such a defence is, the greater scope for Margaret's eloquence and wit. If it were not that I fear to be tedious and to digress too much from the task I have undertaken of writing More's life, I would print the speeches both of Margaret and of Quintilian, either in this place or in an appendix.

In another of More's letters to his daughter he extols her learning in unmeasured terms, and yet, while we cannot suspect the flattery that might be offered to one in high position or the blandishments that might be offered to a child, he was too good and loving a father to wish to deceive.

In another he speaks of her verses as follows : " I would not only repay each line of it with a golden philippine, as Alexander did the verses of Cherilos, but, if my means were as great as my desire, I would reward each syllable with two gold ounces."

These letters, however, and all the others I will omit, for already my account has become longer than I expected. One more only will I transcribe, but it will certainly show the reader still more clearly the admirable wit of Margaret and the great variety of studies pursued in More's school.

" Thomas More to his most dear daughter Margaret :

" There was no reason, my most sweet child, why you should have put off writing for a day, because in your great self-distrust you feared lest your letter should be such that I could not read it without distaste. Even had it not been perfect, yet the honour of your sex would have gained you pardon from any, while to a father even a blemish will seem beautiful in the face of a child. But indeed, my dear Margaret, your letter was so elegant and polished and gave so little cause for you to dread the judgement of an indulgent parent, that you might have despised the censorship even of an angry Momus.

" You tell me that Nicholas, who is fond of you and so learned in astronomy, has begun again with you the system of the heavenly bodies. I am grateful to him, and I con-

gratulate you on your good fortune; for in the space of
one month, with only a slight labour, you will thus learn
thoroughly these sublime wonders of the Eternal Workman,
which so many men of illustrious and almost superhuman
intellect have only discovered with hot toil and study, or
rather with cold shiverings and nightly vigils in the open
air in the course of many ages.

" I am, therefore, delighted to read that you have made
up your mind to give yourself diligently to philosophy, and
to make up by your earnestness in future for what you have
lost in the past by neglect.   My darling Margaret, I indeed
have never found you idling, and your unusual learning in
almost every kind of literature shows that you have been
making active progress.   So I take your words as an
example of the great modesty that makes you prefer to
accuse yourself falsely of sloth, rather than to boast of your
diligence ; unless your meaning is that you will give yourself so earnestly to study, that your past industry will seem
like indolence by comparison.   If this is your meaning
nothing could be more delightful to me, or more fortunate,
my sweetest daughter, for you.

" Though I earnestly hope that you will devote the rest
of your life to medical science and sacred literature, so that
you may be well furnished for the whole scope of human
life, which is to have a healthy soul in a healthy body, and
I know that you have already laid the foundations of these
studies, and there will be always opportunity to continue
the building; yet I am of opinion that you may with great
advantage give some years of your yet flourishing youth to
humane letters and liberal studies.   And this both because
youth is more fitted for a struggle with difficulties ; and
because it is uncertain whether you will ever in future have
the benefit of so sedulous, affectionate and learned a
teacher.   I need not say that by such studies a good judgement is formed or perfected.

" It would be a delight, my dear Margaret, to me to
converse long with you on these matters : but I have just
been interrupted and called away by the servants, who have
brought in supper.   I must have regard to others, else to
sup is not so sweet as to talk with you.   Farewell, my
dearest child, and salute for me my most gentle son, your

husband. I am extremely glad that he is following the same course of study as yourself. I am ever wont to persuade you to yield in everything to your husband ; now, on the contrary, I give you full leave to strive to get before him in the knowledge of the celestial system. Farewell again. Salute your whole company, but especially your tutor."[1]

From all that we have said, then, the reader will easily judge how admirable a father he was to his children, how numerous were their studies, with what great care, affection, and insatiable zeal he instructed them, and, as Margaret Roper alone is enough to prove, how abundantly he succeeded.

[1] Father Bridgett's translation.

CHAPTER XII

APOTHEGMS, WISE AND DEVOUT SAYINGS OF SIR THOMAS MORE

FROM the details we have already given, the reader will have had no difficulty in appreciating the learning, the wisdom, and the piety of Sir Thomas More. I do not wish the reader, however, to be content with my words : I wish him to have evident, clear and, so to say, tangible proofs of More's great qualities. At this point, then, for the benefit of the Latin reader, I will introduce a number of his sayings, as specimens of his wit or his piety. I will also add similar passages from his English Works, not indeed as many as a closer study would gather together, but such as occurred to me during a recent perusal of his works. These extracts, I think, will conduce not only to More's praise, but also—and this is my especial desire—to the reader's utility and edification. It is in no way unusual in writing the lives of great and saintly men to add their clever sayings or proverbs. Speech reveals the man and "from the abundance of the heart the mouth speaketh."[1] I have not thought it necessary to attempt to connect the various sayings together or to arrange them in logical order : I have merely noted the page on which they occur in the volume of his English Works.

First, then, in his book on the Four Last Things : "Think not that every thing is pleasant which men for madness laugh at. For thou shalt in Bedlam see one laugh at the knocking of his own head against a post, and yet there is little pleasure therein."[2] In saying this, he had in mind the judgements and opinions of worldly men, to follow which he thought the height of folly.

"Our soul can have no place for the good corn of spiritual pleasure, as long as it is overgrown with the barren weeds

[1] Matt. xii 34.   [2] E.W., p. 73.

of carnal delectation."[1] Thus does he account for the fact
that many men find no pleasure in prayer or in divine
worship.

He shows by the following example why so few think of
death or fear it : " By the hope of long life we look upon
death, either so far off that we see him not at all, or but
a fleight[2] and uncertain sight, as a man may see a thing so
far off that he wotteth not whether it be a bush or a beast.
And surely so fare we by death, looking thereat afar off,
through a great long space of as many years as we hope to
live."[3] Thus men do not meditate upon the real nature of
death, its terrors, its bitterness, its horrors, its pains and
its dangers.

By the following comparison he warns us, whatever our
age may be, not to promise ourselves a long life : " If there
were two, both condemned to death, both carried out at
once towards execution, of which two the one were sure
that the place of his execution were within one mile, the
other twenty miles off, yea a hundred an ye will, he that
were in the cart to be carried a hundred miles, would not
take much more pleasure than his fellow in the length of
his way, notwithstanding that it were a hundred times as
long as his fellow's, and that he had thereby a hundred times
as long to live, being sure and out of all question to die at
the end."[4] So a young man cannot promise himself a
longer life than an old man. Every man, that is to say, is
born under sentence of death on account of original sin.
The old man travels to execution by a long route, the young
man by a short one, but until death comes neither knows
how long that route may be.

The vanity of sinners who, in the prison of this world, are
anxious to leave some memorial to their rank and name
he declares to be " as if a gentleman thief when he should
go to Tyburn would leave for a memorial the arms of his
ancestors painted on a post in Newgate."[5]

He constructs the following dilemma to show that no
one ought to consider himself injured even though he suffer
the loss of superfluous wealth : " If ye would have spent it
well, ye have no cause to be sorry of the loss, for God

[1] E.W., p. 74.　　[2] *i.e.*, flitting.　　[3] E.W., p. 79.
[4] E.W., p. 82.　　　　　　　　[5] E.W., p. 84.

accepteth your good will.   If ye would have kept it covet-
ously or spent it naughtily, ye have a cause to be glad, and
reckon that ye have won by the loss, in that the matter and
occasion of your sin is by God's goodness graciously taken
from you."[1]

In the following story he pictures to the life the folly of
the miser, especially if he be old : " I remember me of
a thief once cast at Newgate, that cut a purse at the bar
when he should be hanged on the morrow.   And when he
was asked why he did so, knowing that he should die so
shortly, the desperate wretch said that it did his heart good
to be lord of that purse one night yet."[2]

These passages are taken from an incomplete work.   If
those portions that have been lost could be recovered, we
may be sure that we should have in that book of devotion
many more proofs of More's wit and wisdom.

The folly and even the madness of those who take delight
in secret hoards of money he describes most aptly in the
following comparison.   He writes in the person of the souls
of the dead, now in purgatory, in the little book we have
already mentioned, entitled *The Supplication of Souls* : " The
despiteful sights that our evil angels bring us to behold
abroad, so far augmenteth our torment, that we would wish
to be drowned in the darkness that is here rather than see
the sights that they show us there.   For among they convey
us into our own houses, and there double is our pain with
sight sometimes of the self-same things which, while we
lived, was half our heaven to behold.   There show they us
our substance and our bags stuffed with gold, which when
we now see we set much less by them, than would an old
man that found a bag of cherry stones which he laid up when
he was a child."[3]

We will now quote a few similar passages from the books
of *The Dialogue of Comfort in Tribulation.*

In order that we may not be overmuch perturbed by
adversity, he makes the following paradoxical assertion :
" So blind is our mortality and so unaware what will fall,
so unsure also what manner mind we will ourselves have
to-morrow, that God could not lightly do man a more

[1] E.W., p. 91.   [2] E.W., p. 92.
[3] E.W., p. 336.

vengeance, than in this world to grant him his own foolish wishes."[1]

The fruit of tribulation in this life he shows by the following learned distinction : "Likewise as in hell, pain only serveth for punishment without any manner of purging, because all possibility of purging is past ; and in purgatory punishment serveth for only purging, because the place of deserving is past. So while we be yet in this world in which is our place and our time of merit and well-deserving, the tribulation that is sent us for our sin here shall (if we faithfully so desire), besides the cleansing and purging of our pain, serve us also for increase of reward."[2]

The vanity of those who spend this life in sloth and idleness he illustrates thus : "They that so do, fare like a fond fellow that going towards his own house where he should be wealthy, would for a tapster's pleasure become an ostler by the way and die in a stable and never come at home."[3] That is to say, we are on our journey to the kingdom of heaven, but on the way we cleave to earthly things so that we may enjoy the company of some clown or boon companion.

Against lazy and easy-going pastors of the flock he uses this most apt comparison : "As the mother dealeth sometimes with her child, which when the little boy will not rise in time for her, but lie still abed and slug, and when he is up weepeth because he hath lain so long, fearing to be beaten at school for his late coming thither: she telleth him then that it is but early days and he shall come time enough, and biddeth him go. 'Good son, I warrant thee, I have sent to thy master myself; take thy bread and butter with thee, thou shalt not be beaten at all.' And thus, so she may send him merry forth at the door that he weep not in her sight at home, she studieth not much upon the matter though he be taken tardy and beaten when he cometh to school."[4] So many pastors of souls speak soothing words to those who are rich and luxurious. When such men are near to death and in dread of the pains of hell, these pastors buoy them up with false hopes and promise them that all will be well, telling them either that their sins have not

[1] E.W., p. 1147.
[2] E.W., p. 1152.
[3] E.W., p. 1154.
[4] E.W., p. 1156.

been so grave or that God is merciful and will readily forgive. Nor do they care at all what pains these men may
afterwards suffer in hell, provided that they do not sadden
them in this life but retain their goodwill and continue
to benefit by their liberality.

Elsewhere whilst discussing whether prosperity or adversity is more likely to lead man away from the service
of God, he makes the following distinction : " The prayers
of him that is in wealth, and him that is in woe, if the men
be both nought, their prayers be both like. For neither
hath the one lust to pray nor the other neither. And as
the one is let[1] with his pain, so is the other with his pleasure,
saving that the pain stirreth him sometimes to call upon
God in his grief, though the man be right bad, where[2] the
pleasure pulleth his mind another way, though the man be
meetly[3] good."[4]

Against those who are impenitent and put off their
amendment to the end of their life he tells the following
tale, whether true or fictitious : " They tell of one that was
wont always to say that all the while he lived he would do
what he lust, for three words when he died would make all
safe enough. But then so happed it that long ere he were
old, his horse once stumbled upon a broken bridge, and as
he laboured to recover him, when he saw it would not be,
but down into the flood headlong needs he should : in
a sudden flight[5] he cried out in the falling, ' Have all to the
devil !' And there was he drowned with his three words
ere he died, whereon his hope hung all his wretched life."[6]

Between true and false visions he draws this distinction :
" Likewise seemeth me the manner and difference between
some kind of true revelations and some kind of false illusions,
as it standeth between the things that are done waking, and
the things that in our dreams seem to be done."[7]

He shows the empty fears of some timorous men by this
apt illustration : " Likewise as some man going over a
high bridge waxeth so feared through his own fantasy,
that he falleth down indeed, which were else able enough
to pass over without any danger ; and as some man shall

---

[1] *i.e.*, hindered.   [2] *i.e.*, whereas.   [3] *i.e.*, moderately.
[4] E.W., p. 1163.   [5] *i.e.*, state of agitation.
[6] E.W., p. 1174.   [7] E.W., p. 1192.

upon such a bridge, if folk call upon him, ' You fall, you fall,' fall with the fantasy that he taketh thereof, which bridge, if folk looked merrily upon him and said, ' There is no danger therein,' he would pass over well enough, and would not let[1] to run thereon, if it were but a foot from the ground, thus fareth it in this temptation. The devil findeth the man of his own fond fantasy afeard, and then cryeth he in the ear of his heart, ' Thou fallest, thou fallest,' and maketh the fond man afeard, that he should at every foot fall indeed. And the devil so wearieth him with that continual fear . . . that at the last he withdraweth his mind from due remembrance of God and then driveth him to that deadly mischief indeed. . . . So must a man in this temptation too not only resist it always with reasoning thereagainst, but sometimes set it clear at right nought, and cast it off when it cometh, and not once regard it so much as to vouchsafe to think thereon." [2]

How unstable and fleeting is the prosperity of this world he shows by this comparison : " But surely this worldly prosperity . . . is but even a very short winter day. For we begin, many full poor and cold, and up we fly like an arrow that were shot up into the air. And yet when we be suddenly shot up into the highest, ere we be well warm there, down we come into the cold ground again, and then even there stick we still . . . sometimes not in a very cleanly place, but the pride turneth into rebuke and shame, and there is then all the glory gone." [3]

That wealth and honours bring with them almost the certainty of sin he explained under these images : " For as it is a thing right hard to touch pitch and never file the fingers, to put flare[4] unto fire and yet keep them from burning, to keep a serpent in thy bosom and yet be safe from stinging . . . so is it hard for any person either man or woman, in great worldly wealth and much prosperity, to . . . keep themselves from the deadly desire of ambitious glory." [5]

He warns a man, even though he be raised to the highest

---

[1] *i.e.*, hesitate.   [2] E.W., p. 1197.   [3] E.W., p. 1199.
[4] *i.e.*, a flake of lard, highly inflammable. The term is still used by butchers.
[5] E.W., p. 1200.

dignity, not to be moved to vainglory, and bids him regard even the very beggars as his equals and companions. To drive this lesson home he uses the following illustration: "If here were two men that were beggars both, and afterward a great rich man would take the one unto him, and tell him that for a little time he would have him in his house, and thereupon arrayed him in silk, and gave him a great bag by his side filled even full of gold, but giving him this knot therewith, that within a little while out he should in his old rags again, and bear never a penny with him. If this beggar met his fellow now, while his gay gown were on, might he not for all his gay gear take him for his fellow still ? And were he not a very fool, if for a wealth of a few weeks he would ween himself far his better ?"[1]

For so indeed we have all equally come naked into this world, and equally go forth from it naked. It is only by the free generosity of Almighty God that in the meantime we enjoy possessions, greater or smaller.

"Avarice," he says, "fareth like the fire, the more wood that cometh thereto, the more fervent and the more greedy it is."[2]

He speaks of "a good worshipful man, which when he divers times beheld his wife, what pain she took in strait binding up her hair, to make her a fair large forehead, and with strait bracing in her body to make her middle small, both twain to her great pain, for the pride of a little foolish praise, he said unto her, 'Forsooth, madam, if God give you not hell, he shall do you great wrong.'" He goes on to say : "So help me God, and none otherwise, but as I verily think, that many a man buyeth hell here with so much pain, that he might have bought heaven with less than the one half."[3]

He foresaw only too clearly and foretold the spread of heresy in England. He speaks of the carrying into Hungary of the blasphemies of Mahomet, but in reality he is referring to the coming into England of the doctrines of the Lutherans, Sacramentarians, and other heretics or schismatics. "For like as before a great storm the sea

[1] E.W., p. 1201.
[2] E.W., p. 1202 (printed 1124 in error).
[3] E.W., p. 1203 (printed 1205 in error).

beginneth sometimes to work and roar in itself, ere ever the winds wax boisterous, so methinks I hear at my ear some of our own here among us, which within these few years could no more have born the name of a Turk than the name of the devil, begin now to find little fault therein, yea and some to praise them too, little and little as they may, more glad to find faults at every state of Christendom, priests, princes, rites, ceremonies, sacraments, laws and customs spiritual, temporal and all."[1]

That wealth does not deserve of itself that name of good which it so commonly receives, he shows by this argument : "If the having of strength make a man strong, and the having of heat make a man hot, and the having of virtue make a man virtuous, how can those things be verily and truly good which he that hath them, may by the having of them as well be the worse as the better?"[2]

As to places of honour in the State, he says that a man who has others above him, as have all but the King, has no reason for self-complacency. "And I wist once a great officer of the King's say . . . that twenty men standing barehead before him, keep not his head half so warm as to keep on his own cap. Nor he never took so much ease with their being barehead before him, as he caught once grief with a cough that came upon him by standing barehead long before the King."[3]

The holy and pious sentiments which next we shall quote he chose as a salutary guide to his whole life. "There can not in this world be a worse mind than that a man to delight and take comfort in any commodity that he taketh by sinful means." To confirm this he adds: "And therefore if ye will well do, reckon yourself very sure, that when you deadly displease God for the getting or the keeping of your goods, God shall not suffer those goods to do you good, but either shall he take them shortly from you, or suffer you to keep them for a little while to your more harm."[4]

He shows the folly of those who are avaricious and un- willing to give alms by this illustration : "And therefore like as if we saw that we should be within a while driven

[1] E.W., p. 1212.
[2] E.W., p. 1218.
[3] E.W., p. 1224.
[4] E.W., p. 1231.

out of this land, and fain to fly into another, we would ween
that man were mad which would not be content to forbear
his goods here for the while, and send them into that land
before him, where he saw he should live at the remnant of
his life, so may we verily think yet ourselves much more
mad . . . if the fear of a little lack or the love to see our
goods here about us, and the loathness to part from them
for this little while which we may keep them here, shall be
able to let[1] us from the sure sending them before us into the
other world, in which we may be sure to live wealthily with
them if we send them thither, or else shortly leave them
here behind us, and then stand in great jeopardy there to
live wretches for ever."[2]

To console himself for the loss of his liberty in the Tower,
he used to say that the whole world was nothing more than
a prison, for men were banished from paradise and detained
in the world for their sins, and from it they were summoned
daily one by one to stand their trial.[3]

These wise sayings I have selected from his books : those
which follow have been gathered from the recollection of
those who were intimate with him.   The first is well-known
and was frequently upon his lips.   " It may easily be that
a man should lose his head and yet come to no harm "
—i.e., when it is in the cause of truth and right.

Here is another of his witty sayings : " Usually the world
has no desire to reward good deeds as they deserve, but even
if it had the desire it would not have the power."

Of heretics he said : " They have done with hypocrisy
and have substituted impudence.   Whereas before they
affected an appearance of religion, now they glory in their
impiety."

He often prayed as follows : " O Lord, my God, help me
to labour zealously to obtain those gifts for which I am
wont to ask thee in my prayers."

If ever, when he was entertaining his guests at home, he
heard any word against God's honour, any word disloyal
to authority or uncharitable to other men, he would interrupt the conversation by saying : " Let others think and
say what they will, but for my part I consider that this

[1] i.e., hinder.   [2] E.W., p. 1233.
[3] cf. E.W., p. 1245.

gallery is of the greatest elegance and convenience "; and then he would go on to talk of other things.

Of ingratitude he said : " We write in the sand the benefits we receive, but injuries upon marble."

We will now give a few extracts from the books he wrote against the heretics.

The heretics utterly rejected the use of reason in matters of faith, but More argued as follows against so obvious and superstitious a folly : " I cannot see why ye should reckon reason for an enemy to faith, except ye reckon every man for your enemy, that is your better and hurteth you not. Thus were one of your five wits enemy to another.   And our feeling should abhor our sight because we may see further by four miles than we may feel."[1]   Later on he shows by an illustration that reason far from being an enemy to faith is a most useful ally to it.   " But likewise as if a maid be suffered to run on the bridle, or be cup-shotten,[2] or wax too proud, she will then wax copious and chop logic with her mistress, and fare sometimes as she were frantic ; so if reason be suffered to run out at riot, and wax over high-hearted and proud, she will not fail to fall into rebellion towards her mistress faith.   But on the other side, if she be well brought up and well guided and kept in good temper, she shall never disobey faith, being in her right mind.   And therefore let reason be well guided, for surely faith goeth never without her."[3]

More was certainly most happy in choosing apt similes, and clever in applying them.   That the dissensions of the heretics are nothing but a conspiracy of wicked men to deceive the world, he shows by this witty illustration : " Now these heretics be almost as many sects as men, and never one agreeth with other, so that if the world were to learn the right way of them, that matter were much like as if a man walking in a wilderness that fain would find the right way toward the town that he intended, should meet with a many of lewd mocking knaves, which when the poor man had prayed them to tell him the way, would get them into a roundel turning them back to back, and then speak all at once, and each of them tell him, ' This way,' each of

[1] E.W., p. 152.   [2] i.e., drunk.
                    [3] E.W., p. 153.

9

them pointing forth with his hand the way that his face standeth."[1]   For like these rogues do the heretics of the day mock the enquirer.

That the unlearned should not read the books of the heretics he shows thus : " Howbeit, though every shop were full of treacle, yet were he not wise, I ween, that would wilfully drink poison first to drink treacle after, but rather cast the poison to the devil, and let the treacle stand for the some that should happen to need it."[2]

Of heretical versions of the Bible, and of the unwisdom of reading them even when corrected, he wrote as follows : " The faults be so many in Tyndall's translation of the New Testament, and so spread through the whole book, that likewise as it were as soon done to weave a new web of cloth, as to sew up every hole in a net, so were it almost as little labour and less, to translate the whole book all new, as to make in his translation so many changes as needs must be ere it were made good ; besides this that there would no wise man, I trow, take the bread which he well wist was of his enemy's hand once poisoned, though he saw his friend after scrape it never so clean."[3]   Especially when he had at hand other bread that never had been poisoned.

Such was the readiness of his wit in discovering analogies in nature with which to refute the arguments of the heretics.

From the texts, " Of his own will hath he begotten us by the word of truth," and " By grace you are saved through faith, and that not of yourselves, for it is the gift of God "[4] the heretics tried to show that it was by his own goodwill that God saved us, but not by our own : " he did not beget us after our own will, nor as it pleased us."   More replied : " If I desired a man to give me a thing, and laboured much to him therefore, and much endeavoured myself in many things to please him, to the intent that he should give it me, and that he thereupon so did, this were then but a poor argument to say thus : ' This man willingly gave me this thing, and after his own will, and as it pleased him, ergo he gave it me not after my own will and as it pleased me.'   For as ye see, it both pleased him to give it me and also it pleased me that he so should, or else I would never

[1] E.W., p. 707.   [2] E.W., p. 356.
[3] E.W., p. 224.   [4] Jas. i 18 and Eph. ii 8.

have desired it, nor never have laboured therefore."[1] For thus penitent sinners obtain from God pardon, and the just many gifts of grace.

It was taught by the heretics that fasting should be practised for no other purpose than the taming of the flesh. If this were so, he replied, " Then many wedded men should need few fasting days to their pain, having their remedy so pleasant and so present always ready at hand, and then would many an honest maiden be ashamed to fast any day at all, lest she should seem thereby to give young men warning that she were wax warm and bid them, if they will speed, speak now."[2] Other extracts of a like kind we will give in the next chapter.

He used to say that he who was filled with an ardent desire to see the face of God would readily be admitted by God to his presence ; whilst, on the contrary, no one would ever be permitted to enjoy the vision of God who had not longed for it with the greatest fervour.

Let these few examples of his prudent and devout sayings suffice as specimens from which to judge his learning, his wisdom, and his piety. We will now go on to give some quotations to illustrate, not only his learning and his piety, but also his ready humour which, though so brilliant and amusing, never wounded anyone. Thus we trust that the reader may be able to know better the admirable character and talents of this incomparable man.

[1] E.W., p. 860.   [2] E.W., p. 368.

CHAPTER XIII

HIS KEEN HUMOUR

SIR THOMAS MORE, of whom Erasmus, his intimate friend, writes that his heart was purer than snow, though his wisdom was profound, his life strict, and his reserve impenetrable, yet was in the ordinary intercourse of life extraordinarily pleasant, witty, and amusing. The seriousness of his character was much in evidence in the multifarious public business in which he was engaged, but he tempered it ever with kindliness and humour. It is not easy to decide which was more admirable, his wisdom as a Councillor or his geniality as a friend. He often introduced humour even into most serious business, without the slightest change in his features or the gravity of his demeanour. He was never angry, but always pleasant; nor did he ever appear light or frivolous, but always serious and self-possessed. Often, indeed, even by his most intimate friends he was thought to be speaking in earnest when he was simply joking. Even when in his writings he is giving a most convincing reply to an opponent, often it is a humorous one. Nowhere in his works will you find sarcasm, jeering, or bitter irony. He confutes the heretic, parrying his attacks and answering his objections, but in a playful way. In a word, whether he is pressing his opponent or being pressed by him, whether he is striking or defending, he does so with humour, so wittily and cleverly indeed that you will be at a loss to decide whether you should admire more his cleverness or his easy manner, his keen logic or his eloquence.

But it will be better for us now to give examples of all these qualities, partly from his writings and partly from what we have gathered from trustworthy witnesses. First, then, from his writings.

Luther claimed it as a miracle that in so short a time such

a large body of Christians had joined his sect. More replied : "That the people should hasten to accept the offer of freedom to live licentiously, is as strange a miracle as that stones should fall to earth." And again : "If the monastic life is, as you strive to show, against the Gospel, then the evangelical life is contrary to the monastic life, and one should live in luxury, eat well, drink well, sleep well, give full rein to lust and all other pleasures." Such an answer is as clever and witty as it is weighty and serious. Of the same nature is the following : "If good works are the necessary result of faith" (for so they assert in order to give some moral covering to their doctrine of justification by faith alone), "when you argue against good works, what else do you do but babble against the fruit of faith ?" Also the following, where More replies to the heretics who condemn as mercenaries those who hold that there is a reward for good works : "These gentry are so noble-minded that rather than allow themselves to be hired to work for one penny in the vineyard, they would prefer to be hanged outside." One more example : "Whereas you are constantly attacking scholastic theology on the ground that it is dangerous to move doubts against the truth, you on the contrary attack truth by asserting falsehoods as indubitable facts."[1]

Now let us turn to his English Works, for all his other Latin writings are contained in the Latin volume and are in everybody's hands.

When the writings of the heretics were praised for their brevity, he replied : "Since that of all their whole purpose they prove in conclusion never a piece at all, were their writing never so short, yet were their whole work at last too long by all together."[2] In another place he expresses it yet more cleverly : "Like as no man can make a shorter course than he that lacketh both his legs, so can no man make a shorter book than he that lacketh as well words as matter."[3]

<hr/>

[1] All the extracts just given are from More's Latin letter against Pomeranus (Bugenhagen), which was published by John Fowler, Louvain, 1568, but is not contained in More's collected works (Bridgett, p. 218 n.).

[2] E.W., p. 848.   [3] E.W., p. 931.

To a heretic who said that More ought not to blame in his writings those who stirred up schisms and dissensions, unless he could provide some remedy for these same dissensions, he replied : " It is much like as if he would say that there ought no man to blame him that would burn up another man's house, but he that would build it up again."[1]

The following passage is yet more clever and witty. A heretic in attacking More had said that he ought to prove his point by an explicit text of Scripture and not by his unwritten dreams. More answered : " He giveth my dreams, I thank him of his courtesy, much more authority than ever I looked for. For while he rejecteth none of therein but such as are unwritten, he sheweth himself ready to believe them, if I would vouchsafe to write them."[2]

He used to say that the heretics concocted weak and fallacious arguments and pretended that these were the arguments of the Catholics, which then they proceeded to confute without any difficulty, " as," he said, " children make castles of tile shards, and then make them their pastime in the throwing down again."[3]

Of the abuse the heretics showered upon him he said : " I was not so far unreasonable as to look for reasonable minds in unreasonable men."[4]

The heretics were angry at these and similar pleasantries of More, and blamed them, though, as I believe, it was rather because they envied his wit than because they felt themselves hurt. " I can scant believe," he says, " that the brethren find any mirth in my books. For I have not much heard that they very merrily read them."[5]

He regarded it as a great mistake and defect for theologians to be versed in scholastic theology alone, to neglect the reading of Holy Scripture and the Fathers, and to be content with Peter Lombard or Gratian and the extracts cited by them from the Fathers. On this matter he spoke as follows in his letter to Martin Dorpius :

"Theologians of this kind, who read nothing of the Fathers or of the Scriptures except in the Sentences, and the commentators on the Sentences, seem to me to act as if one were to set aside all the authors who have written in

[1] E.W., p. 935.   [2] E.W., p. 1117.   [3] E.W., p. 1131.
[4] E.W., p. 930.   [5] E.W., p. 927.

Latin, and, gathering the rules of grammar from Alexander, try to learn all else from the *Cornucopia* of Perottus and from Calepinus, being convinced that all Latin words will be found there. Well, most words will be found there, and the choicest words, and the sentences from ancient poets and orators, some of whom are no longer extant elsewhere. Yet such a method will never make a good Latinist. And so also, though in your Summists and Masters of Sentences you will find many sayings of the ancients quoted as authorities, yet the study of these things alone will never make a good theologian."[1]

But not only in his writings—in which, as he tells us, he used to insert merry sayings, like a sauce to the meat—but still more in his manner of acting and in familiar conversation humour played a gracious part. Often indeed he would turn aside a matter of grave offence with a joke.

ESCAPE OF THE HERETIC CONSTANTINE FROM MORE'S HOUSE.

When he was Chancellor he had in his custody a heretic named Constantine. This man managed to escape from More's house. Calling the porter, More bade him to "see the stocks mended and locked fast that the prisoner shall not in again." The heretics were jubilant over the escape of their friend, and spread about the story that the Chancellor was so vexed at this mishap that because of his anger he could scarcely eat for three days. More replied : " I could him in good faith good thank. For never will I for my part be so unreasonable as to be angry with any man that riseth if he can, when he findeth himself that he sitteth not at his ease."[2]

The never-broken serenity of his mind was doubtless due to the constant peace and joy of his conscience. The merriness of his speech and a clever wit were most helpful to More in most difficult circumstances, and were a sure protection to his innocence and his constancy. I will now give a few examples so that his ready humour may be seen, and, at the same time, his noble freedom and serenity of soul.

[1] Father Bridgett's translation.   [2] E.W., p. 902.

More turns aside the Anger of Wolsey.

When he was Speaker in Parliament, by his eloquence, wisdom, and perseverance he defeated certain unjust proposals of Cardinal Wolsey, who at that time was all-powerful with the King. When the Session was at an end, the Cardinal summoned More—in order, no doubt, to rebuke his boldness—to attend him at the magnificent new palace which he had lately built for himself. When, after keeping More waiting for a long time, the Cardinal at length appeared, he said to More in the hearing of many gentlemen, "Would to God you had been at Rome, Mr. More, when I made you Speaker." Instantly More replied, "Your Grace not offended, so would I too, my Lord ; for I should then have seen for the first time a beautiful city of which I have heard much." He said no more, but at such an unexpected reply the Cardinal was struck dumb and walked by More's side for some time in silence. At length, feeling some shame at so long a silence in the presence of so many noblemen and gentlemen, and thinking how he might break so awkward a pause, More began to speak of the beauty and the magnificence of the palace and so on. The Cardinal had imagined that More would beg his pardon and submit himself utterly to him, but seeing his composure he gave no answer but suddenly broke away and hastened to his room. This incident shows More's boldness and freedom, but the following shows also his clever and ready wit, whereby without giving offence he was able to parry successfully a bitter attack.

He opposes Wolsey's Ambitious Proposals.

Soon after More's entry into the Privy Council, Wolsey brought forward a proposal that a Supreme Constable should be created to represent the person of the King in the whole kingdom. Such a magistracy was almost unparalleled in England, but Wolsey, whose ambition brought so much ruin on our country, doubtless hoped that he would be appointed to the new office. He strongly urged his suggestion and was meekly followed by all the Dukes,

Counts, and other nobles who formed the King's Council. No one dared to contradict or to suggest any objection until More's turn came to speak. He spoke last and in a contrary sense : but he supported his view with so many powerful arguments that the Council wavered and declared that the matter needed fuller deliberation. The Cardinal was angry and thus addressed More : " Are you not ashamed, Mr. More, being the lowest of all in place and dignity, to dissent from so many noble and prudent men ? You show yourself to be a stupid and foolish Councillor." " Thanks be to God," replied More instantly, " that the King's Majesty has but one fool in his Council." He said no more, but the question was postponed and the plan finally rejected. More's answer was as wise as it was humble, and witty as well. Enough of this subject.

More and the Cut-Purse.

The incident which I shall now relate was not only a proof of his cleverness, but also very amusing. It took place in open court ; for, as we shall see, not only in the law-courts, but even in prison and on the scaffold, More's humour would burst out.

One day, when More was on the bench of magistrates, some pickpockets were brought before them. Those whose purses had been stolen were complaining of the losses they had sustained, when one of the magistrates, a very dignified old gentleman, with some asperity began to lecture them for not guarding their purses more carefully, and for providing, by their negligence and thoughtlessness, an opportunity for rogues of this kind to exercise their trade. Thus did he inveigh against those for whom he should have given judgement. A speech of this nature was little to More's taste, and accordingly, as the case was adjourned, he had one of the thieves brought from the prison privately to him that night, and arranged with him that at the next session he should steal the purse of the magistrate who had thus inveighed against the innocent, as he sat in court. The thief was quite willing, and More promised him his favour for this one occasion. When, then, More and the other magistrates were again assembled in court, the thief

was one of the first to be called upon to answer the charge
made against him. He replied that he could clear himself
if he were allowed to whisper some secret information to
one of the magistrates. Being asked to choose whichever
one he wished, he fixed upon that particular old gentleman.
Coming close to him to whisper his story into his ear, he
skilfully cut off the well-filled purse which was hanging at
his side. When he had finished what he had to say, he
returned to his place and gave a sign to More that he had
succeeded. A little while after More suggested that help
should be given to some poor fellow who was in danger
of death and permitted a public collection to be made on
his behalf. It began with him and his magistrates. The
old gentleman, wishing to give an alms, then discovered
that he had lost his purse : with shame and annoyance he
averred that he certainly had had it when he took his place
on the bench. More then suggested that he should not be
too severe on others who suffered a like misfortune and bade
the thief restore the purse. All who were present enjoyed
the joke and appreciated the wisdom that was intertwined
with More's humour. To incidents of this nature More
was referring, I imagine, when in his Epitaph he wrote :
" He was neither odious to the nobility, nor unpleasant to
the people." For by his kindness and cheerfulness he made
himself pleasing to all, and of all did he gain the goodwill.
Although there was never any bitterness or malice in his
humour, yet often with the greatest cleverness he turned
the laugh against pretentious vanity.

He confounds a Flemish Braggart.

When he was at Brussels on an embassy to the Emperor
Charles V it chanced that some braggart in that illustrious
Court affixed to the wall a paper in which he issued a
challenge to all and sundry. He professed himself ready to
answer any question or dispute upon any point in law or
literature. Seeing the man's vanity, Thomas More proposed the following question in English Law, " Whether
cattle taken in withernam be irrepleviable?" adding that
one of the suite of the English ambassadors desired to
dispute upon that subject. The braggart could of course

make no answer to a question of which he did not even understand the terms, and was forced to acknowledge his vanity in thus issuing a general challenge, becoming the laughing-stock of the whole Imperial Court.

But as in most serious matters he tried always to be pleasant and humorous, so in the midst of his jokes he kept so grave a face, and even when all those around were laughing heartily, looked so solemn, that neither his wife nor any other member of the family could tell from his countenance whether he was speaking seriously or in jest, but had to judge from the subject-matter or the circumstances. . . .[1]

"MADAM, MY LORD IS GONE."

The following instance shows his prudence and modesty no less than his ready wit. After he had resigned the Chancellorship, whilst as yet no one knew what had occurred, he came from London to his home and went at once to the church, where Vespers were being sung. Out of respect for his rank, his wife had a private closed pew. At the end of the office he went to the place and said to his wife, as usually one of his servants would say, " If you please, Madam, my Lord Chancellor is gone." Seeing him making the announcement in person, she thought he was joking. " No doubt it pleases you, Mr. More," she said, " to joke in this fashion." He replied : " I speak seriously and it is as I say : my Lord Chancellor is gone and is no longer here." In great astonishment she rose at once, and when she had learned the whole truth of the matter, woman-like she was in great distress at her husband's loss of position. By this humorous way of making the announcement, More wished both to soften the blow for his wife and to show what little account he made of his high honour.

---

[1] We omit here an anecdote which, though perfectly innocent, is very trivial and would repel rather than amuse the modern reader. Cresacre More thought it worth preserving (Bk. VII, § 3, 1st edition).

OTHER WITTY SAYINGS.

He married twice, and each of his wives was short in stature. When asked the reason he answered, " Of two evils one should choose the less."

At his imprisonment, on his entry into the Tower, when according to custom he was asked by the porter for his upper garment he handed him his cap. (" This certainly," he said, " rests in the highest place.") What the porter really demanded, with the warrant of custom, was his cloak.

When he was in the Tower, he was entertained at the table of the Lieutenant, according to his rank and position, as is the custom. (The Lieutenant, as is nearly always the case in the Tower, was a Knight.) Once the Lieutenant was politely apologising for the fare set before him. More answered, " If any one of us " (the others present were his fellow-captives) " is not satisfied with his fare, then I think you should turn him out of house and let him go and be hanged."

When later on the rigour of his confinement was increased and all his books and papers were taken away, he kept the blinds of his windows drawn down day and night. His gaoler asked why he acted thus. He answered : " Now that the goods and the implements are taken away, the shop must be closed."

When he was going up on to the scaffold where he was to die, he stretched out his hand for help : " I pray you," he said, " see me safe up : as for my coming down I will not trouble anyone."

When the executioner according to custom asked his pardon, " I am sorry," he replied, " that my neck is so short, for you will find it difficult to cut off my head creditably."

Many other witty sayings of a similar kind are related, but there is no need to recount them all here, nor is there reliable authority for all of them. His rivals and the heretics took offence at what they called his foolish levity in laughing and joking at so solemn a time. Edward Hall, the chronicler, for example, calls More therefore a foolish sage or a wise fool. The insulting gibe of this trifler has been well answered by one of our writers in a Greek couplet which may be rendered thus :[1]

> To thee, fond Hall, seems More both fool and wise :
> A fool to men may wise be in God's eyes.

It was not, indeed, through any levity or folly that More intermingled his jokes even with most serious business, but deliberately and on principle he gave play to his nimble wit. The reason which moved him so to act he explains by an apt comparison in the following passage : " Some man if he be sick can away with no wholesome meat, nor no medicine can go down with him, but if it be tempered with some such thing for his fantasy as maketh the meat or the medicine less wholesome than it should be. And yet while it will be no better we must let him have it so."[2] As men, then, will not endure to listen to long serious discourses unless they be enlivened by " merry tales," right reason justifies the use of such anecdotes. This is his apology for his common practice of intermingling humour and witty stories even with his most weighty arguments. It was the same with his conversation.

The following passage contains another justification for his practice : " God sent men hither to wake and work, and as for sleep and gaming . . . it must serve but for a refreshing of the weary and fore-watched body, to renew it unto watch and labour again. . . . For rest and recreation should be but as a sauce. . . . And therefore likewise as it were a fond feast that had all the table full of sauce and so little meat therewith that the guests should go thence as empty as they came thither, so is it surely a very mad ordered life that hath but little time bestowed in any fruitful business, and all the substance idly spent in play."[3] Similarly that life is sad and monotonous, dry and insipid, which has no admixture of joy and laughter. If this is generally true, it is especially so in the case of a man like More, married, a courtier, and occupied with all manner of public business.

[1] Stapleton gives a Latin as well as a Greek couplet.
[2] E.W., p. 1171. [3] E.W., p. 1048.

These, then, are a few samples, out of the many that might
be quoted, of his clever sayings and witty answers.

COMPARISON WITH CATO.

As I look back upon all that I have so far written about
Sir Thomas More, as I consider the high offices he filled in
the State and his blameless conduct throughout the whole
of his brilliant career ; his skill in letters and his wide
learning ; his gifts as poet, orator, philosopher, and even
theologian ; his numerous writings, his virtue and piety ;
his care of his children and his whole household ; his contempt of wealth and honours ; his many wise and witty
sayings ; his powerful mind, ready memory, and kindly
manners ; his constant geniality, sweetness, and lowliness
in the midst of such great talents, such high honours, and
such favour with his sovereign—as I recall all this and
ponder upon it, I am reminded of Livy's description of
M. Portius Cato Censorius.[1]   Indeed, the picture seems to
me to fit Sir Thomas More more truly and exactly than
Cato. " He possessed such powers of mind and intellect
that in whatever position he had been born he would
certainly have risen to the highest eminence. He lacked
no quality that makes for success in either private or public
life. With the affairs of the town and of the country-side
he was equally familiar. Some men attain high honours
by their legal skill, others by their eloquence, others by their
virtue : this man's genius was so many-sided that whatever
line he might have adopted, he would have been thought
by all to have been following his natural bent." From his
zeal for virtue you would have thought him a monk rather
than a courtier. Also he was a writer of great fame. " In
knowledge of the law he was most skilled : in pleading he
was most eloquent. The eloquence he displayed " on the
platform, in the courts, in Parliament, as a barrister, a
judge, or Speaker of the House of Commons " did not die
with him. Of eloquence alone, indeed, no lasting record
is possible, but his inspired words still live and are still
powerful in writings of every kind," Latin, Greek, secular

[1] Bk. XXXIX, ch. xl.

and religious. If he had to go on embassies, he was un-
surpassed in skill and success. If he was called upon for
advice in grave matters of State, his prudence was unrivalled. No one more freely spoke his mind. Averse to
all deceit and vain flattery, he expressed himself clearly,
simply, and always wittily.

Livy writes of Cato : " It is true that his disposition was
harsh, and his tongue bitter and unrestrained, but he was
sternly upright and unmoved by cupidity : wealth and
honours he despised." Such a description could not,
indeed, apply to Sir Thomas More, for his heart was bright
and gay : he was a Christian, not a Stoic : from Christ
he had learnt to be " meek and humble of heart."[1] He
knew that " the Lord is not in the wind . . . nor in the
earthquake," but that " the whistling of a gentle air "[2] is
the sign of his presence. He remembered that it was
foretold of Christ, " He shall not cry out . . . he shall not
be sad nor troublesome."[3] Of More, then, it could not be
said that " his disposition was harsh and his tongue bitter
and unrestrained." The rest of the description, however,
applies perfectly : "he was sternly upright and unmoved
by cupidity : wealth and honours he despised," as what we
have already related has shown and what we have still to
relate will show yet more clearly. We shall see how More
sacrificed all the favour of his prince, an ample fortune, and
the highest honours to be sternly upright, to be unconquered
by cupidity, to keep unsullied the purity of his conscience.

Cato, again, through the harshness of his disposition,
" harshly attacked the patricians and was as bitterly
attacked by them, so that it is not easy to decide whether
they caused him or he caused them more annoyance."
But Sir Thomas More was born to kindliness and gentleness : never did he engage in rivalries with others either
publicly or privately, nor did he bear ill-will to any. As he
wrote in his epitaph, " he had thus gone through this course
of offices or honours, that neither . . . was he odious to
the nobility nor unpleasant to the people, but yet to thieves,
murderers and heretics grievous." Hostile to vice, grievous
to criminals, More was like Cato in his seriousness, his

[1] Matt. xi 29.   [2] 3 Kings xix 11.
[3] Isa. xlii 4.

incorruptibility, his strict uprightness ; but to these qualities he added a constant courtesy of manner, sweetness, and meekness. He rendered, indeed, Cato's severe virtues amiable by his wit and cheerfulness. In no way, then, was he inferior to Cato in intellect, eloquence, knowledge, virtue, or integrity, whilst in kindliness of manner he excelled him.

But now we must pass on to consider in More gifts yet higher and nobler.

CHAPTER XIV

THE ORIGIN OF THE KING'S ANGER AND VENGEFUL PROCEEDINGS AGAINST SIR THOMAS MORE

I COME now to that part of the life of Thomas More which chiefly induced me to undertake the whole narrative. For I have written his Life not to draw his portrait as a man of rank, learning, wit, or high position, not as a good father, a wise ruler of a household, a just judge, or a man of letters, but above all as a saint and a glorious martyr for truth and right. For all that I have hitherto written of his public life and the favour of his prince, of his many friendships, his happy home life, his learning, etc., enhances the merit of his sacrifice. For when he laid his head upon the block, he could look back upon many years of public life, when he enjoyed the highest honours ; and for many future years he could have held the same positions of eminence, high in his King's favour, if he would but by a hair's-breadth have gone aside from the truth.

Martyrdom indeed is always glorious : so noble in the sight of men and so dear to God that even the vilest and most abandoned of men, if they sincerely repent and suffer death bravely for justice' sake, will receive the praise they deserve : they will be honoured by the Church of God and rewarded abundantly by God himself. But as in the Church Triumphant "there are many mansions,"[1] and "star differeth from star in glory,"[2] so also in the Church Militant there are various merits and degrees of honour. The more numerous and severe the temptations the martyr overcomes, and the more glorious the martyrdom, so much the more powerful will be his good example, and so much the greater praise will the Church's judgement ascribe to him. The

[1] John xiv 2.   [2] 1 Cor. xv 41.

Apostle had good reason to note that " not many wise according to the flesh, not many mighty, not many noble "[1] had in his days embraced the Cross of Christ. So although the Church honours all the martyrs, yet in her public litanies it is chiefly those of noble rank that we find commemorated. Thus, Sebastian, an officer of high rank in the household of Diocletian ; John and Paul, brothers and nobles so high in the public estimation that they were put to death secretly ; Cosmas and Damian, illustrious by their skill in medicine and intimately acquainted with the Emperors Diocletian and Maximian ; Gervasius and Protasius, also noble and wealthy, who prepared to meet their persecutor by distributing their goods to the poor and freeing their slaves. Thus, too, St Paulinus, because, although a rich and noble senator, he gave up everything to become a minister of the Church and to devote his energies to her cause, is lauded to the skies by his contemporaries, Ambrose,[2] Augustine,[3] and Jerome.[4]

My reason for dwelling in such detail upon Sir Thomas More's worldly honours, his skill in letters, his charming character, his most dear family, etc., is that the sufferings that afterwards he bore for the glory of God and for conscience' sake may appear as glorious as in reality they were. For I should not have praised these matters so highly in More, nor indeed should I have thought it right to do so, if they had not all served the cause of truth, and all been sacrificed at the call of God's will. It is indeed true that the end crowns the work and that the fine fruit of a good work is perseverance : but it is of the greatest importance to note that the truest praise and highest glory of the learned man, the man of high public office, the good citizen, the good father, is to be as ready to bear persecution bravely as to do good in prosperity. For we who are Christians and true servants of God "in our patience we possess our souls ";[5] "we shall receive a reward according to our labour ";[6] we call those " blessed who mourn," " who bear their cross after Christ," " who suffer persecution for

[1] 1 Cor. i 26.   [2] Epist. 36 (S.).
[3] Epist. 32 and *De Civ. Dei*, I, 10 (S.).
[4] *In Epist. ad eundem*, tom. i (S.).
[5] Luke xxi 19.   [6] 1 Cor. iii 8.

justice' sake,"[1] especially those who resist unto blood. For " greater love than this no man hath, that a man lay down his life for his friends,"[2] and if this be so in the case of friends, what are we to say of one who dies for God, who is to be loved above all ?

So now let us speak of More, the great and glorious martyr. But as it is not the death but the cause that makes the martyr, we will be at great pains to make the cause clear, all the more that hitherto it has not been thoroughly understood by foreign writers. We shall therefore describe the matter from the very beginning, put before the eyes of our readers all the charges that were made or rather trumped up against More, and make his innocence and unsullied honour clearer than the noonday sun.

The Divorce Question.

When, about the year 1528, first arose that unhappy question about Henry VIII's marriage with Catharine, his brother Arthur's widow, Thomas More was indeed a member of the King's Council, but was not invited by him to discuss or examine the matter. The examination was entrusted to theologians and canonists alone, and much was said on either side. Some asserted that the Bull of Dispensation was defective in juridical form by the omission of certain clauses, others brought forward an Apostolic Brief to remedy that defect. Afterwards the Pope's power of dispensation was brought into question, not in general, but for this particular impediment, which to some appeared, from the words of Leviticus, to be a matter of the Divine Law.[3]

At the time More happened to be abroad on an embassy to Flanders and was entirely ignorant of what was taking place. When he returned from this embassy and had given his account of all that had been done, the King called him aside and opened to him the matter of his divorce. He got a Bible and pointed out to More the texts of Leviticus and Deuteronomy, with the arguments that weighed with him and, as he said, many other learned men. Then he

---

[1] Matt. v 5 and 10, Luke xiv 27.   [2] John xv 13.
[3] *cf*. E.W., p. 1422.

asked More for his opinion. Thus appealed to, More said candidly what his view was of that text of Scripture. His opinion was not pleasing to the King, but Henry seemed to take it in good part, and bade him consult with Nicholas Fox, a doctor of theology, who was afterwards Bishop of Winchester, but then the King's Almoner. Also he bade him read a certain book, which was already in preparation, upon the question. He did as the King desired, but then a second time declared to him his opinion, which was unchanged.

A little later the King held at Hampton Court an assembly of a large number of learned men, but More was not present. Little business was done at this meeting, beyond settling the form in which was to appear the above-mentioned book on the divorce.

Soon afterwards this book was read through in the presence of Cardinal Wolsey and certain other Bishops and theologians, and was thought by them all to contain grounds sufficient to cause misgiving to the King as to the validity of his first marriage. They expressed the opinion that the King would do best to submit his difficulty to the judgement of the Church for solution.

Thereupon began the legal process before the two Apostolic Legates, Wolsey and Campeggio, an Italian. All this time More had no part whatever in the matter: indeed, as he writes, he was not qualified to do so, as the case was one for theologians and canonists. Indeed, while the Legates were continuing the sessions, More was a second time sent by the King on an embassy to Cambrai, to conclude peace between Charles the Emperor, Ferdinand the King of the Romans, Henry, King of England, and Francis, King of France—an embassy crowned with complete success. While More was away, the case dragged on for some months (on this point see Polydore), so that at last the King got angry and on October 18, 1529, deprived Wolsey of the dignity of Chancellor. On the 26th day of the same month this dignity was conferred on More, who had just returned from his successful mission to Cambrai.[1]

[1] The Great Seal was taken from Wolsey on October 19 and given to More on October 25. On the next day, October 26, More took the oath and was solemnly installed at Westminster (see Chapter III)

HENRY'S ATTEMPTS TO GAIN MORE'S SUPPORT.

Now that More was Chancellor, the King once more bade him make a new and more careful study of the marriage question. He was to put aside all prejudice in his investigation. If he came to the conclusion that he could give his consent to a divorce, the King would very gladly avail himself of his help in conjunction with the others to whom he had entrusted the business.

It is clear that the King hoped by the grant of this new and unprecedented honour to bring More entirely round to his side. " The course of events," writes Cardinal Pole, " shows clearly enough that the King made More Chancellor with the intention of bribing him, that he might allow himself to be a party to the King's designs."

At the time, however, the King bade More, in treating the question, say nothing and do nothing but what his conscience dictated, and place before his eyes God in the first place, and only in the second place the King. It may be that the King up to this time was really indifferent in the matter, although, taking into account the fall of Wolsey and other matters soon to be mentioned, we do not consider this probable. Or it may be that knowing More's utter sincerity he thought there was no other way of dealing with him.

MORE'S LOYALTY TO KING AND TO CONSCIENCE.

More, anxious, as in duty bound, to obey the King and to make a thorough examination of the whole case, begged him to deign to name some others who might help him in his investigations. For this purpose the King appointed Cranmer, afterwards Archbishop of Canterbury, Lee, afterwards Archbishop of York, Richard Fox, and Nicholas,[1] an Italian, all of whom were doctors of theology or canon law. More now discussed the matter thoroughly with these learned doctors : he read through and through all that he could find upon the matter, by whomsoever written, and studied the question as deeply as he could. He allowed

---

[1] *i.e.,* de Burgo.

no prejudice to influence him, but looked at the matter impartially and conformed himself to the judgement of the others as far as reason allowed, as the doctors we have mentioned afterwards testified to the King. But after all his study his opinion remained the same. Again he opened his mind to the King, protesting that he would far more willingly have followed the royal desire in the matter than receive any honours or revenues whatsoever from him, either those he had already received or those he might hope to receive in the future. The King, whether sincerely or not, received More's reply and protestation with the greatest kindness. For the future, however, those only did he admit to treat of the affair of his marriage, those only did he employ whose consciences he saw could without any scruple approve of the divorce.[1] But More and the many others whose consciences forbade approval he made use of in other affairs of State, for up to this time he forced the conscience of no man and made no trouble or difficulty with anyone in this matter.

After this More acted so loyally in the matter of the divorce that although he read gladly all the books that were published on the King's part, yet he would never so much as look at any published against the divorce, although many men at home in English and abroad in Latin had written against it. A certain book, written by the Bishop of Bath against the divorce at the time when the Papal Legates were holding their Court, More afterwards found amongst his papers ; but he delivered it up to the flames.

The details I have here transcribed are taken from a letter which after his resignation of the Chancellorship More wrote to Thomas Cromwell, then of the King's Council. My purpose has been to show what may have been the first cause of the King's annoyance with More, although at this time it was in no way apparent ; to show how loyally, wisely, and sincerely More behaved so that he might offend neither against the King nor against his own conscience ; and finally to show how anxious the King was to draw More over to his side.

For the whole time during which More was Chancellor

[1] Hence it is clear that the King deliberately favoured the divorce (marginal note, S.).

the affair of the divorce remained undecided. As the King, however, continued to follow his desire or rather his lust, and wished at all costs to satisfy it, More, who foresaw only too well the troubles that afterwards occurred, by earnest and repeated prayers, obtained from the King permission to resign the dignity and the burden of the Chancellorship, after he had borne that great charge with the highest integrity for a period of two and a half years. It was on October 26, 1529, that he was appointed, and on May 15, 1532, he resigned.[1]

[1] In reality it was on May 16 (Rymer, XIV, 433).

CHAPTER XV

THE FIRST ATTACK UPON MORE

MORE now lived at home in retirement, giving his time to prayer and study as he had always desired to do. But, as befitted the future noble confessor of the truth, and the spotless mirror of virtue and fortitude, he was attacked by various calumnies. Some of these may have been suggested to his creatures by the King himself, for he now began to appear disgusted with More's strict conscientiousness. Some may have been invented by his rivals in order to inflame the King's anger against an innocent man.

A few months after More's resignation—in August of the same year—William Warham, Archbishop of Canterbury, died. In his place was appointed Thomas Cranmer, Anne Boleyn's chaplain, a man after the King's own heart, ready to curry favour at any cost. After the King had determined to throw off the authority of the Apostolic See rather than remain any longer debarred from the union he lusted for, it was this same Cranmer (as can be seen more fully in the book on the origin of the Anglican Schism[1]) who, as Primate of England and Metropolitan, pronounced the divorce—that divorce which the King had so ardently desired—which was to be polluted with so much innocent blood, and was to be the foundation of so unhappy a schism.

More accused of Writing against the Divorce.

Immediately after the divorce a book was issued by the authority of the King's Council, giving the reasons for it. Amongst other things it was said that the King did not await the judgement of the Holy See because he was

---

[1] *i.e.*, Dr. Nicholas Sander's well-known work.

appealing from it to a General Council. A rumour immediately was spread abroad that More had published an answer in refutation of this book. From this calumny More clears himself in a letter to Thomas Cromwell, then a member of the King's Council and high in influence, asserting that he had never written nor wished to write against that book, and showing by many arguments that the whole story was utterly improbable.

THE " HOLY MAID OF KENT."

Having cleared himself on one calumny, he was attacked by another. Not long afterwards a certain nun called Ann Barton,[1] under divine inspiration as it was thought, prophesied evil to the King and to the realm. Consequently she fell under suspicion of treason, and after a long imprisonment she was executed together with some other religious. More had examined her at the command of the King, and it was made a matter of accusation against him that in addition to this examination he had had secret conferences with her and that they had exchanged letters. On this ground a charge was brought against More in Parliament, the King's attorney himself adding his name to the bill of attainder. But More entirely cleared himself from this base and odious calumny in another letter to Cromwell and in a letter to the King himself, with the result that Parliament dropped the charge.

As More had been able to defend himself against these two false accusations, he did not have to stand his trial. But nevertheless the second of the two charges had sunk deep into the King's mind, and his suspicions were increased by More's continued opposition to the divorce.

MORE REFUSES THE OATH OF SUCCESSION.

Meanwhile, the divorce being pronounced, and publicly proclaimed in the official book of which we have spoken, the King had contracted the marriage he had so greatly longed for. It was in October, 1532, that he secretly took Anne Boleyn to wife, but few then knew it. Even up to

[1] Commonly called Elizabeth Barton, the " Holy Maid of Kent."

Easter of the following year there had been no public celebration of this ill-omened marriage. But on April 12, 1533, Anne was proclaimed Queen by royal edict, and on July 5 of the same year Queen Catharine was in the same manner declared to be the widow of Prince Arthur. In April of the next year, when Anne's child, wicked progeny of a wicked mother, was now eight months old, Henry, for the fuller security of his divorce, disinherited Princess Mary, the daughter of Catharine, and desired all to swear allegiance to Anne's child, Elizabeth, as the King's sole legitimate offspring and heir to the kingdom, and at the same time to abjure the Pope's authority in England. When this twofold oath first began to be administered in London, all the clergy were summoned to take it on a certain day before Cranmer, Archbishop of Canterbury, and most of the King's Council. More alone of the laity was called upon to attend and was the first to be asked his opinion. His replies I prefer to give in his own words. On his imprisonment in the Tower of London he wrote the following letter to his daughter Margaret :

"When I was before the Lords at Lambeth . . . after the cause of my sending for declared unto me (whereof I somewhat marvelled in my mind, considering that they sent for no temporal men but me), I desired the sight of the oath, which they showed me under the Great Seal. Then desired I the sight of the Act of Succession, which was delivered me in a printed roll. After which read secretly by myself, and the oath considered with the Act, I answered unto them that my purpose was not to put any fault either in the Act or any man that made it, or in the oath or any man that sware it, nor to condemn the conscience of any other man : but as for myself, in good faith my conscience so moved me in the matter, that though I would not deny to swear to the succession, yet unto that oath that there was offered me I could not swear without the jeoparding of my soul to perpetual damnation. And that if they doubted whether I did refuse the oath only for the grudge of my conscience or for any fantasy, I was ready therein to satisfy them by my oath which if they trusted not, what should they be the better to give me any oath ? And if they trusted that I would therein swear true, then trusted I that of their goodness they would not move me to swear the oath that they offered me, perceiving that for to swear it was against my conscience.

" Unto this my Lord Chancellor said, that they all were very sorry to hear me say thus, and see me thus refuse the oath. And they said all, that on their faith I was the very first that ever refused it, which would cause the King's Highness to conceive great suspicion of me and great indignation towards me. And therewith they showed me the roll and let me see the names of the Lords and the Commons which had sworn and subscribed their names already. Which notwithstanding, when they saw that I refused to swear the same myself, not blaming any other man that had sworn, I was in conclusion commanded to go down into the garden."

Meanwhile the whole of the London clergy, pastors, doctors, and all the other priests, with some Bishops, among them the Bishop of Rochester, were called in to take the oath. With the exception of the Bishop of Rochester and Doctor Wilson, every single one took the oath and subscribed his name without the slightest delay or difficulty. More continues :

" When they had played their pageant and were gone out of the place, then was I called in again. And then was it declared unto me, what a number had sworn ever since I went aside, gladly without any sticking. Wherein I laid no blame in no man, but for mine own self answered as before. Now, as well before as then, they somewhat laid unto me for obstinacy, that whereas before, since I refused to swear, I would not declare any special part of that oath that grudged my conscience, and open the cause wherefore. For thereunto I had said unto them, that I feared lest the King's Highness would, as they said, take displeasure enough towards me for the only refusal of the oath. And that if I should open and disclose the causes why, I should therewith but further exasperate His Highness, which I would in nowise do, but rather would I abide all danger and harm that might come towards me, than give His Highness any occasion of further displeasure, than the offering of the oath unto me of pure necessity constrained me.

" Howbeit, when they divers times imputed this to me for stubbornness and obstinacy, that I would neither swear the oath, nor yet declare the causes why, I declined thus far towards them, that rather than I would be accounted for obstinate, I would upon the King's license, or rather his such commandment had, as might be my sufficient warrant, that my declaration should not offend His Highness nor put me in the danger of any of his statutes, I would be content to declare the causes in writing, and (over that) to give an oath in the beginning, that if I might find those causes by any man in suchwise answered, as I might think mine own conscience satisfied, I would after that with all my heart swear the principal oath too.   To this I was answered, that though the King would give me license under his letters patent, yet would it not serve me against the statute.   Whereto I said, that yet if I had them, I would stand unto the trust of his honour at my peril for the remnant.   But yet thinketh me, lo ! that if I may not declare the causes without peril, then to leave them un-declared is no obstinacy.

" My lord of Canterbury taking hold upon that that I said, that I condemned not the consciences of them that swear, said unto me, that it appeared well, that I did not take it for a very sure thing and a certain, that I might not lawfully swear it, but rather as a thing uncertain and doubtful.   ' But then,' said my lord, ' you know for a certainty, and a thing without doubt, that you be bound to obey your sovereign lord your King.   And therefore are you bound to leave off the doubt of your unsure con-science in refusing the oath, and take the sure way in obeying of your prince, and swear it.'   Now all was it so, that in mine own mind methought myself not concluded,[1] yet this argument seemed me suddenly so subtle, and namely with such authority coming out of so noble a prelate's mouth, that I could again answer nothing thereto, but only that I thought myself I might not well do so, because that in my conscience this was one of the cases in which I was bounden that I should not obey my prince, since that (whatsoever other folk thought in the matter,

---

[1] *i.e.*, Although I considered that this reasoning was not conclusive.

whose conscience or learning I would not condemn nor take upon me to judge), yet to my conscience the truth seemed on the other side. Wherein I had not informed my conscience neither suddenly nor slightly, but by long leisure and diligent search for the matter.[1] And of truth, if that reason may conclude, then have we a ready way to avoid all perplexity; for in whatsoever matter the doctors stand in great doubt, the King's commandment, given on whether side he list, solveth all the doubts.

"Then said my lord of Westminster to me, that howsoever the matter seemed unto mine own mind, I had cause to fear that mine own mind was erroneous, when I see the great Council of the realm determine of my mind the contrary, and that therefore I ought to change my conscience. To that I answered that if there were no more but myself upon my side, and the whole Parliament upon the other, I would be sore afraid to lean to mine own mind only against so many. But, on the other side, if it so be that in some things for which I refuse the oath, I have (as I think I have) upon my part as great a council and a greater too, I am not then bounden to change my conscience and conform it to the Council of one realm against the general council of Christendom.

"Upon this Master Secretary, as he that tenderly favoureth me . . . " said he was deeply grieved and in many words gave expression to his grief. He urged against me the indignation of the King's Highness, " to which I said that . . . whatsoever should mishap me, it lay not in my power to help it without the peril of my soul.

"Then did my Lord Chancellor repeat before me my refusal unto Master Secretary, as to him that was going unto the King's Grace; and in the rehearsing his lordship repeated again that I denied not but was content to swear unto the succession. Whereunto I said, that as for that point I would be content, so that I might see my oath in that point so framed, in such a manner as might stand with my conscience. Then said my lord : ' Marry, Master Secretary, mark that too, that he will not swear that neither but under some certain manner.' ' Verily no, my lord,'

[1] Stapleton refers to the letter to Cromwell (E.W., p. 1422) on which he has drawn so largely in Chapter XIV.

quoth I, ' but that I will see it in such wise first as I shall
myself see that I shall neither be forsworn nor swear against
my conscience.' '' [1]

This was his first examination, this the beginning of his
persecution, this the first act of the tragedy that brought
such shame to the King, but such glory to More.   The
reader may see how wise, sincere, and modest were his
replies ; how careful he was not to wound the conscience of
any man ; how anxious not to offend the King ; how cleverly,
like a stag surrounded by baying hounds, he kept his
pursuers at bay—in a word, how pious and Christ-like was
his demeanour.   It is noteworthy that amongst so many
laymen, learned, wise, influential, of high rank, More alone
was summoned, and, even before the clergy, examined and
tempted.   We have already seen what efforts the King made
to draw this one man over to his side.   Now we see the whole
of the King's Council, the Chancellor, the Archbishop,
the Abbot, the Secretary, sometimes in common, sometimes separately, striving in vain to seduce him.   Nothing
could show more clearly the honour and respect that More
enjoyed in the eyes of the King, the Parliament, and the
people, and at the same time his firmness and constancy
in the cause of God and the truth.

How More had prepared Himself.

At this place it is well that I should show the reader how
carefully and religiously the brave soldier of Christ prepared himself for the combat.   After laying down his high
office, he betook himself to his home, free at last from the
slavery of the Court and public life.   He gave himself up
to the task of defending in numerous learned writings the
Catholic faith against the heresies that then were rising
up in England ; and with greater strictness and severity
than before he attended to religious exercises, prayer, and
the mortification of the flesh.   He cut down rigorously the
number of his household, although he took care that the
servants he dispensed with, amongst them his fool, should
be provided with other suitable situations.   All his gold
and silver plate, which was worth more than £400, he sold,

[1] E.W., p. 1428.

lest it should be seized by the royal treasury, as indeed happened to his property later on. He settled his children, all now married and blessed with children of their own, in various places, keeping only Margaret and her husband with him in the same village of Chelsea, though no longer under the same roof. Very often (as he writes in one of his letters to Margaret from his prison)[1] he would lie awake almost the whole night, although his wife thought him asleep, thinking over the various sufferings that might come upon him, even death itself ; and with many prayers and tears he overcame the weakness of the flesh, although, as he writes elsewhere, it was so tender and frail that it could scarce bear a fillip.[2]

The Hired Apparitor.

He played a strange trick upon his family after he had resigned his office of Chancellor. He hired one of the King's officers to come to his house when all the family were at table, to knock suddenly at the door, to come in, and to cite him in the King's name to appear next day before the royal commissioners. All were thrown into confusion by the unexpected message, but whilst some wept and lamented, others showed a brave resignation. The latter he praised, but the former he reprimanded. In such ways did he prepare himself and his dependants for future misfortune.

As I recall More's trick, I am reminded of John the Almsgiver, Patriarch of Alexandria, who prepared himself for death by a similar stratagem. He ordered a monument to be built for himself but to be left unfinished. Those who were building it were to come every feast day to him as he was sitting with his clergy, and to say : " Your monument, my lord, is still unfinished. Give orders for its completion, for the hour of death is uncertain."[3]

But how necessary so much forethought and preparation were even to so saintly a man, the course of events and the temptations he had to meet will show.

---

[1] E.W., p. 1442. [2] E.W., p. 1448.
[3] Surius, in his Life of this saint, tom. 1 (S.).

The Summons to Lambeth.

More happened to be in London on Palm Sunday[1] with Roper his son-in-law to hear the sermon at St Paul's. When it was over he went to the house of John Clements. There one of the King's officers came to him and cited him to appear the following morning before the royal commissioners at the Archbishop's palace at Lambeth. He returned home at once, and that evening bade farewell to all his dear ones. The next morning he received Holy Communion. Then as he was leaving his house his wife and children, who were in tears, wished to accompany him to the riverside. He would not, however, allow them to do so, but, shutting the gate, went on his way with no companion save Roper. Sitting in the boat that was taking him to London, he was silent and sad, as if he were sharing Christ's agony in the garden, filled with fear and saying: "My soul is sorrowful even unto death."[2] But at length he turned a bright and cheerful countenance to his son-in-law and said: "Son Roper, I thank our Lord, the field is won." Thus More, on the way to his examination, from which he saw that his death might follow, "was in an agony and prayed the longer";[3] but, relying on the promised help of Christ, "Have confidence, I have overcome the world,"[4] he also gained the victory over the world. For unless Christ had first been victorious, how could his members have hoped to be so? Or rather we may say, with St Augustine, "He would not have conquered the world, if the world were to conquer his members."[5] For if he conquers, we conquer, because through him we conquer. This, then, was More's first persecution, his first examination, the first temptation in connection with his future passion, his first victory.

[1] This is a mistake for Low Sunday (Bridgett, p. 350 n.).
[2] Matt. xxvi 33.   [3] Luke xxii 43.
[4] John xvi 33.   [5] *Tract. 103 in Johannem* (S.).

CHAPTER XVI

HIS IMPRISONMENT AND HIS CONSTANCY UNDER TRIAL

AFTER More had refused and rejected, as we have seen, the twofold oath of the Royal Supremacy and the Succession, he was for a few days committed to the charge of the Abbot of Westminster. Soon he was thrown into the Tower of London, condemned to perpetual imprisonment and to the loss of all his possessions.

MORE'S CHEERFULNESS UNDER IMPRISONMENT.

As soon as he was cast into the Tower, while he was guarded with the utmost rigour, he wrote with a coal a short letter to his daughter Margaret, which I will now give in order that the reader may see the cheerfulness with which, from the very first, he accepted the dirt and discomforts of prison.

" Mine own good daughter, our Lord be thanked I am in good health of body, and in good quiet of mind : and of worldly things I no more desire than I have. I beseech him make you all merry in the hope of heaven. And such things as I somewhat longed to talk with you all, concerning the world to come, our Lord put them into your mind, as I trust he doth and better too by his Holy Spirit : who bless you and preserve you all. Written with a coal by your tender loving father, who in his poor prayers forgetteth none of you all, nor your babes, nor your nurses, nor your good husbands, shrewd wives, nor father's shrewd wife neither, nor our other friends. And thus fare ye heartily well for lack of paper.

" P.S.—Our Lord keep me continually true, faithful, and plain, to the contrary whereof I beseech him heartily never to suffer me live. For as for long life (as I have often told thee, maid) I neither look for, nor long for, but am well contented to go, if God calls me hence, to-morrow. And I thank our Lord, I know no person living, that I would have one fillip for my sake : of which mind I am more glad than of all the world beside.

" Recommend me to your shrewd Will, and mine other sons, and to John Harris my friend, and yourself knoweth to whom else, and to my shrewd wife above all, and God preserve you all and make and keep you his servants all."[1]

Such were his dispositions at his entry into prison : his thoughts were with his dear ones, but he did not allow the affection he bore them, or his longing for their presence, to move him from his duty to God.

Margaret urges him to take the Oath.

Soon after began a long series of trials, for the King tried every means to bend More to his will, but, aided by the divine assistance, the brave soldier of Christ overcame them all. In the first place Margaret Roper, his dearly beloved daughter, whom, as is clear from what has gone before, he loved beyond all others, urged him not to scruple to take an oath which so many great men throughout England, esteemed for their learning and piety, had taken. Whether or not she expressed her true sentiments, it is certain that More took her words seriously. That the trial was a painful one is clear from the following letter in reply : " If I had not been, my dearly beloved daughter, at a firm and fast point I trust in God's great mercy this good great while before, your lamentable letter had not a little abashed me surely far above all other things, of which I hear divers times not a few terrible toward me. Surely they all touched me never so near, nor were so grievous unto me, as to see you, my well-beloved child, in such vehement piteous manner, labour to persuade unto me, that thing wherein I have of pure necessity for respect unto mine own soul so often given you so precise answer before. Wherein as touching the points of your letter, I can make none answer. For I doubt not but you well remember, that the matters which

[1] E.W., p. 1430.

moved my conscience (without declaration whereof I can nothing touch the points) I have sundry times showed you that I will disclose them to no man. And therefore, daughter Margaret, I can in this thing no further, but like as you labour me again to follow your mind, to desire and pray you both again, to leave of such labour, and with my former answers to hold yourself content. A deadly grief unto me, and much more deadly than to hear of mine own death (for the fear thereof I thank our Lord, the fear of hell, the hope of heaven, and the passion of Christ daily more and more assuage), is, that I perceive my good son your husband, and you, my good daughter, and my good wife, and mine other good children and innocent friends in great displeasure and danger of great harm thereby. The let[1] while it lieth not in my hand, I can no further but commit all to God. For ' as the divisions of waters, so the heart of the King is in the hand of the Lord : whithersoever he will he shall turn it.' "[2]

How bitter a trial to the brave confessor was the piteous letter of his sweet daughter is clear from this reply. He was the best of fathers : his love for his children was tender and strong, as has been shown above : but with the greatest fortitude of spirit he overcame the temptation and gained the victory.

A second trial to More was his meeting with this same beloved daughter in his prison. In her discourse with her father she adroitly brought forward, as though uttered by others, all the arguments alleged by men, great and small, against More's rejection of the oath, an action in which he stood almost alone. It will not be out of place to enumerate briefly these arguments, together with More's prudent and conscientious replies. Thus will More's action, based as it clearly was on motives of religion and conscience, be defended against the sneers and sophistries of the world, and the reader be instructed how to deal with similar cases which are not of rare occurrence in the State.

These, then, are briefly the objections Margaret urged. First, that one who was under such great obligations to the King and had received so many honours from him was

[1] i.e., hindrance.
[2] Prov. xxi 1. More quotes the text in Latin.

bound beyond all others to conform himself to the royal will except in matters clearly and obviously contrary to the commandments of God. That in this matter (and this was the second argument) so general was the consent of the whole kingdom, of men of such number and weight, that it was scarcely credible that all would wish to disobey Almighty God. Third, that the Bishop of Rochester stood alone and that More should beware of following his single authority or imitating his obstinacy. Fourth, that whereas those who had taken the oath were so high in rank and character, bishops, doctors, parish priests, religious, nobles, and other men of eminence and prudence, More was but a layman and not of the highest rank in the nobility. Not only, then, could he, without rashness or danger to salvation, accommodate his conscience to theirs, but indeed he was bound so to do. Fifth and last, that as the matter was settled in public session of Parliament and received the assent of all ranks, it was the general opinion that More was bound even in conscience to acknowledge and approve this public decree. As he was almost alone in refusing the oath, some loudly accused him of rashness and inconsideration, others of folly, others of wickedness and obstinacy.

More's answers to these various arguments were on the following lines. First, that certainly no man in the whole kingdom would more willingly take the oath than he, who was, as he acknowledged, indebted in so many ways to the King's Majesty, if by so doing he should not grievously offend God. That he had not lightly or carelessly dealt with the matter but had given it his close study for seven[1] years after the appearance of the King's book against Luther, in reading which book he first realised that the Primacy of the Roman Pontiff was by divine right. That he had read all the Fathers, both Latin and Greek, that he could find upon the subject and—to use his own words— " I have found in effect the substance of all the holy doctors, from St Ignatius, disciple to St John the Evangelist, unto our own days, both Latins and Greeks, so consonant and agreeing in that point, and the thing by such General Councils so confirmed also, that in good faith I never neither read nor heard anything of such effect on the other side

[1] See note on p. 38.

that ever could lead me to think that my conscience were well discharged, but rather in right great peril, if I should follow the other side, and deny the primacy to be provided by God.

"Which if we did, yet can I nothing (as I showed you) perceive any commodity that ever could come by that denial. For that primacy is at the leastwise instituted by the corps of Christendom, and for a great urgent cause in avoiding of schisms, and corroborate by continual succession more than the space of a thousand years at the least (for there are passed almost a thousand years since the time of the holy St Gregory). And therefore since all Christendom is one corps, I cannot perceive how any member thereof may, without the common consent of the body, depart from the common head."

As to the offence the King has taken in this matter "albeit that I have for my own part such opinion of the Pope's Primacy[1] . . .[2] never have I in any book of mine put forth among the King's subjects in our vulgar tongue,[3] advanced greatly the Pope's authority. And albeit that a man may peradventure so find therein that, after the common manner of all Christian realms, I speak of him as primate, yet never do I stick thereon with reasoning and proving of that point. . . . But whereas I had written thereof at length in my *Confutation* before, and for the proof thereof had compiled together all that I could find therefor, at such time as I little looked that there should fall between the King's Highness and the Pope such a breach as is fallen since ; when I saw the thing likely to draw towards such displeasure between them I suppressed it utterly, and never put word thereof in my book, but put out the remnant without it. Which thing well declareth, I never intended anything to meddle in that matter against the King's gracious pleasure whatsoever mine own opinion were therein."[4] . . . But now by the oath that is tendered to me I see that I am thrust into these straits, that I must

---

[1] So in the MS. Rastell prints " Supremacy " in E.W., p. 1426.

[2] The words which Stapleton omits are : " yet never thought I the Pope above the General Council."

[3] He had done so in Latin.

[4] E.W., p. 1426 (*i.e.*, More's letter to Cromwell).

necessarily offend either God or the King, that I must expose myself either to the greatest perils in this world (all of which, however, I have long foreseen and considered) or to the sentence of eternal damnation.

To the second argument he replied that he wished in no way to discuss or judge the consciences of other men, but that many things might induce them to take the oath.   To use his own words : " That the keeping of the prince's pleasure, and the avoiding of his indignation, the fear of the losing of their worldly substance, with regard unto the discomfort of their kindred and their friends, might hap make some men either swear otherwise than they think, or frame their conscience astretch to think otherwise than they thought, any such opinion such as this is, will I not conceive of them.   I have better hope of their goodness, than to think of them so.   For if such things should have turned them, the same things had been likely to make me do the same : for, in good faith, I knew few so faint-hearted as myself."[1]

We may well admire the humility of this holy man.   He proceeds : " And some might hap to frame himself a conscience, and think that while he did it for fear, God would forgive it.   And some may peradventure think that they will repent and be shriven thereof, and that so God shall remit it them.   And some may be peradventure of that mind, that if they say one thing and think the while the contrary, God more regardeth their heart than their tongue, and that therefore their oath goeth upon that they think, and not upon that they say."[2]   To such dangers I dare not expose myself, nor do I consider it safe to shield myself in such excuses.

As to the third objection he pointed out how improbable it was, because he refused the oath before the Bishop of Rochester had been summoned to take it, and because the latter was " content to have sworn of that oath either somewhat more, or in some other manner than ever (More) minded to do."   " For albeit," he said, " that of very truth I have him in the reverent estimation, that I reckon in this realm no one man, in wisdom, learning and long-approved virtue together, meet to be matched and com-

[1] E.W., p. 1440.   [2] E.W., p. 1437.

pared with him, yet . . . I never intend to pin my soul at another man's back.''[1]

As to the fourth objection he wrote : '' I nothing doubt at all, but that though not in this realm, yet in Christendom about, of those well learned men and virtuous that are yet alive, they be not the fewer part that are of my mind. Besides that, that it were ye wot well possible that some men in this realm too, think not so clear the contrary, as by the oath received they have sworn to say. . . . But go me now to them that are dead before, and that are I trust in heaven, I am sure that it is not the fewer part of them, that all the time while they lived, thought in some of the things the way I think now. I am also . . . of this thing sure enough, that of those holy doctors and saints . . . there thought in some such things as I think now. I say not that they thought all so, but surely such and so many as will well appear by their writings, that I pray God give me the grace that my soul may follow theirs.''[2]

To the fifth and last argument he replied : '' As to the law of the land, though every man being born and habiting therein is bounden to the keeping in every case upon some temporal pain, and in many cases upon pain of God's displeasure too, yet there is no man bound to swear that every law is well made, nor bound, upon the pain of God's displeasure, to perform any point of the law as were indeed unlawful.'' He pointed to doubtful and controverted doctrines of the Church, for example, whether or not the Blessed Virgin was conceived in original sin, saying : '' If it so hap that in any particular part of Christendom, there be a law made that be such as . . . some that are good men and cunning . . . think some one way, and some other of like learning and goodness think the contrary, in this case he that thinketh against the law, neither may swear that law lawfully was made, standing his own conscience to the contrary, nor is bounden, upon pain of God's displeasure, to change his own conscience therein, for any particular made anywhere, other than by a General Council,''[3] or universal legislator. He went on to say that in matters which have been clearly decided by General

[1] E.W., p. 1437.   [2] *Ibid.*
[3] E.W., p. 1439.

Councils or by the unanimous consent of the Church, it was not allowable for anyone who wished to be a Christian and to save his soul to think or to speak otherwise or to form his conscience in any other way at the bidding of any civil law, however many learned men should do so and strive to draw others by their example.

So did Sir Thomas answer the arguments brought against him, and the criticisms men passed on his action. We have translated and brought together on this head various passages from his English Works, but especially from a letter in which his daughter Margaret wrote the words she had heard from his own lips to her sister, Lady Alington, wife of Sir Giles Alington, Knight.

In several other ways also, as we can see in this same letter, did Margaret, without wishing to lead her father into sin, yet tempt his courage and constancy. Always, however, did More answer with the greatest prudence and piety, showing himself ready, in the true spirit of a martyr, to suffer every possible hardship on behalf of the truth. I will give briefly his replies, so that the reader may see that he was guided in all this matter by religion, sincerity, and wisdom, and not by rashness, vanity, self-will, or obstinacy. He had given to the subject the deepest and most serious consideration, and his one desire was, not to appear wiser than others or to offend the King, but to avoid offending God. When Margaret, then, saw that her father had replied so effectually to all her arguments, " But yet, father," she said, " by my truth I fear me very sore, that this matter will bring you in marvellous heavy trouble. You know well that, as I showed you, Master Secretary sent you word, as your very friend, to remember that the Parliament lasted yet."[1]

MORE READY FOR ANY EXTREMITY.

In these words she hinted to her father the danger that existed of his being by name condemned to death in Parliament itself, as is not infrequently the case in England. To this he replied that he had thought well beforehand of every extremity, and that nothing perilous could happen to him

[1] E.W., p. 1441.

which he was not long before in mind and will prepared
to suffer. "Albeit," he said, "I know well that if they
would make a law to do me any harm, that law could never
be lawful, but that . . . no man shall do me hurt but if
he do me wrong. . . . And notwithstanding also that
I have good hope, that God shall never suffer so good and
wise a prince, in such wise to requite the long service of his
true faithful servant, yet since there is nothing impossible
to fall, I forgot not in this matter the counsel of Christ in
the Gospel, that ere I should begin to build this castle for
the safeguard of mine own soul, I should sit and reckon
what the charge would be. I counted . . . what peril
were possible for to fall to me, so far forth I am sure that
there can come none above. . . . But yet . . . I never
thought to change, though the very uttermost should hap
me that my fear ran upon."

"No father (quod Margaret) it is not like to think upon
a thing that may be, and to see a thing that shall be, as ye
should (our Lord save you) if the chance should so fortune.
And then should you peradventure think, that[1] you think
not now, and yet then peradventure it would be too late."

"Too late daughter (quod More) Margaret? I beseech
our Lord, that if ever I make such a change, it may be too
late indeed. For well I wot the change cannot be good for
my soul, that change I say that should grow but by fear.
And therefore I pray God that in this world I never have
good of such change. For so much as I take harm here,
I shall have at the leastwise the less therefore when I am
hence. And if it so were that I wist well now, that I should
faint and fall, and for fear swear hereafter, yet would I wish
to take harm by the refusing first : for so should I have the
better hope for grace to rise again. And albeit, Margaret,
that I wot well my lewdness hath been such : that I know
myself well worthy that God should let me slip, yet can
I not but trust in his merciful goodness, that as his grace
hath strengthened me hitherto, and made me content in
my heart, to lose goods, land, and life too, rather than to
swear against my conscience, and hath also put in the King
toward me that good and gracious mind, that as yet he hath
taken from me nothing but my liberty, wherewith (as help

---

[1] *i.e.*, what.

me God) his grace hath done me great good by the spiritual profit that I trust I take thereby, that among all his great benefits heaped upon me so thick, I reckon, upon my faith, my prisonment even the very chief. I cannot, I say, therefore distrust the grace of God, but that either he shall conserve me and keep the King in that gracious mind still, to do me none hurt, or else if his pleasure be, that for mine other sins I shall suffer in such a case in sight as I shall not deserve, his grace shall give me the strength to take it patiently, and peradventure somewhat gladly too, whereby his high goodness shall (by the merits of his bitter passion joined thereunto, and far surmounting in merit for me all that I can suffer myself) make it serve for release of my pain in purgatory, and over that for increase of some reward in heaven. Mistrust him, Meg, will I not, though I feel me faint. Yea and though I should feel my fear even at point to overthrow me too, yet shall I remember how St Peter with a blast of a wind began to speak for his faint faith, and shall do as he did, call upon Christ and pray him to help. And then I trust he shall set his holy hand unto me, and in the stormy seas, hold me up from drowning. Yea and if he suffer me to play St Peter further, and to fall full to the ground, and swear and forswear too (which our Lord for his tender passion keep me from, and let me lose if it so fall, and never win thereby), yet after shall I trust that his goodness will cast upon me his tender piteous eye, as he did upon St Peter, and make me stand up again, and confess the truth of my conscience afresh, and abide the shame and the harm here of mine own fault.

" And finally, Margaret, this wot I very well, that without my fault he will not let me be lost. I shall therefore with good hope commit myself wholly to him. And if he suffer me for my faults to perish, yet shall I then serve for a praise of his justice. But in good faith, Meg, I trust that his tender pity shall keep my poor soul safe and make me commend his mercy. And therefore mine own good daughter, never trouble thy mind, for anything that ever shall hap me in this world. And I make me very sure that whatsoever that be, seem it never so bad in sight, it shall indeed be the best."[1]

[1] E.W., p. 1442.

So spoke More in prison to his daughter.   How he wins our admiration as we gaze on him, not only ready to suffer every extremity, but (what is more and is indeed the strongest safeguard to fortitude and all other virtues) humble, thinking little of himself, conforming himself in everything to God's will, just, holy, simple, upright, and God-fearing.

Letters to Dr. Wilson.

I feel that to meet the persuasions, the objections, and the anxieties of this most dear daughter must have been More's greatest trial.   But he gained the victory, and then came another temptation of no slight force.   Nicholas Wilson, a doctor of theology, was a man much esteemed for his wisdom and learning.   He was often employed by the King and was an intimate friend of More's, with whom he had studied closely the questions of the divorce and the supremacy.   When all the clergy were summoned to take the oath, as we have related, besides the Bishop of Rochester, Dr. Wilson also refused to swear.   Afterwards, however, having been imprisoned, he weakened and changed his mind, promising to take the oath.   Before he did so he wrote to Sir Thomas More asking whether he too was going to swear.   More replied as follows : " Whereas I perceive that you would gladly know what I intend to do, you wot well that I told you when we were both abroad, that I would neither therein know your mind nor no man's else : nor you nor no man else should therein know mine. For I would be no part taker with no man, nor of truth never I will : but leaving every other man to their own conscience, myself will with God's grace follow mine own. For against mine own to swear, were peril of my damnation. . . .   And whereas I perceive by sundry means that you have promised to swear the oath, I beseech our Lord give you thereof good luck.   I never gave any man counsel to the contrary in my days, nor never used any ways to put any scruple in other folk's conscience concerning the matter."[1]

Dr. Wilson asked for a more definite answer, and in his

[1] E.W., p. 1443.

lengthy reply More repeats almost all that he had said in
his letter to Thomas Cromwell and in his discussion with
Margaret Roper, of which we have spoken above. Among
much else he writes as follows : " I am not so bold or pre-
sumptuous to blame or dispraise the conscience of other
men, their truth nor their learning neither : nor I meddle
of no man but of myself, nor of no man's conscience else
will I meddle with but of mine own. And in mine own
conscience (I cry God mercy) I find of mine own life
matters enough to think upon. I have lived methinketh
a long life, and now neither I look nor I long to live much
longer. I have since I came in the Tower, looked once or
twice to have given up my ghost ere this : and in good
faith mine heart waxed the lighter with hope thereof. Yet
forgot I not that I have a long reckoning and a great to
give account of. But I put my trust in God, and in the
mercies of his bitter passion, and I beseech him give me and
keep me the mind, to long to be out of this world and to be
with him. For I can never but trust, that whoso long to be
with him, shall be welcome to him ; and, on the other side,
my mind giveth me verily, that any that ever shall come to
him, shall full heartily wish to be with him, ere ever he shall
come at him." [1]

Thus More, strong in wisdom divine and human, was in
no way moved by the example and the fall of so great a
man, nor shaken in his own resolution, although certainly
the example of so excellent a theologian might well have
been a grave scandal to a layman. But More was no
ordinary layman.[2]

Many other tests also to his constancy did More have to
meet during his imprisonment ; for the King, More's
friends, and his enemies too, did all in their power to make
him yield. His friends desired to save his life ; his enemies
to bend him to their will, for they were greatly annoyed
that such a man as More, and he alone, should refuse an
oath that almost all others had taken.

[1] E.W., p. 1445.
[2] . . . but," adds Stapleton, " above τὸν λάον." The same play
upon words occurs at the end of the letter from Budé quoted in the
middle of Chapter V.

Threatened Proceedings against More.

A rumour, therefore, was industriously spread abroad and zealously brought to More's ears, to the effect that if he persisted in his obstinacy the King would be forced to take advantage of the continued session of Parliament to pass a new law against him.   Of this rumour, and the new temptation or rather threat that it implied, he wrote thus to his daughter Margaret :

" I cannot let[1] such a law to be made.   But I am very sure that if I died by such a law, I should die for that point innocent before God. . . ."   I did not leave " that point unthought on, but many times more than one, resolved and cast in my mind before my coming hither, both that peril and all other that might put my body in peril of death by the refusing of this oath.   In devising whereupon, albeit (mine own good daughter) that I found myself (I cry God mercy) very sensual, and my flesh much more shrinking from pain and from death, than methought it the part of a faithful Christian man, in such a case as my conscience gave me, that in the saving of my body should stand the loss of my soul.   Yet I thank our Lord, that in that conflict, the spirit had in conclusion the mastery, and reason with help of faith finally concluded, that for to be put to death wrongfully for doing well . . . it is the case in which a man may lose his head and yet have none harm, but instead of harm inestimable good at the hand of God.

" And I thank our Lord (Meg), since I am come hither, I set by death every day less than other.   For though a man lose of his years in this world, it is more than manifold recompense by coming the sooner to heaven.   And though it be a pain to die while a man is in health, yet see I very few that in sickness die with ease.   And finally, very sure am I that whensoever the time shall come that may hap to come, God wot I, soon, by which I should lie sick in my deathbed by nature, I shall then think that God had done much for me, if he had suffered me to die before by the colour of such a law.   And therefore my reason showeth me (Margaret) that it were great folly for me to be sorry to

---

[1] *i.e.*, hinder.

come to that death, which I would after wish that I had died. Beside that, that a man may hap with less thank of God, and more adventure of his soul, to die as violently and as painfully by many other chances, as by enemies or thieves.

" And therefore, mine own good daughter, I assure you (thanks be to God) the thinking of any such, albeit it hath grieved me ere this, yet at this day grieveth me nothing. And yet I know well for all this mine own frailty, and that St Peter which feared it much less than I, fell in such fear soon after, that at the word of a simple girl he forsook and forsware our Saviour. And therefore am I not (Meg) so mad as to warrant myself to stand. But I shall pray, and I pray thee mine own good daughter to pray with me, that it may please God that hath given me this mind, to give me the grace to keep it.

"And thus have I, mine own good daughter, disclosed unto you the very secret of my mind, referring the order thereof only to the goodness of God, and that so fully, that I assure you, Margaret, on my faith, I never have prayed God to bring me hence nor deliver me from death, but referred all things whole unto his only pleasure, as to him that seeth better what is best for me than myself doth. Nor never long I, since I came hither, to set my foot in mine own house : but gladly would I sometime somewhat talk with my friends, and specially my wife and you that pertain to my charge. But since that God otherwise disposeth, I commit you all wholly to his goodness, and take daily great comfort, in that I perceive you live together so charitably and so quietly : I beseech our Lord continue it."[1]

In writing this letter to his daughter upon hearing the rumour of which we have spoken, More was certainly less anxious about himself than about the possible distress of his family.

REBUTS CHARGE OF OBSTINACY.

In addition to the trials we have mentioned, he had to suffer distress on another score. It was brought as a grave objection against him and as a proof, obvious to all and

[1] E.W., p. 1447.

particularly to the King, of his obstinacy and stubbornness,
that during the whole period of his imprisonment he wrote
no letter to the King nor petitioned him for any kind of
grace or pardon. To this objection he replied in a letter
to a devout priest. " In good faith," he writes, " I do not
forbear it of any obstinacy, but rather of a lowly mind and
a reverent, because that I see nothing that I could write,
but that I fear me sore, that His Grace were likely rather to
take displeasure with me for it than otherwise, while His
Grace believeth me not that my conscience is the cause,
but rather obstinate wilfulness."[1] Such a persuasion he
could not remove from the King's mind by letters, nor,
while it remained, did he hope that he might be able to
do any good by writing.

TREACHERY OF SIR RICHARD RICH.

Not long before More received the sentence of death,
there came to him in prison Richard Rich, who held the
high post of Solicitor-General, in the guise of a friend, but,
as the event showed, with the intention of finding matter for
accusation. For the whole of the conversation between
them was reproduced, word for word, in the indictment.

In trying to persuade More, by many arguments, to
conform to the laws of the kingdom, he used the following
comparison. " Now if," he said, " in the Parliament of
the realm, I, Richard Rich, by a decree accepted by all
were declared King of England, and by the same decree
anyone who should deny Richard Rich to be King were
declared a traitor, would not you, being a citizen of England,
be bound to give your consent to this decree ? Would you
not commit a crime if you did not acknowledge as King
him whom Parliament had declared to be such ?" To this
More replied that in such a case he would be bound to
give consent, " but," he added, " the case you propose is
easy; I will put before you a harder one. What if it were
declared in Parliament that God were not God ? If you,
Richard Rich, were asked whether God were God, would
you deny it because of the decree of Parliament ?" To
this Rich replied : " Of course I would not deny it, for such

[1] E.W., p. 1450. Letter to Master Leder.

a case is utterly impossible. But as you have given me such an extreme case, I will give you another that is more reasonable. You know that our King has been declared by decree of Parliament to be the Supreme Head on earth of the Church of England. Why do you not conform yourself to this decree and give it your consent, just as in the other case I proposed you said you would conform yourself?" More's answer was : " There is a broad and evident distinction. The King can be created or deposed by authority of Parliament and all English subjects are bound to obey. But by no decree of the kingdom can the King be lawfully declared Head of the Church of England, for outside the realm of England, all other kings and princes shrink from a primacy of this kind. All the other provinces of the Christian world contradict this prerogative of the King. For to be Head of the Church, and to judge in ecclesiastical causes, is a matter of faith and religion, not within the competence of the civil power."

This was More's answer, at least as it appeared in his indictment. And if he had uttered those words, they would have been in no way blameworthy or deserving of death, they would have asserted openly the true and orthodox opinion. But as up to this time he seems never to have spoken so openly, perhaps the account of his words given in the indictment is not altogether true.[1] However that may be, the indictment itself bears witness that the Solicitor-General used every means to move More from his purpose, but entirely in vain.

His Wife's Visit to the Tower.

Nothing, then, could move More from his purpose or cause him any fear. His wife then was sent into prison to tempt her husband, to weaken his resolution by soft words and womanly wiles, or to move him to pity for his family. She came, and after greeting him entreated him with all earnestness not to sacrifice his children, his country, and his life, which he might yet enjoy for many years. As she kept on pleading, and harping upon a long life, he

[1] More at his trial took a solemn oath that he had not spoken the words which Rich charged upon him.

interrupted her : " And how long, my Alice, shall I be able to enjoy this life ?" " A full twenty years," she replied, " if God so wills." " Do you wish me, then," said More, " to exchange eternity for twenty years ? Nay, good wife, you do not bargain very skilfully. If you had said some thousands of years, you would have said something, but yet what would that be in comparison with eternity ?" Thus did More wittily and effectually silence the persuasions of his wife.

" I HAVE CHANGED MY MIND."

But the following anecdote is especially amusing, and yet a remarkable witness to his utter tranquillity and peace of heart in prospect of imminent death. Many men of high position used to visit him in prison, either of their own accord, or sent by the King. The latter is more probable, for access to the prisoners in the Tower of London is usually not so easy. Amongst these visitors was one whose attempts to move More were vehement rather than prudent. His warnings, his pleadings were incessantly repeated. He begged More to change his opinion, and not to be obstinate, and yet in all that he said there was no word of the divorce or the oath. More, either out of fun, or to rid himself of the man's importunity or to rebuke his want of courtesy, at length answered him with apparent seriousness. " Indeed, my lord, I will tell you how the matter stands. After giving everything most careful consideration, I have changed my opinion and I intend to act quite differently from the manner I had proposed." The good man, hearing this, waited for nothing further, but showed himself delighted at More's words and begged him to remain firm in the new course he had chosen. In all haste he went to the King and announced to him that More had changed his opinion. The King readily believed what it gave him such pleasure to hear, but wishing for complete certainty, " Return," he said, " to More, and say that I am delighted to hear that he has conformed his opinion to mine. I ask one thing only, that he should put into writing the change of his mind and intention, so that as many as have been scandalised by his obstinacy may now be edified by his retractation." The foolish man returned to More in prison and acquainted him with the King's words and good pleasure. On hearing him, More professed the greatest astonishment. " Have you, then, been to the King ?" he said. " Have you reported to the King's Majesty the words we here privately interchanged?" " Why should I not report," said the other, " what I knew would be so pleasing to the King's Majesty?" " But at least," said More, " you should have understood my words better before you carried them to any one else, most of all to the King." " But I understood what you said quite clearly," replied the other, " that after most careful consideration you had changed your opinion." " Indeed," said More, " you have done a ridiculous thing. I have indeed changed my opinion, and told you so in familiar conversation, and I would have finished what I had to say if you had waited to hear it ; but as regards the grave matter of the oath that was offered to me I have not changed my opinion. On that subject you did not speak to me, nor did I refer to it." " In what other way, then," asked the other, " have you changed your opinion ?" " I will tell you clearly," answered More. " You know that during all the time I have been at Court, I have always been clean-shaven like the other members of the King's Council, and as is the custom amongst lawyers. But while I have been in prison my beard has grown long, as you see, and for some time now I had determined to shave it before going to execution so that I should not appear strange to those who know me. But now I have entirely changed my mind, and I intend to allow my beard to suffer the same fate as my head." The other was filled with confusion, as the King had ordered him to return to inform him of the matter. " So," said the King, " does this man still mock us with his jests."

Thus, then, was More tempted and gravely tempted again and again in prison, but nevertheless he was always merry and cheerful. Almost every day he sang psalms to himself, showing thus the deep and perpetual peace of his soul, according to the words of St James : " Is any one cheerful in mind ? Let him sing."[1] In short, he said to his

[1] Jas. v 13.

daughter Margaret, on his faith, that never had he received a greater benefit from the King than his imprisonment in the Tower, on account of the incredibly great spiritual progress that, as he hoped, he was there making. We end this chapter by giving some verses he composed in prison.

LEWIS THE LOST LOVER.

By flattering fortune, look thou never so fair,
Or never so pleasantly begin to smile,
As though thou wouldst my ruin all repair,
During my life thou shalt not me beguile.
Trust shall I God to enter in awhile
His haven of heaven sure and uniform.
Ever after thy calm look I for a storm.

DAVY THE DICER.

Long was I, lady Lucke, your serving man,
And now have lost again all that I gat,
Wherefore when I think on you now and then,
And in my mind remember this and that,
Ye may not blame me though I beshrew your cat,
But in faith I bless you again a thousand times
For lending me now some leisure to make rhymes.[1]

---

[1] E.W., p. 1432. Stapleton's Latin version of these verses is very free.

CHAPTER XVII

HIS TWO EXAMINATIONS IN THE TOWER

MORE'S position in England was very high and his influence enormous. He had received the greatest marks of the royal favour: his unblemished life, his wide learning, his many services to the State had won him the popular esteem. Now all eyes were turned upon him as being the only layman in the kingdom who refused to approve of the divorce and the royal supremacy. It is easy to understand, then, that the King used every possible effort to draw him over, somehow or other, to his own opinion. The attempts that the King had made for this purpose during the preceding years in so many various ways will be fresh in the reader's memory. But as none of the King's devices to tempt More had succeeded as he desired, he sent twice to him during his imprisonment men chosen from his Council to examine him again on the matter and if possible to extort his consent. We must now relate More's conduct under these two examinations and describe his prudence, his piety, and his constancy. All that took place in his prison More was accustomed to communicate by letter to his beloved daughter Margaret, partly for her comfort and that of his whole family, and partly to give her a true account of what occurred, in order to correct the false rumours that at this time were constantly being spread abroad about him.

MORE'S FIRST EXAMINATION.

It was about the middle of April, 1534, that More was first cast into prison after having refused the oath tendered to him. He had now been a prisoner for a year, but neither by the monotony of confinement, nor by the entreaties of his friends, nor by the various trials of which we have spoken, could he be moved from his resolution. At length, on May 7, 1535,[1] there came to him in the Tower, by command of the King, five of the Privy Council, the Secretary, the Attorney, the Solicitor, and two doctors of law. They took their seats and summoned More before them : they asked him to sit down, but he refused and remained standing. Then the Secretary began as follows: "Since it is now by Act of Parliament ordered that His Highness and his heirs be, and ever of right have been, and perpetually shall be, Supreme Head on earth of the Church of England under Christ, the King's pleasure is that these of his Council here assembled shall demand your opinion and what your mind is therein." More answered : "In good faith I had well trusted that the King's Highness would never have commanded any such question to be demanded of me, considering that I ever from the beginning well and truly from time to time declared my mind unto His Highness ; and since that time unto your mastership, Master Secretary, also, both by mouth and by writing" (*i.e.*, in the letter to the Secretary—Thomas Cromwell—from which a few pages back we have quoted at some length). "And now I have in good faith discharged my mind of all such matters, and neither will dispute Kings' titles nor Popes' ; but the King's true, faithful subject I am and will be, and daily

---

[1] Stapleton's words imply that this was More's first examination by members of the King's Council. He speaks of two examinations only, on May 7 and June 3. Roper and Harpsfield also seem to know of these two examinations only. In entire accord with Stapleton is the indictment (Bridgett, p. 117), for it quotes More's words as spoken on May 7 and on June 3, and gives the same names of the councillors as Stapleton does for the two occasions. More, who gives such detailed accounts of what occurred in his letters to his daughter Margaret, also speaks of only two such examinations. A difficulty, however, arises as to dates. Stapleton quotes his account of what happened at this first examination from a letter (E.W., p. 1451) in which More describes what occurred "on Friday the last day of April in the afternoon." I cannot resist the inference that in transferring all that More says happened on April 30 to a week later Stapleton means to imply that More has made a mistake in his date. Father Bridgett (p. 404) supposes that there was an examination both on April 30 and on May 7, although he has no details of the latter as distinct from the former. In this he has been followed by later writers—*e.g.*, Hutton, *Life of More*, p. 256 ; Dom Bede Camm, *English Martyrs*, p. 217 ; Sidney Lee in the *Dictionary of National Biography*, etc.

I pray for him, and all his, and for you all that are his honourable Council, and for all the realm.   And otherwise than this I never intend to meddle.   Whereunto Master Secretary answered, that he thought this manner of answer should not satisfy nor content the King's Highness, but that His Grace would exact a more full answer.   And his mastership added thereunto, that the King's Highness was a prince, not of rigour, but of mercy and pity.   And though that he had found obstinacy at some time in any of his subjects, yet when he should find them at another time conformable and submit themselves His Grace would show mercy ; and that concerning myself, His Highness would be glad to see me take such conformable ways, as I might be abroad in the world again among other men, as I have been before.   Whereunto shortly (after the inward affection of my mind) I answered for a very truth, that I would never meddle in the world again, to have the world given me. And to the remnant of the matter I answered in effect as before, showing that I had fully determined with myself neither to study nor meddle with any matter of the world, but that my whole study should be upon the Passion of Christ " (on which, as we have said, he wrote while in prison a most beautiful treatise) " and mine own passage out of this world.

" Upon this I was commanded to go forth for a while, and after called in again.   At which time Master Secretary said unto me, that though I were a prisoner condemned to perpetual prison, yet I was not thereby discharged of mine obedience and allegiance to the King's Highness.   And thereupon demanded me, whether that I thought that the King's Grace might not exact of me such things as are contained in the statutes, and upon like pains as he might upon other men.   Whereto I answered that I would not say the contrary.   Whereunto he said, that likewise as the King's Highness would be gracious to them that he found conformable, so His Grace would follow the course of his laws towards such as he shall find obstinate.   And his mastership said farther, that my demeanour in that matter was a thing that of likelihood made other so stiff therein as they be.   Whereto I answered, that I gave no man occasion to hold any point one or other, nor never gave any man advice or counsel therein one way or other. And for conclusion I could no farther go, whatsoever pain should come thereof. ' I am ' (quoth I) ' the King's true, faithful subject and daily bedesman, and pray for His Highness, and all his, and all the realm. I do nobody no harm, I say none harm, I think none harm, but wish everybody good. And if this be not enough to keep a man alive, in good faith I long not to live. And I am dying already, and have, since I came here, been divers times in the case that I thought to die within one hour. And I thank our Lord I was never sorry for it, but rather sorry when I saw the pang past. And, therefore, my poor body is at the King's pleasure. Would God my death might do him good.' "

The Secretary, who certainly seems to have been a friend to More, according to the flesh, hereupon interposed : " Well, ye find no fault in that statute; find you any in any of the other statutes after ?" He wished, that is to say, that even if More was unwilling to approve the statute, at least it might appear as if he did not disapprove of it, and even gave by his silence what might be interpreted and accepted as a tacit approbation. A similar kindness did some of the servants of King Antiochus wish to show to the aged Eleazar.[1] But More openly and honourably replied : " Sir, whatsoever thing should seem to me other than good in any of the other statutes, or in that statute either, I would not declare what fault I found, nor speak thereof." Whereupon the Secretary said kindly to More that nothing of what he had said to them should be used to his prejudice, but that a report would be made to the King that his gracious pleasure might be known.

This, then, was the result of his first examination in the Tower. The King's Councillors did not succeed in their endeavour, and More was in no way moved from his resolution or shaken in his constancy. Not for a moment did he waver in his witness to the truth.

THE SECOND EXAMINATION.

On June 3 following another group of noblemen came by order of the King to examine him in the Tower and to

[1] 2 Mac. vi 18.

attempt to gain his consent.   We give the account in More's own words :[1]

" Here sat my Lord of Canterbury, my Lord Chancellor, my Lord of Suffolk, my Lord of Wiltshire, and Master Secretary. And after my coming Master Secretary made rehearsal in what wise he had reported unto the King's Highness what had been said by His Grace's Council to me, and what had been answered by me to them, at mine other being before them here last, which thing his mastership rehearsed in good faith very well, as I knowledged and confessed, and heartily thanked him therefore. Whereupon he added thereunto that the King's Highness was nothing content nor satisfied with mine answer ; but thought that by my demeanour I had been occasion of much grudge and harm in the realm, and that I had an obstinate mind and an evil towards him, and that my duty was, being his subject (and so he had sent them now in his name upon mine allegiance to command me), to make a plain and a terminate answer, whether I thought the statute lawful or not. And that I should either knowledge and confess it lawful that His Highness should be Supreme Head of the Church of England, or else utter plainly my malignity. Whereto I answered that I had no malignity, and, therefore, I could utter none. And as to the matter, I could none other answer make than I had before made, which answer his mastership had there rehearsed. Very heavy I was that the King's Highness should have any such opinion of me. Howbeit if there were one that had informed His Highness many evil things of me that were untrue, to which His Highness for the time gave credence, I would be very sorry that he should have that opinion of me the space of one day. Howbeit, if I were sure that other should come on the morrow by whom His Grace should know the truth of mine innocency, I should in the mean while comfort myself with consideration of that. And in likewise now, though it be great heaviness to me that His Highness hath such opinion of me for the while, yet have I no remedy to help it, but only to comfort myself with this consideration, that I know very well that the time shall come when God shall declare my truth towards His Grace before him and

[1] E.W., p. 1452.

all the world. And whereas it might haply seem to be but small cause of comfort, because I might take harm here first in the mean while, I thanked God that my case was such here in this matter, through the clearness of mine own conscience, that though I might have pain, I could not have harm. For a man may in such a case lose his head and have none harm. For I was very sure that I had no corrupt affection, but that I had always from the beginning truly used myself, looking first upon God, and next upon the King, according to the lesson that His Highness taught me at my first coming to his noble service, the most virtuous lesson that ever prince taught his servant. . . .

" To this it was said by my Lord Chancellor and Master Secretary both, that the King might by his laws compel me to make a plain answer thereto either the one way or the other. Whereto I answered that I would not dispute the King's authority what His Highness might do in such a case. But I said that verily, under correction, it seemed to me somewhat hard. For if it so were that my conscience gave me against the statute (wherein how my conscience giveth me I make no declaration), then I nothing doing nor nothing saying against the statute, it were a very hard thing to compel me to say, either precisely with it against my conscience to the loss of my soul, or precisely against it to the destruction of my body." If therefore there be danger either way and this law be like a two-edged sword which cuts both ways, it were hard that I who have neither done nor said anything against this law should now be forced to declare my mind concerning it.[1]

" To this Master Secretary said, that I had, ere this, when I was Chancellor, examined heretics, and thieves, and other malefactors, and gave me great praise above my deserving in that behalf. And he said, that I then, as he thought, and at the least wise bishops, did use to examine heretics, whether they believed the Pope to be Head of the Church, and used to compel them to make a precise answer thereto. And why should not then the King, since it is

---

[1] This sentence is not in the letter from which we are quoting, but its substance is implied in the preceding sentence. In the indictment More was said to have uttered these words on this occasion (Bridgett, p. 417).

a law made here that His Grace is Head of the Church here, compel men to answer precisely to the law here, as they did then concerning the Pope? I answered and said, that I protested that I intended not to defend my part or stand in contention. But I said there was a difference between those two cases, because at that time, as well here as elsewhere through the corps of Christendom, the Pope's power was recognised for an undoubted thing ; which seemeth not like a thing agreed in this realm and the contrary taken for truth in other realms. Whereto Master Secretary answered, that they were as well burned for the denying of that as they be beheaded for the denying of this ; and, therefore, as good reason to compel them to make precise answer to the one as to the other. Whereto I answered, that since in this case a man is not by a law of one realm so bound in his conscience, where there is a law of the whole corps of Christendom to the contrary in a matter touching belief, as he is by a law of the whole corps, though there happen to be made in some place a law local to the contrary, the reasonableness or unreasonableness in binding a man to precise answer standeth not in the respect or difference between beheading and burning, but because of the difference in change of conscience, the difference standeth between beheading and hell. Much was there answered unto this, both by Master Secretary and my Lord Chancellor, over long to rehearse.

" And, in conclusion, they offered me an oath by which I should be sworn to make true answer to such things as should be asked me on the King's behalf, concerning the King's own person. Whereto I answered, that verily I never purposed to swear any book oath more while I lived. Then they said, that I was very obstinate, if I would refuse that, for every man doth it in the Star Chamber and everywhere. I said that was true ; but I had not so little foresight, but that I might well conjecture what should be part of mine interrogatories, and as good it was to refuse them at the first as afterwards. Whereto my Lord Chancellor answered, that he thought I guessed truth, for I should see them. And so they were showed me, and they were but twain : the first, whether I had seen the statute ; the other, whether I believed that it were a lawful made statute or not. Whereupon I refused the oath."

This, then, was the result of his second and last examination in the Tower. The reader will easily perceive the King's anxiety to win More's support for his impiety, using every endeavour to this end, and sparing no device or labour. He will realise, on the other hand, with what constancy, prudence, moderation, and piety More strove to defend the truth. The King's efforts show how much he esteemed More : More's firmness shows how deserving he was of esteem. Moreover, these two careful and detailed examinations are a clear and evident proof of his innocence. It was just because it was clear that no crime worthy of death had been committed by him that they examined him at such length and in such detail, trying to fix some charge upon him and to prove him guilty of some crime. As the refusal to take an oath that had not been sanctioned by any law, but had been imposed by the sole will of the King, was evidently not a sufficiently just cause of death, and as More had not offended against the law in prison, they tried to extort from him at least an expression of his disapproval of the law. As they could not obtain his approval of the law and would not permit him to remain silent, they wanted to be able to punish him as an enemy to the laws of the State. Although if they had been able to get from him such an expression of disapproval, not spread abroad among the people, not uttered spontaneously or maliciously, not pertinaciously defended, but given in answer to the question of a judge at the request of the King, how could it possibly afford a proof or even a suspicion of crime ? But More wished to remain blameless and as far as possible to avoid offending the King, therefore out of respect to the King he would not condemn the law, but he could not approve of it because he feared God. Such was his piety, his prudence, and his constancy. But in spite of all this, as it was a capital crime to oppose the King, and the royal anger was unappeased, by hook or by crook an innocent man had to be delivered up to death. The manner of this we must now describe : we shall see fraud and deceit on the side of the King, on More's side piety and constancy.

Meanwhile I will record for the reader only one more

circumstance.   After this examination More was kept far
more strictly confined, like one condemned to death.   He
could foretell without difficulty how the matter would end.
At this time he wrote with a coal a letter to his trusty friend
Antonio Bonvisi, an Italian merchant.   In this beautiful
and affectionate letter he pours out his gratitude to his
friend for his fidelity in time of adversity.   I would insert
it here were it not to be found in print in More's Latin
Works.

CHAPTER XVIII
HIS TRIAL AND CONDEMNATION

MORE had now been in the Tower for some fifteen months, straitly confined in a place commonly used for men guilty of the gravest crimes. For nearly the whole period he had not been permitted to receive visits from friends and relatives : his trials had been varied, frequent, and severe : twice he had been examined. Yet nothing could ever induce him to act against his conscience, to approve an impious decree, or to betray by any dissimulation the Catholic faith.

THE CHARGES AGAINST MORE.

At length on July 1, 1535, he was brought from the Tower to Westminster Palace, the chief tribunal in the kingdom, to be formally indicted by the King's Attorney.[1] He was cited to stand his trial for his life in that very place where not long before he had taken his place as judge with supreme power amidst the unbounded joy of the whole kingdom. He walked the long way, leaning on his staff, weakened not so much by age as by the sufferings of his imprisonment, but his countenance betokened no anxiety. The indictment that was read against him was long and involved. So diffuse was it, indeed, and so interminable were its clauses that More, whose memory was as good as any man's, had to confess that he could remember scarcely the third part of all the charges preferred against him. All that could have been charged upon the most abandoned criminal,

---

[1] As his authorities for the account of More's trial Stapleton quotes Cardinal Pole, *De Unitate Ecclesiae* ; Cardinal Nicholas of Capua, *Letters of Princes*, translated into French by Belleforest ; Erasmus, Covrinus Nucerinus, Philip Montanus, in pamphlets on the death of Thomas More, published in 1536 at Paris and Antwerp. Stapleton dates the trial June 1—an obvious misprint.

upon one who had betrayed his country, and contemned all its laws, was massed together, in order that, we must suppose, More might not be able to make a satisfactory answer to such a multitude of charges, and that thus the listeners would at least suspect very strongly that he was really guilty.   No doubt they hoped that More would be overwhelmed by the torrent of words, dumbfounded by the length of the indictment, or confused by the complexity of the language and consequently quite unable to make an adequate reply.   The whole aim and purpose of the Attorney's speech was to prove that More had obstinately and traitorously rejected the new statute concerning the royal supremacy over the Church of England.   In proof was adduced the twofold examination of More in the Tower by the King's Councillors, of which we have spoken above.   The conversation, also, with Richard Rich, which we have reproduced some pages back in full, was brought forward.   In addition it was alleged that from his prison he had written a letter to the Bishop of Rochester in which he had said that the new statute was like a two-edged sword which would ruin a man either way.   "For if he approve it it will confound his soul, if he disapprove of it, it will confound his body."   Again, too, was maliciously brought forward the old controversy concerning the King's second marriage.   The conclusion to which the Attorney came was that More obstinately rejected the statute of the realm, that he refused to submit to the authority of the King and so was guilty of treason.

After the close of the accusation, before More could reply, the Chancellor, who had succeeded him, and the Duke of Norfolk addressed him in the following terms : " You see, Mr. More, from the charges which we have brought forward, and you cannot deny, that you have gravely offended the King's Majesty. Nevertheless, if you will repent, put aside your obstinacy and correct your opinion, we trust that you will receive pardon of the King's clemency."   See here how the Serpent repeats his blandishments as of old, to the same refrain, " Ye shall not die the death !"[1]   But More was skilled in the warfare of the spirit and not to be deceived by the wiles of the Old Serpent.

[1] Gen. iii 4.

He answered, therefore : " My Lords, I thank you from my heart for this kindness, but I earnestly pray Almighty God to strengthen me in my just opinion and enable me to persevere in it even unto death." See how ready he is ! He does not forget the duty of courtesy : he earnestly calls upon God : he stoutly maintains the justice of his cause. In these few words he gives an example of three virtues, courtesy, piety, and constancy : he acts as a good citizen, a devout Christian, and a noble confessor. After this brief preface he comes to his defence.

HIS DEFENCE.

" Considering the length of the indictment and the gravity of the charges against me, I fear that I shall not have the wit, the memory, or the power of speech to reply to each one because of the great bodily weakness which a sickness contracted in prison and still upon me, has produced." At this point, by order of the judge, a seat was placed for him. After he was seated he went on with his speech. " If I mistake not, there are four main counts in the indictment : I will deal with them in order. As to the first charge that I have always maliciously opposed the King's second marriage, I freely confess that I have always made clear to His Majesty my disapproval of this marriage. I cannot say or think in this matter otherwise than I have hitherto thought or said, for the direction given me by my conscience has never changed. I have never wished to hide from the King's Majesty my conscientious opinion, nor was it right to hide it when it was asked. But in this matter there can lurk no suspicion of treason. On the contrary, being consulted by my Sovereign on a matter so vital to his honour and to the peace of the realm, if I had hidden the truth in order to curry favour I should truly have deserved to be charged, as I now am, with malice, perfidy and treason. But yet for this error, if it be an error to say the truth in answer to a question from my Sovereign, I have already been severely punished. I have suffered the loss of all my goods and been condemned to perpetual imprisonment, which I have already sustained for some fifteen months.

" The second and the principal charge against me is that I have incurred the penalty for violating the statute of Parliament, in that whilst in prison, I am alleged to have refused, maliciously, perfidiously and treasonably, to give to the King the honour that is due to him by virtue of this statute—*i.e.*, the new title by which he is declared to be Supreme Head on earth of the Church of England. I am said to have refused and denied this new prerogative because when I was twice questioned by Mr. Secretary and others His Majesty's Councillors as to my opinion of the statute, I would give no other answer but that this law, whether just or unjust, was no concern of mine, because at law I was civilly dead, and was under no obligation to give my opinion of laws which I was debarred from using. I went on to say that however much I might be concerned with that law, yet I had never done or said anything which might show disapproval of it, and therefore I could not rightly be condemned by a law against which no word or act of mine could be alleged.   I said that for the future I wished to meditate upon the bitter Passion of Christ my Saviour and my departure out of this life and to put aside all other cares.   Such do I freely acknowledge to have been my reply.   But I maintain that by such a reply I violate in no way any law or statute nor commit any capital offence. For laws punish deeds or words, but silence cannot be condemned either by this your law, or by all the laws of the whole world.   Of secret thoughts God alone is Judge."

As More's argument seemed to be impressing the court, the King's Attorney here interrupted him.   " Even though," he said, " we should have no word or deed to charge upon you, yet we have your silence, and that is a sign of your evil intention and a sure proof of malice.   For no subject in the whole realm who is well disposed towards his Sovereign will refuse, when questioned about this statute, to state his opinion categorically."

To this More replied as follows : " My silence is no proof of malice, as His Majesty can well know by many other tokens, nor is it shown to be any disapproval of your law.   Indeed it should be taken rather as a mark of approval than of disapproval, in accordance with the common legal rule ' he who is silent seems to consent.'   You speak of the duty of a good subject, arguing from the example of all the subjects in England ; but I consider that the duty of a good subject is to obey God rather than men, unless he wishes to be a good subject at the price of being a bad Christian. He is bound to have greater care of his conscience and the salvation of his soul than of any other thing whatsoever, especially when his conscience does not raise any offence, scandal or sedition against his prince. Such certainly is my conscience, for I solemnly affirm that I have never discovered what is in my conscience to any person living.

" I come now to the third article of the charge, that I am shown to have infringed this statute and act of Parliament, to have maliciously attempted, traitorously endeavoured and perfidiously practised against it (as the indictment speaks) because I wrote eight letters in the Tower to the Bishop of Rochester, in which I am said to have urged him to disobey the law and to have encouraged him in his obstinacy. I heartily wish that these letters could be produced here and read either for my condemnation or for my acquittal. But since, as you say, the Bishop has burnt them, I will make no difficulty about telling you the whole truth in the matter. Some of them treated of our private affairs, for we were old and intimate friends. One was a reply to a letter in which the Bishop desired to know how I had answered the King's Councillors as regards the new statute. As to this I said nothing more than that I had settled my conscience and he must settle his own. So may God love me and save my soul, but I wrote nothing else in that letter. As God is my witness I assert that this and nought else is the truth. On this count, then, I have done nothing against your law worthy of death.

" The fourth and last charge against me is that when I was being examined concerning this law in the Tower, I said that it was like a two-edged sword, for by contradicting it I should lose my head, by assenting to it I should lose my soul. Since the Bishop of Rochester gave a similar reply, it is argued that clearly we conspired together. To this I answer that when I used those words in the Tower before the Lords of the Council it was only conditionally. Thus, if there be danger either way, whether I approve or condemn this law, and if therefore it be like a two-edged sword that cuts whichever way it is turned, then it seems to me a very hard thing that it should be offered to me who have never contradicted it in word or deed. This is what I said : what the Bishop of Rochester answered I do not know. If his reply was similar to mine, it did not arise from any conspiracy between us, but rather from the likeness of our dispositions and opinions. In fine, you may be assured that never to any living man did I speak against this statute, although perhaps the King's Majesty has falsely been told the contrary."

Such was More's answer. The indictment was long, in sound serious and grave, in matter empty and false. The reply was short and clear : the defence just and true. Against such clear evidence of truth and innocence the Attorney had no reply, but the word " malice " remained in the minds of all those present, and as a proof of it, in default of any word or deed, silence alone was accepted.

The Jury's Verdict.

Twelve men were then summoned, whose duty it is, according to the custom of our nation, to listen to the evidence and decide upon it in all capital cases. The indictment was given to them in writing and they were ordered to consult together upon it, and afterwards to give their verdict whether Thomas More had maliciously contravened the aforesaid statute. After withdrawing for only a quarter of an hour, for there is no need for long discussion when not justice but the royal will is in question, they returned and gave their verdict " Guilty "[1]—i.e., worthy of death. For these twelve men do not give any grounds or arguments for their judgement, but with a single word they decide between life and death. No intermediate verdict, such as " not clear," is permitted. The twelve summoned in this case were of noble rank, like More. Two were knights, two esquires, and the eight others of gentle birth. For the twelve chosen are of the same rank as the accused. I might give the names and surnames of

---

[1] Guilty, spelt by Stapleton " gilty," is the only English word he introduces into his text throughout the whole book.

each, but, because of their infamous verdict, I prefer to pass them over in silence and hide the ignominy of such honoured families.

The Sentence.

Having received the verdict, the Lord Chancellor, who presided, pronounced sentence of death in these words : " Our sentence is that Thomas More shall be taken back from this place by William Kingston, the Constable, to the Tower and thence shall be dragged right through the City of London as far as the gallows at Tyburn. There he shall be hanged, cut down while yet alive, ripped up, his bowels burnt in his sight, his head cut off, his body quartered and the parts set up in such places as the King shall designate."

Such was the noble sentence pronounced against Sir Thomas More as a penalty for keeping silent. Such was the condemnation of one who had rendered the highest services to King and State, because he would not be untrue to his conscience. Such was the honourable reward conferred upon a faithful Councillor who had nobly served his King, because he would not give approval to filthy lust or barter his honour for gain. Not undeservedly does Paul Jovius for this one crime call Henry another Phalaris.[1]

This ferocious sentence, which was usually carried out only upon the very worst criminals, was indeed afterwards changed to the milder one of simple beheading. But this was rather because the Kings of England are accustomed to choose this manner of execution for those who are illustrious by birth or office, than through any clemency on the part of Henry. The only benefit conferred is like that conferred by highwaymen, who make a merit of granting life to those of their victims whom they do not murder. Wherefore when word was brought to More that the King of his clemency had been so gracious to him as to commute his sentence into beheading only, he replied : " May God avert such royal clemency from all my friends." But of this more hereafter. Now it is our duty to relate what More did and said after sentence of death had been pronounced.

[1] *Praises of Famous Men*, tit. 89 (S.).

MORE'S OPEN PROFESSION OF FAITH.

After the judge had sentenced him, More knew that he was called to the grace of martyrdom, for hitherto he had been in doubt whether Almighty God would bestow upon him the favour of so high a vocation. Whereas he had, therefore, up to this time refused to say what he thought, now with bold and fearless conscience he spoke as follows: " Seeing that I am condemned, and God knows how justly, for the discharge of my conscience I will now speak freely of your statute. When I saw, from the way the affairs of the realm were tending, that it would be necessary to seek out the source of the origin of the Pope's authority, I confess that I turned my studies to that matter for a full seven years. But never could I find in any writing of the Doctors whom the Church approves that a layman ever had been, or ever could become, head of the spirituality."

At this point the Chancellor interrupted More's speech, saying, " So then, Mr. More, you wish to be thought wiser and more conscientious than all others, that is to say, all the Bishops, all the nobility and the whole kingdom."

More replied: " My Lord Chancellor, for one Bishop whom you may produce for your side, I will bring forward a hundred saintly and orthodox prelates who subscribe to my opinion: for your one Parliament, and God knows of what sort it is, I have on my side all the councils that have been held in the whole Christian world for more than a thousand years: and for your one kingdom of England I have with me all the kingdoms of Christianity."

With these grave words did More with the full weight of his authority silence the trivial and frivolous interruption of the Chancellor. But the Duke of Norfolk, first in noble rank after the King as the Chancellor was first in office, was displeased and thus addressed More: " Now, Mr. More, you show us clearly the malice of your mind."

At once More replied: " Noble Lord, no malice has moved me to speak as I have done, but a necessity in justice for me to discharge my conscience in this judgement hall. God, who alone is the searcher of heart and reins, is my witness that I have been urged by no other motive. As to the law, by which I have been condemned, I have some observations to make. You, my Lords, the Peers of the realm, explicitly promised, and confirmed your promise with an oath, that you would maintain the rights of the Church inviolate. Therefore I say that you have done very wrong in passing this law, for in this realm you stand alone, in opposition to the unanimous consent of Christendom. Your law has dissolved the unity, the peace and the concord of the Church, although the Church is, as all know, a body which is one, universal, whole and undivided, and therefore in matters of religion nothing can be decided without the general consent of the whole. Yet I know full well what has been the chief cause of my condemnation : it is that I would never give my approval to this new marriage.

" In this world there will ever be discord, and variety of opinion. But I trust that as Paul persecuted Stephen even to death and yet both are now united in heaven, so we too who are now at variance in this world and differ in our opinions, may be one in heart and mind for ever in the world to come. In this hope, I pray God to preserve you all, and especially my lord the King, and to deign always to send him faithful counsellors."

EVIL COUNSELS OF WOLSEY.

These were the last words of Sir Thomas More at that famous tribunal. They were jealously treasured up by those who heard them, and they were put into print at Paris a long time ago, when the memory of the affair was still fresh. What words could be more worthy of a noble martyr of Christ ? He stoutly confesses the truth ; he shows no anger at an unjust sentence ; and, most noble of all, his thoughts turn to St Stephen, and in imitation of him he prays for his persecutors. Not only does he pray, but he puts his finger, so to say, on the source of all the evil when he expresses his hope that the King may have good counsellors. The great calamity of our land, or rather of the whole earth, was that the King gave ear to evil advice. The King had no thought at all of a new marriage until Cardinal Wolsey first suggested it to him through another

person.[1]   The Cardinal had not received from the Emperor
Charles the support he had fully expected in his candida-
ture for the Papacy.   Deprived of his ambition and wishing
to be revenged on Charles and to win again the friendship
of the French King, he insinuated to Henry a doubt as to
the validity of a marriage in which he had remained for
twenty years without scruple, in order that, if this marriage
were annulled, he might arrange a new one between Henry
and the sister of Francis I of France.   But to none was this
evil counsel more harmful than to him who gave it.   The
King's new marriage, not with a French Princess, but
with Anne Boleyn, was the signal for the ruin, first of Wolsey
himself, and afterwards of the whole spirituality and even
of religion itself in England.   But if at that time all the
members of the King's Council had been like Sir Thomas
More, and all the Bishops like the Bishop of Rochester, they
would have dealt with the matter justly and conscien-
tiously: they would have answered truly to the King: they
would have tried, not to curry favour, but to utter faithfully what truth and their conscience dictated.   Then that
unhappy marriage would not have brought upon England
such torrents of blood, and the new-fangled and anti-
Christian title of the King would not have brought religion
in England to such universal ruin.

Thus, then, did Sir Thomas More make his answer to the
charges brought against him, not only like a noble confessor and eloquent defender of the orthodox faith, but also
as a most prudent counsellor of the King.

[1] This would seem to refer to the fact, vouched for by Nicholas Sander
(i. 3) and Harpsfield (*Treatise of Marriage*, ii, p. 93), that Wolsey
first approached John Longland, Bishop of Lincoln, the King's confessor.
It is clear that Wolsey was ambitious of the Papacy, but the Catholics
of the next generation, who blamed him as the author of all their misfortunes, may sometimes by their bitterness against him have been led
into exaggeration.   (See E. L. Taunton's *Cardinal Wolsey, Legate
and Reformer*.)

CHAPTER XIX

AFTER THE CONDEMNATION

S IR THOMAS MORE'S speech was interrupted by his judges rather than brought to its natural conclusion. For they were no more able to endure the wisdom and the boldness of so learned and eloquent a man than were the stiff-necked Jews able to bear the attack of St Stephen. More thereupon was led back from the bar to his prison once more, whilst an axe was carried before him with its edge turned towards him as a sign of his condemnation.

PARTING FROM MARGARET ROPER.

Now was seen a spectacle more piteous and more astonishing than his very condemnation. John More, his only son, threw himself at his father's feet as he passed on his way, and on his knees begged with many tears his father's blessing. This, however, was quite in accordance with the custom of our country, and therefore it aroused less comment, although the father, in a letter which we shall afterwards quote, wrote that his son's dutiful affection, at such a time and place, had given him no little consolation. But when More had got some little distance away from the judgement hall,[1] his daughter Margaret Roper met him. So dear to him was this beloved child, as is clear from what we have already said, that if More's strength had not been superhuman, he might well have been moved from his resolution. She had mingled with the crowd in order to see her father and bid him farewell; but now her love gave

---

[1] Stapleton is mistaken in saying that the meeting with Margaret Roper took place near Westminster (" paulo extra judicii locum "). Roper, who could not be wrong on such a point, states that Margaret awaited the return of her father at the Tower Wharf.

her more than a man's strength, and she pushed her way through the crowd, breaking through the armed guard that surrounded him until she reached his side. Although she was a lady of great delicacy and reserve, yet on this occasion her shyness and timidity were entirely forgotten in her uncontrollable grief, or, as I prefer to believe, in the immensity of her love. For she fell upon the neck of her beloved father and pressed him to her bosom in a long embrace, unable to utter a word beyond " Oh, my father." Few in the crowd could remain unmoved. But how could More withstand the love of his dear daughter expressed at such a time, a love so strong and fearless ? Surely he would not only have been moved by it, but even somewhat shaken in his constancy, unless the power of divine grace, which had enabled him to hear without flinching the sentence of death and afterwards to speak and to act with still greater courage, had not now also strengthened him not to give way to nature or to waver in his resolution. That a daughter so noble, so worthy of such a father, so richly endowed with all nature's gifts, should lavish every mark of affection which it can delight parents to receive from their children, should force her way to him when scarcely a man could have pressed through the crowd, should no sooner see him than clasp him in a close embrace, cannot have failed to pierce More's heart through and through with grief. Much as he loved all his children, he reserved his most special affection for Margaret. How his sorrow must have been deepened when she clung to his embrace with grief too great for words, when she would not be torn away from him ! At last she was separated from him, but again love surged up impetuously and she rushed back to his embrace, not to be torn away save with far greater difficulty than before. What was then his grief and anguish of soul ! How great was his need of spiritual strength and divine consolation when the consolation of natural affection could but cause him a grief more bitter than any death.

But yet More did not allow himself to be overcome : he stood firm, a noble victor. His voice, his countenance, his manner showed that nature tempted him in vain, and that he had conquered all things under heaven that can cause grief to men. His words were as firm as ever. He said gravely to his daughter that although he was innocent, yet his sufferings were permitted by God, who knew the secrets of his heart. He bade her submit her natural affection to the will of God and be patient in their common affliction. This was at their first embrace. But when after having gone ten or a dozen paces she returned and a second time clung around his neck, no word was heard, for tears choked his speech. Even so his countenance betrayed no sign of any weakening in his purpose. One behest only did he make, that she should pray for her father's soul.

Another one, too, at the same time embraced and kissed him. This was Margaret Gigs, his daughter, not by birth, but by adoption, and afterwards the wife of Doctor Clements. John, too, his son, after receiving his father's blessing, kissed him and received his kiss in return. All of these afterwards bore witness that from the mouth of More, as they kissed him, they perceived a marvellous sweet fragrance. Amongst those who witnessed this piteous meeting, these embraces and kisses, there were many of the crowd who could not refrain from weeping, and some even of the soldiery. We shall not wonder at this when we read the words of Cardinal Pole : " Strangers who had never known More were so moved to grief by his death that, in reading the written accounts of it that were circulated, they could not refrain from tears, bewailing a man unknown to them except by his noble fame. Not because of any especial personal intimacy with him, but because of his goodness and virtue and because of his splendid services to his and my country, I honour and love him so much that even now, as from so distant a land I write of his death, my tears rise unbidden (God is my witness) hindering my writing and often blotting out the letters I form so that I can scarcely proceed."[1]

Thus More was more severely tempted on his way back to the Tower than he was in the judgement hall, and the victory he gained was all the more meritorious.

[1] *De Unitate Eccles.*, Bk. III (S.).   Written at Rome.

More's Last Letter.

Returned to his prison and " knowing that his hour was come that he should pass out of this world to God,"[1] on the fourth day after his condemnation, which was the fifth of July and a Monday, he wrote his last letter with a coal (for a pen was denied him) to his sweetest and dearest daughter, Margaret Roper.   I will quote it in full, because it is the last thing he ever wrote, and because while steeped in human affection it breathes forth the spirit of a Saint.

" Our Lord bless you, good daughter, and your good husband and your little boy, and all yours, and all my children, and all my god-children, and all our friends. Recommend me when you may to my good daughter Cecily, whom I beseech our Lord to comfort.   And I send her my blessing, and to all her children, and pray her to pray for me.   I send her an handkercher: and God comfort my good son her husband.   My good daughter Dauncy hath the picture in parchment, that you delivered me from my lady Coniers, the name is on the back side.   Show her that I heartily pray her, that you may send it in my name to her again, for a token from me to pray for me.   I like special well Dorothy Colley,[2] I pray you be good unto her.[3] I would wit whether this be she that you wrote me of.   If not I pray you be good to the other, as you may in her affliction, and to my good daughter Jane Aleyn[4] too.   Give her, I pray you, some kind answer, for she sued hither to me this day to pray you be good to her.

" I cumber you, good Margaret, much, but I would be sorry if it should be any longer than to-morrow.   For it is

---

[1] John xiii 1.

[2] Afterwards the wife of John Harris, the secretary of Sir Thomas More, and still living at Douai when Stapleton wrote. (In order not to break the continuity of this beautiful and touching letter I am placing in the notes the information which Stapleton encloses in parentheses.)

[3] She was Margaret Roper's maid and was often sent by her to the Tower to carry her gifts to her father.

[4] Another one of Margaret Roper's maids who received her education with More's family and is therefore called his daughter.

St Thomas' even,[1] and the utas[2] of St Peter : and therefore to-morrow long I to go to God : it were a day very meet and convenient to me.

" I never liked your manner toward me better, than when you kissed me last. For I love when daughterly love and dear charity hath no leisure to look to worldly courtesy.

" Farewell, my dear child, and pray for me, and I shall for you and all your friends, that we may merrily meet in heaven. I thank you for your great cost. I send now to my good daughter Clements[3] her algorism stone, and I send her and my godson and all hers God's blessing and mine. I pray you at time convenient recommend me to my good son John More. I liked well his natural fashion.[4] Our Lord bless him and his good wife my loving daughter, to whom I pray him be good as he hath great cause : and that if the land of mine come to his hand, he break not my will concerning his sister Dauncy. And our Lord bless Thomas and Austin[5] and all that they shall have."[6]

This last letter of Sir Thomas More is clearly filled with the spirit of God and with a wisdom more than earthly. His mind is entirely peaceful and vexed with no anxiety. He forgets none of his dear ones. To his very last breath he is faithful to all the duties of a good father and a noble confessor of Christ. His spirit is entirely Christ-like : he utters no bitter word, but begs the blessing of God upon one and all. As Jacob on his bed of death blessed his children and grandchildren, so does More from his prison invoke blessings and spiritual favours upon all. From all, too, he begs prayers for himself, for to the very end of his life he retained the spirit of humility and the fear of the Lord as a most sure guarantee of all the other virtues.

---

[1] i.e., the eve of the feast of the Translation (of the relics) of St Thomas of Canterbury, which was kept on July 7 in England, and observed throughout Christendom, though on another day. The feast is still kept in some English dioceses.

[2] i.e., Octave-day of the Feast of SS Peter and Paul, June 29.

[3] Margaret Gigs, the wife of John Clements, M.D.

[4] i.e., when he fell upon his knees before his father after his condemnation to beg his blessing.

[5] These were the two sons already born to John More.

[6] E.W., p. 1457.

His Knowledge of the Future.

Did he not also possess the spirit of prophecy and a special intimacy with God ?   For notice how in this letter he foretells the day of his death.   " I cumber you much, but I would be sorry if it should be any longer than to-morrow."   On that morrow he suffered.   Why should he fix on the morrow rather than some later day as the day of his death, unless he had received some enlightenment from God ?   Why did he wait until the fourth day after his condemnation to write his last letter ?   For daily after sentence of death had been passed his daughter Margaret sent her maid Dorothy to him, nor did the jailer, a friend to More, at this time refuse access.   But it was only on the fourth day that he bade farewell to his dear ones, and no other day than the fifth did he designate for his passion.

Fitness of the Day of his Death.

At least it is certain that More especially longed for that day, whether he had received knowledge from God or had offered special prayers in regard to it.   " It were a day very meet and convenient to me."   Why ?   Because it was the feast of the Translation of the relics of St Thomas of Canterbury, which although not a public holiday was yet celebrated with much solemnity in the churches.   It was also the Octave-day of St Peter, the Prince of the Apostles. With sweet graciousness did God grant to his martyr that day so fittingly desired by him on which the Church was celebrating the memory of his patron saint and of that Apostle for whose primacy he was shedding his blood. For More, devout Catholic as he was, did not doubt that he would enjoy the special intercession of those glorious saints on the day on which all Catholics were united in begging their help.   He knew well that honour is paid to the saints with this end in view—" that it may be available to their honour and our salvation : and that they may vouchsafe to intercede for us in heaven, whose memory we celebrate on earth."[1]   Familiar indeed were these words

---

[1] From the Ordinary of the Mass.

to More, who, though by vocation a layman, showed ever in his life the holiness and spotlessness of a priest. If, then, the saints are honoured in order that they may intercede for us, doubtless on those days when the Church pays them special honour she receives a more abundant fruit from their prayers.

Great, then, was the desire of Sir Thomas More that on that day he might " be dissolved and be with Christ,"[1] and, as the Church sings in her office for martyrs, "the Lord gave him the desire of his heart."[2] Naturally did he hope that on that day, of the saints who were his peculiar patrons, he would receive the special help and intercession that he might enter upon eternal bliss. Who is there amongst the faithful who does not look for help from God more abundant and more certain on the feast of his patron saint? Who does not know that the Spaniards on the feast of St James, their national patron, fight with greater confidence and often have gained signal victories? So, too, the English and the French, when both those nations were entirely Catholic, often performed prodigies of valour on the feasts of St George and St Denis.

MORE DIES FOR THE PRIMACY OF THE POPE.

It was, then, meet that on the day of the glorious Translation of St Thomas the Martyr, his patron, Sir Thomas More should wish to be " translated " from darkness to light and receive the crown of martyrdom. One giving his life for Christ might well wish to die on the day of our Saviour's birth, of his Passion, his Resurrection, or his Ascension. Many indeed, as we read in the Acts of the Martyrs, have been butchered by heathen persecutors and have given a noble witness to Christ, actually on Easter Day or Passion Sunday.[3] But St Peter was appointed by Christ himself to be the first Prince of the ecclesiastical order and state. St Chrysostom calls him " the ruler of the whole earth,"[4]

---

[1] Phil. i 23. [2] Ps. xx 3.
[3] Stapleton in a note instances the hundred Christians martyred on a Good Friday by Sapor, King of the Persians (see Sozomen, Bk. II, ch. x).
[4] Homily No. 55 on St Matthew (S.).

and St Damascene, also a Greek, says that " he received authority over the whole Church."[1]   But Henry in England sacrilegiously claimed for himself St Peter's primacy.   For this primacy More was going to lay down his life and make his glorious confession.   Was it not fitting, then, that he should wish to do so on the Octave-day of St Peter? This, then, was his desire, and the Lord " did not withhold from him the will of his lips."[2]   These words, applied by the Church to all the martyrs, are peculiarly applicable to More.

This last letter of More, then, gives evidence of a knowledge of the future, or at least of an intimate understanding of the divine will.   Every word of the letter betokens the peace of his soul : he gives loving directions about various matters, not as if he were a prisoner condemned to die on the morrow, but as if he were at home in full enjoyment of his liberty and about to set out on a journey.   He is thoughtful for his dear ones, as was Christ on the Cross, when he entrusted the care of his Mother to the beloved disciple.

He sends back his Instruments of Penance.

Together with this last letter he sent to his daughter Margaret, wrapped in a cloth, his hair-shirt and the scourge with which he had been wont to give himself the discipline.

He was not warned by the King, his judges, or his gaoler, for normally he would not have received notice until after another full day,[3] yet he was sure of receiving the crown of martyrdom on the morrow, either through a heavenly message or because of his confidence in the divine goodness. Certain, then, that the struggle was ending and glorious victory at hand, he laid down the weapons of his spiritual warfare.   He had several reasons for sending away his instruments of penance.   He was unwilling that they should

---

[1] In his sermon on the Transfiguration (S.).

[2] Ps. xx 3.

[3] This seems to be the meaning of the puzzling sentence : " non a custode . . . monitus, neque enim hoc fieri solet nisi sub vesperam sequentis diei."

come into the hands of any but his loved ones ; he wished to hide his secret habit of mortification from all strangers ; he feared that if these penitential weapons should be left in his prison they would give occasion to scorn and derision or to a suspicion of hypocrisy or affected holiness. So much, then, on More's condemnation to death and what followed thereon.

CHAPTER XX

HIS HAPPY DEATH AND GLORIOUS MARTYRDOM

AFTER receiving sentence of death and being led back to the Tower on July 1, 1535, Thomas More prepared himself for approaching death. He was in no way cast down or anxious in mind : he was not only quite resigned, as we have seen, but even cheerful and merry, according to his wont. Of this we shall soon have proof. But not for a moment did he put aside the fear of the Lord. " Blessed is the man that is always fearful."[1] During those last days, within the narrow limits of his prison, he would walk up and down clad in a linen sheet, like a corpse about to be buried, and severely discipline himself. Mark the holiness of the man who had, though innocent, suffered for so long such heavy punishment, but was as unrelenting towards himself as if he had ever lived in pampered luxury and had committed the grossest crimes. Woe to us who live delicately, who are puffed up with pride, green with envy, mean, avaricious, gross, impure, but yet are unwilling to bear any hardship for Christ's sake or for our own good. But " the kingdom of heaven suffereth violence, and the violent bear it away."[2] Thomas More had learnt this lesson thoroughly, and to the last day of his life he willed to be harsh and to do violence to himself. He knew that in the race the strong runner, as he approaches his goal, increases his efforts and his speed.

THE WAY TO THE SCAFFOLD.

When the day had arrived which was to bring to More death, or rather life, he was led out of his prison. His beard was long and disordered, his face was pale and thin from the rigour of his confinement. He held in his hand

---

[1] Prov. xxviii 14.   [2] Matt. xi 12.

a red cross and raised his eyes to heaven. His robe was of the very poorest and coarsest. He had decided to make his last journey in a better garment and to put on the gown of camlet, which Bonvisi had given him in prison, both to please his friend and to be able to give it to the executioner. But through the avarice or wickedness of his gaoler, he, so great and renowned, he who had held such high office, went out clad in his servant's gown made of the basest material that we call frieze.[1] But this was for Thomas More a fitting nuptial garment: by it he was made like to Christ, who willed to be poor : clothed in it he hastened to drink the Chalice of Christ and to celebrate the Nuptial Feast of the Lamb.

Margaret Gigs, the wife of John Clements, once showed me a life-like image, made with great skill, of More going out to the place of execution, and in accordance with that image I have described here his appearance and demeanour. She was present at More's death and assisted the other Margaret, Roper's wife, to bury him.

As he was passing on his way, a certain woman offered him wine, but he refused it, saying, " Christ in his passion was given not wine, but vinegar, to drink."

Another woman shouted at him and demanded to know what he had done with certain documents which she had entrusted to him while he was Chancellor. " Good woman," he replied, " as for your documents, have patience, I beseech you, for the space of one short hour. For then from the care of your documents and from every other burden, the King's Majesty in his goodness will give me complete relief."

He was again interrupted by another woman, who perhaps felt she had a grievance or perhaps was suborned by others, and now cried out that he had done her a grave injury while he was Chancellor. " I remember your case quite well," he gravely replied, " and if I had to pass sentence again, it would be just the same as before."

Our readers will remember, too, the man of whom we spoke in Chapter VI, who appealed to him now for advice and prayers.

[1] Stapleton adds " vel griseam "—a word probably connected with the French " gris."

THE CROWN OF MARTYRDOM.

When he arrived at the place of execution and was about to mount the scaffold, he stretched out his hand for assistance, saying, " I pray you see me safe up, and for my coming down let me shift for myself." On the scaffold he wished to speak to the people, but was forbidden to do so by the Sheriff. He contented himself, therefore, with saying : " I call you to witness, brothers, that I die the faithful servant of God and the King, and in the faith of the Catholic Church." Such were his words ; and in truth no one in the kingdom could be matched with him for fidelity to the King : God he served with the greatest zeal and holiness of life : he died not only in the Catholic faith but on its behalf. After that, kneeling down, he recited aloud the fiftieth Psalm : " Have mercy on me, O God."

The Bishop of Rochester in the same circumstances had said the *Te Deum*. He was filled by God with joy and exultation : he had hastened to the scaffold, casting aside the staff of his old age. On the day he was to die, he had slept peacefully in bed until an advanced hour of the morning, and had asked for milk for his breakfast.

More, however, was filled with the spirit of humility and holy fear : he chose to recite a prayer for forgiveness and not a hymn of praise. The dispositions of each were from God and pleasing to God. For the Apostle tells us that " the fruit of the spirit is joy,"[1] and David reminds us that " a sacrifice to God is an afflicted spirit."[2] Although the Bishop of Rochester was no more destitute of holy fear than More was destitute of holy joy. For after saying the Psalm and finishing his prayer, he rose briskly, and when according to custom the executioner begged his pardon, he kissed him with great love, gave him a golden angel,[3] and said to him : " Thou wilt give me this day a greater benefit than ever any mortal man can be able to give me. Pluck up thy spirits, man, and be not afraid to do thine office. My neck is very short : take heed, therefore, thou

[1] Gal. v 22.   [2] Ps. l 19.
[3] Roper says that More *sent* the money.

strike not awry for saving of thine honesty." But, even
before, he had asked his daughter and other friends to do
whatever acts of kindness they could to his executioner.
Then the executioner wished to bind his eyes, but he said,
"I will cover them myself." He covered his face with
a linen cloth he had brought with him, and joyfully and
calmly laid his head on the block. It was at once struck
off, and his soul sped to heaven.

By binding his eyes he had just cut himself off from the
sight of men, but now at once he reaches the open vision of
God and the angels. How happy his soul, raised, by one
single blow, to the everlasting joys of heaven! Now did he
experience the truth of a saying he often uttered : " A man
may very easily lose his head, but come to no harm." He
was beheaded, but in what way was he harmed? He was
old and in bad health : suffering a few moments of pain he
exchanged what remained to him of this life for the never-
ending life of heaven. In the eyes of the world he died
a shameful death, but what loss was that to him who now
enjoys not only the glory of heaven, but perpetual honour
even amongst men ? For a moment he was parted from
those he loved, but how could that be painful to him when
he knew that as a reward for his sacrifice he would be for
ever happily reunited with them ? He died robbed of
his honours and his wealth, but in return he has received
an abundant reward in heaven, for Christ, who is the very
truth, said of such as More : " Be glad and rejoice, for your
reward is very great in heaven."[1]

MORE DIES FOR THE PRIMACY OF THE POPE.

Thomas More, then, gladly suffered imprisonment, the
loss of his goods, and death itself for the Primacy of the
Pope, the one Supreme Head of the Church. And truly
upon this Primacy and Supremacy the whole peace, order,
and unity of the Church depend, for if it is rejected a way
is opened to all the heresies, and the wolves ravage the flock
with impunity, as the example of England alone may well
teach other nations.

Thus More, his toils and sorrows past, reigns gloriously in

[1] Matt. v 12.

heaven, and on earth enjoys the praise not only of the good but even of the wicked themselves. All bewail his death as most unjust : none can be found, except perhaps a few sycophants of the impious King, to approve of it.

THE KING'S EMOTION AT HIS DEATH.

For even King Henry himself, when the news was brought to him that the supreme penalty had been exacted of Thomas More—he happened to be playing with dice at the time—was greatly upset. " Is he then dead ?" he enquired. Hearing that it was so, he turned to Anne Boleyn, who was sitting by him, and said : " You are the cause of that man's death." And rising at once he retired to another room and shed bitter tears.

There is no doubt that from youth upwards Henry was fond of Thomas More. There was not a great difference in their ages, More being only seven[1] years the King's senior. The King was eighteen when he came to the throne, and at that time More wrote an excellent epigram to convey his congratulations on his accession. The King was not the first-born of his father, but succeeded to the throne owing to the death of his elder brother Arthur. He had, consequently, been educated with especial care, and himself devoted to literature and philosophy, he had a great affection for those whose tastes were similar. In the fifth or sixth year, then, of his reign, he took More, who then was Under-Sheriff of London, into his diplomatic service and soon after made him a member of his Privy Council. For more than twenty years—it was in the twenty-seventh year of the reign that More was executed— More was so dear to the King, so faithful, that his advancement was continuous and unprecedented. His violent and shameful death, therefore, against all the rules of justice, after such a long friendship and so many years of faithful service, could not but be displeasing even to the tyrant himself. But love of Anne Boleyn and the boundless lust of the flesh gained the victory. The King, indeed, as is stated by many, wished to keep More in perpetual imprisonment. But Anne Boleyn could not rest until, like another

[1] About thirteen.

Herodias, she saw More's head severed from his body. Yet her joy was short-lived, for before another year had passed, in that same place where More had suffered for justice and truth she was beheaded for adultery and incest.

MORE'S HEAD RECOVERED BY MARGARET ROPER.

But now, before we come to relate the laments of others besides ourselves over the death of Thomas More, we will record what happened to the head and the body of the blessed martyr. The former, by order of the King, was placed upon a stake on London Bridge, where it remained for nearly a month, until it had to be taken down to make room for other heads. For the King's thirst for blood, once gratified, grew apace. The head would have been thrown into the river, had not Margaret Roper, who had been watching carefully and waiting for the opportunity, bribed the executioner whose office it was to remove the heads and obtained possession of the sacred relic. There was no possibility of mistake, for she, with the help of others, had kept careful watch; and, moreover, there were signs so certain that anyone who had known him in life would have been able now to identify the head. A tooth was missing, which he had lost in life, and his countenance was almost as beautiful as before. One remarkable fact that his friends noted was that his beard, which before his death was almost white, now appeared to be of a reddish-brown colour. Margaret Roper as long as she lived kept the head with the greatest reverence, carefully preserving it by means of spices, and to this day it remains in the custody of one of his relatives.

BURIAL OF THE BODY.

His body was buried by Margaret Roper and Margaret Clements in the little Chapel of St Peter in the Tower, by permission of the Lieutenant. In regard to this burial an incident occurred which may well be regarded as miraculous. Margaret Roper from earliest morning had been going from church to church and distributing such generous alms to the poor that her purse was now empty. After her father's execution she hastened to the Tower to bury his body, for the Lieutenant had promised to allow this with the permission of the King, which was readily given. In her hurry she forgot to replenish her purse and found that she had no winding-sheet for the body. She was in the greatest distress and knew not what to do. Her maid Dorothy, afterwards the wife of Mr. Harris, suggested that she should get some linen from a neighbouring shop. "How can I do that," she answered, "when I have no money left ?" "They will give you credit," replied the maid. "I am far away from home," said Margaret, "and no one knows me here, but yet go and try." The maid went into a neighbouring shop and asked for as much linen as was needed : she agreed on the price. Then she put her hand into her purse as if to look for the money, intending to say that unexpectedly she found herself without money, but that if the shopkeeper would trust her she would obtain the price of the linen as quickly as possible from her mistress and bring it back. But although the maid was quite certain that she had absolutely no money, yet in her purse she found exactly the price of the linen, not one farthing more nor less than the amount she had agreed to pay. Dorothy Harris, who is still living here in Douai, has told me these details again and again.

With this winding-sheet, so strangely obtained, the two Margarets and Dorothy most reverently buried the body.

The shirt in which he died, stained with his blood, Margaret Clements showed me whole and entire, and gave me a large portion of it. I am not sure whether she was allowed by the other Margaret from the beginning to keep it, or whether it only came to her after her death (for Margaret Roper died many years before Margaret Clements).

PROCEEDINGS AGAINST MORE'S FAMILY.

But, soon after, the weight of the King's anger was felt by More's whole family. His widow Alice was turned out of her house ; and from all More's property, which was now confiscated to the royal treasury, she was allowed no

more than a pension of £20 a year, on which she managed
to continue to live, although in straitened circumstances,
in the village of Chelsea.

Margaret Roper was brought before the King's Council,
and charged with keeping her father's head as a sacred
relic, and retaining possession of his books and his writings.
She answered that she had saved her father's head from
being devoured by the fishes, with the intention of burying
it : that she had hardly any books and papers but what had
been already published, except a very few personal letters,
which she humbly begged to be allowed to keep for her
own consolation. By the good offices of friends she was
released. Although there were many women in More's
household, she was the only one to be troubled. But every
one of the men—John More, John Clements, William Roper,
Giles Heron, and John Dauncy—was cast into prison for
refusing the oath. But all of them, sooner or later, were
released through the influence of powerful friends.

MORAL EFFECT OF MORE'S DEATH.

But now let us return to More himself. As the only
layman, and he one of the highest honour and reputation,
to give his life for the cause of religion at that first period
when it began to be attacked, by his example he was of more
profit to our country than could easily be believed. The
death of so many Carthusian Fathers and other monks,
and even the death of the Bishop of Rochester himself,
eminent in holiness and learning as he was, though no
doubt equally precious in the sight of God, did not impress
men of every rank so deeply as did the death of More alone.
The others all belonged to the clergy, and evil-minded men
might suspect that from some human motive they were
defending the privileges of their class. But no such suspicion could be formed of More. The others were eminent
for piety and learning alone, but More in addition was
a successful man of affairs, a brilliant lawyer, who had
occupied, with the praise of all, the highest offices in the
State. All this enhanced his constancy in the cause of
religion. I can remember quite well, and many others
will bear me out, that when we were boys, More's fame and

his illustrious martyrdom were constantly the subjects of our talk and fired our zeal for the Catholic faith.   More's wisdom was held in such high esteem that he was regarded as England's oracle, not only when he delivered judgement in the law-courts, but also in those two matters of the gravest importance, the royal divorce and the Primacy of the Pope.   And this not only whilst he enjoyed freedom and high position in the State, but all hung upon his words even when he was imprisoned.   Laymen and priests, among others Dr. Wilson and John Fisher, Bishop of Rochester, wrote to him to know his opinion about these matters. How eagerly Henry VIII tried, by repeated attempts, to bring More, above all others, over to his side, has been sufficiently shown in what has preceded.

Blessed Germain Gardiner and John Larke.

Eight years later Germain Gardiner,[1] a noble layman of great learning, suffered martyrdom for the same cause, the Primacy of the Pope.   At the place of execution he would give to the people no other reason why he suffered death for such a cause than that the simple piety of the Carthusians, the wide learning of the Bishop of Rochester, and the profound wisdom of Thomas More convinced him that he was in the right.   Multitudes, through More's example, persevered in the faith and obedience of the Roman Church : many even suffered death for their faith. His own parish priest, John Larke,[1] followed the example of his distinguished parishioner and nobly suffered martyrdom, as our annals testify.   And thus we reach the end of our account of More's life and happy death.

More's Personal Appearance.

More was not tall in stature, but well-formed and of perfect proportions.   His complexion tended to phlegmatic. In colour he was white and pale.   Of joyous countenance, his expression was cheerful and amiable ; yet his refined and handsome face was thoroughly in keeping with the

[1] Blessed Germain Gardiner and Blessed John Larke suffered at Tyburn on the same day, March 7, 1544.

responsible positions he held. His eyes were grey and somewhat small : although not brilliant, they were kindly. His
forehead was broad. His hair was straight and uncurled,
in colour between black and yellow. His neck was short
and thick. His hair was dressed after the manner of the
nobility and gentry of that day. These details as to his
personal appearance have been handed down to us by
eye-witnesses.

CHAPTER XXI

THE VERDICT OF FAMOUS SCHOLARS UPON MORE'S DEATH

I THINK it will not be out of place if I record here the judgements that have been passed upon the death of More by famous men of learning outside England.

CARDINAL POLE.

Reginald Pole, Cardinal of the Holy Roman Church, was living in Rome when the persecution broke out in England. He wrote a book against Henry VIII, in defence of the Unity of the Church, in which, referring to the regret expressed everywhere abroad for the death of More, he thus apostrophises England :[1] " Thy father, England, thy honour, thy glory has been led out in thy sight to execution, although he was innocent. By birth he was thy son, in rank thy citizen, but in good deeds thy father, for he has given more proofs of his paternal affection towards thee than the most indulgent father has ever given to an only and well-beloved son. But never did he show himself more truly thy father than in his death, for he died for thee and that he might not betray thy highest interests. It is written in the history of the Greeks, that after Socrates had been executed, as now More in thee, through unjust processes of law, it happened that the people were witnessing a play in the theatre, and that one of the actors uttered the words " Ye have put to death him who was the noblest of all the Greeks." At once such bitter remorse for the death of Socrates filled the hearts of the people (although the poet's words had quite a different reference) that the

---

[1] Bk. III, p. 66. The apostrophe is in Pole's work made not to England but to London, as indeed appears in the latter portion of the passage.

whole theatre was filled with sobs and tears. The people ordered an enquiry to be made as to the authors of his death, and those who could be found were executed, the others punished with exile. A statue, also, was erected to his memory in the market-place. If, then, those citizens, when those words were uttered in the theatre, were justly moved to anger against the authors of the crime, and to pity for the victim—a man of unblemished life and noble character—how much more justly wilt thou, O City of London, now be moved to anger and pity when thou art forced to hear those same words uttered, not once as a coincidence by an actor, but as a grave and serious charge, made against thee constantly by men of the most sober judgement throughout the Christian world. ' Ye have put to death him who was the noblest of all the English.' "

Pole, the writer of the above passage, on account of his noble birth (for he was connected with the royal family), his ecclesiastical dignity, his wide learning, his upright and virtuous life, and the extraordinary grace and courtesy of his manners, enjoyed the friendship of the greatest men in Europe, and consequently his account of the judgement they passed upon More's death is entirely reliable. It is, too, borne out to the letter by the other testimonies we shall quote.

Erasmus.

We shall first give the words of Erasmus. Although he wrote anonymously, for he still had friends in England whom he desired to keep, the style most clearly points him out as the author, and moreover we find almost the same phrases elsewhere among his letters.[1] " It is abundantly clear that More and Fisher were guilty of no ill-will towards the King, but, if they erred, it was by following their conscience in all sincerity. It was their firm persuasion and deep conviction that the opinion they defended was holy,

---

[1] Stapleton refers to a pamphlet printed by John Stelsius at Antwerp in 1536 bearing the title *The Death of Thomas More*, and written as from P. M. to Caspar Agrippa. The pamphlet was reprinted by Episcopius at Basle in 1563, when the name of the writer was given as G. Covrinus Nucerinus and the name of the person addressed as Philip Montanus. It was also reprinted amongst the letters of Erasmus, Appendix, 378.

pious, honourable to the King, and salutary to the State.
They wished to keep silence if they could : but with calm-
ness and resignation they suffered death, offering their
prayers for their King and their country. Even in the
greatest crimes, the guilt is extenuated by a simple and
upright conscience and an intention of doing what is right.
Moreover, even amongst savage nations honour is often
paid to noble virtue and exceptional learning. Plato would
have been executed in Ægina, according to the laws of that
state, had he not borne the name of philosopher. Diogenes
made his way with impunity into the camp of Philip, the
King of Macedon. He was brought before the King as
a spy and used the occasion to upbraid him, in no measured
terms, for his madness in not being content with his own
kingdom and running the risk of losing all he had. He
was not only allowed to depart unharmed, but even rewarded, for no other reason than because he was a philosopher. As the generosity of monarchs towards learned
men has greatly enhanced their fame, so harsh treatment
of the learned has brought the deepest shame upon them.
Who does not hold in horror the conduct of Antony, who
caused Cicero to perish by the sword ? Who does not
loathe Nero, who put Seneca to death ? The fame of
Octavius Caesar has suffered no little detriment for his
having sent Ovid into banishment among the Getae.

"When Louis XII of France came to the throne he
attempted to get a divorce from the daughter of Louis XI.
Many good men were angry, and two of them, John Stan-
dock and his disciple Thomas, publicly said that prayer
ought to be offered to God that he might inspire the King
with good counsel. Words of such a nature to the people
were accounted seditious and a violation of the royal
edict. But the King confiscated none of their goods and
imposed no penalty but exile. And when he had brought
his negotiations to a successful conclusion he recalled
them. By such moderation the King avoided unpopularity
and at the same time forwarded his own cause, for both
were theologians and both enjoyed a reputation for
sanctity.

"But More's death is deplored even by those whose
views he combated with the greatest possible vigour. So

attractive was his openness, his courtesy, his kindness. Was there ever a man with any pretence to learning whom More did not reward ? Was there ever a stranger to whom he did not try to be a benefactor ? Many help none but their own : the French will assist a Frenchman, the Germans a German, the Scottish a Scot. But he was a friend to all, whether Irish, French, German, or Scottish. His goodness of heart endeared him so much to all that they grieve for his death as they would for a father or a brother. I myself have seen many shed tears who had never seen More nor had any intercourse with him. And even as I write these lines, in spite of my efforts tears rise unbidden to my eyes. The sword that beheaded More wounded many noble hearts."

That Erasmus wrote the above is confirmed by a passage that follows shortly after. Forgetting the part he was playing, he betrays himself by these words : " Wherefore to those who congratulate me on having a friend so dear and so high in position " (for More was Lord Chancellor of England) " I am wont to reply that I will not congratulate him upon his promotion until he himself bids me do so." Erasmus here clearly speaks in his own person, and hence there is no doubt that the whole composition is his work. For I have never heard any report or come across any written evidence of any friendship between More and G. Covrinus Nucerinus or P. Montanus.[1]

JOHN COCHLAEUS.

John Cochlaeus, a learned German theologian, immediately after the martyrdom of More and Fisher wrote in their defence against an Englishman, Richard Sampson, who supported the King's cause. It was against this same writer that Cardinal Pole published his books in defence of the unity of the Church. Cochlaeus, then, in this book, amongst much else in eloquent praise of Sir Thomas More, has the following passage on his death. He is addressing Henry's nobles and councillors, for he prefers to impute More's death to them rather than to the King himself. " What praise or favour did you expect to gain from the cruelty you exercised against Sir Thomas More ? All men

[1] See preceding note.

knew and admired his noble and lovable character, his
courtesy, his kindness, his affability, his wit, his eloquence,
his wisdom, his unblemished life, his intellectual powers,
his learning. In rank he was Lord Chancellor, coming
next after the King, ever in the public eye, employed constantly in affairs of State since his youth with the applause
of all, taking part in important embassies, and now verging
upon old age and venerable for his grey hairs. Having
obtained from the King permission to resign with all honour,
he lived in the privacy of his home with his wife, children
and grandchildren, guilty of no crime nor even suspected
of one, to no one hurtful or troublesome, but gentle and
kind, ready to do a service to any. Through your evil
counsel he was taken from his home, where all lived together
so pleasantly in the pursuit of learning and piety, for no
other cause than that he refused to approve of your im-
pieties, because his conscience forbade, he feared God
and he wished to save his soul. Do you suppose that your
deed of blood has ever won or will ever win the approval
of any, of whatever age or sex ? Not so. You have injured
yourselves rather than him. You have stamped yourselves
for ever as murderers, guilty of innocent blood. To him,
in the sight of God, of all the hosts of heaven and of men,
you have given the most honourable and glorious crown
of martyrdom. He will live and reign with God for all
eternity : you can never efface the stain of your infamous
guilt. For it is written : ' He knoweth both the deceiver
and him that is deceived. He bringeth counsellors to a
foolish end, and judges to insensibility. He looseth the belt
of kings, and girdeth their loins with a cord.' "[1]

PAUL JOVIUS.

To this I will add the testimony of Paul Jovius, the Bishop
of Nocera, a famous writer who in his *Praises of Famous Men*[2]
speaks of Sir Thomas More and his unjust death as follows :
" Fortune, fickle and, as is her custom, inconstant and ever
unpropitious to virtue, if ever she has played the part of
a proud and cruel mistress, has done so lately under Henry
in England with fierce rage, overthrowing before our eyes

[1] Job xii 16.   [2] Tit. 89 (S.).

Thomas More, whom the King, so shortly before a fervent admirer of lofty virtue, had raised to the highest honours. The sovereign, however, by fatal madness changed into a wild beast, with fierce cruelty cast him down headlong, for the reason that More, being a man of high principle and eminent sanctity, would not flatter the evil lusts of his furious prince. For whilst the latter was urgent to repudiate his wife, bring in a concubine, and to her great shame disinherit his daughter, More, Lord Chancellor, guilty only for his piety and innocence, was forced to plead his cause before the royal tribunal, was condemned most unjustly to die, like a robber, a most barbarous death, whilst his loving family was forbidden even to bury his severed members. But Henry, by this one crime alone the equal of Phalaris, has not been able to hinder More's name from enjoying everlasting praise because of the *Utopia*, and has branded his own with the perpetual infamy of a monstrous injustice." It will be noted that Paul Jovius here describes not the actual death that More suffered, but that mode of execution to which he was sentenced. We mentioned above the reason why the sentence was changed to a milder one.

WILLIAM PARADINUS.

To Erasmus of Belgium, to Cochlaeus of Germany, to Paul Jovius of Italy we will add William Paradinus of France, so that from various parts of Christendom judgement may be pronounced upon the foul and infamous murder of Sir Thomas More. He wrote a narrative of the attacks upon religion in England, in which he says : " The troubles and dissensions had reached in England their second year, when in the month of July John Fisher, Bishop of Rochester, was thrown into prison in London, because he appeared to condemn the divorce and the law recently passed against the Pope's supremacy. Of the same opinion, too, was Thomas More, a viscount [*sic*] of London, famous for his knowledge of languages and for his skill in every kind of literature (somewhat rare in a courtier), and of unblemished life. As these two men considered that they ought to obey God rather than men, and had so strongly fixed themselves in their resolution that

neither entreaties, bribes, promises, much less threats of
death, nor anything else could ever move them from it,
they were condemned to die and underwent their sentence
with great constancy."

It would be tedious to cite here other authors who wrote
in the same sense. All, indeed, who wrote of the events of
that time were greatly grieved at the most unjust death of
Sir Thomas More—Roverus Pontanus, a German, in his
Index of memorable events; Lawrence Surius at considerable length in his commentaries on the year 1535;
John Fontanus also in considerable detail in his French
history of our times; Onuphrius of Padua in treating of
Paul III; Nicholas Cardinal of Capua in his letters of
princes, written in French. John Secundus of Hague wrote
an elegy on the death of Sir Thomas More, but I have not
been able to consult his work.

JOHN RIVIUS.

These were Catholic writers, but even amongst those
opposed to him in religion, some, like Carion and Sleidanus,
spoke honourably of him. Especially would I quote the
words of John Rivius of Altendorf,[1] who speaks as follows
of the King's cruelty and More's conspicuous piety : " One
who is in a King's Court, if ever he is asked his counsel,
ought to say openly and freely whatever he considers to be
for the advantage of his sovereign, and not to flatter or say
merely what will please. He should never blame what is
praiseworthy nor praise what is worthy of blame, even
though he greatly fears that if he openly urges and advises
what is good he will be not rewarded but even punished."
He goes on to give the example of Papinian, a noble lawyer,
who was commanded to defend the parricide of the Emperor
Antoninus, but preferred to die rather than violate his
conscience by defending an evil deed. Then he writes :
" Such a one, recently within our memory, we have in
Sir Thomas More, a man eminent in learning and holiness,
the singular glory and ornament of his country. The King
of England had repudiated his former wife and wished to

[1] Bk. II, on Conscience (S.).

marry another, but this excellent man, who had deserved so well both of the King and of the whole country, refused to act against his conscience by consenting to the new marriage. Secure in the approval of his conscience, he persevered firmly to the very end in his defence of justice, religion and right, and so was put to death by that impious parricide, that most monstrous and bloody tyrant. Such cruelty cannot be paralleled in our century : such ingratitude and impiety on the part of a King were hitherto unknown. More was incorruptible and pious, ever devoted to his sovereign and to the glory and prosperity of his country : he counselled what was right and just and warned against injustice : he was not found guilty or convicted of any crime. Not only was he faultless, but he had served his sovereign long and faithfully : he was indeed the most faithful of all the royal counsellors. But his prince did not forbear to let him waste his strength and pine in prison and finally (alas !) to punish him with death. Are these thy rewards, O King ? Is this thy return for his fidelity and good-will towards thee ? Is this the price of a noble man's toil ? Is this the fruit he receives of his faithful service ? But thou, More, art now happy in the possession of eternal bliss, for thou didst prefer rather to lose thy head than to give any approval thy conscience forbade, and didst esteem right and justice, virtue and religion, more highly than life itself. Thou losest this mortal life but gainest that which is true and never-ending. Thou leavest the society of men but enterest the company of the angels and saints."

The writer of this passage, John Rivius, was a thoroughgoing Lutheran, and yet he bears witness to the truth, for the innocence of Sir Thomas More was as notorious as the barbarous cruelty of the King.

There is no need for more, either to add to More's praise or to the well-deserved shame of Henry. No Catholic Englishman could express them more truly or more forcibly than has done this German Lutheran. So great is the power of truth, the radiance of piety, and the light of justice that sometimes it cannot be hidden even from strangers and opponents.

THE EMPEROR CHARLES.

Finally I will cite a testimony to the same effect which I obtained through trustworthy witnesses. It is a noble tribute and deserves to be for ever remembered. The Emperor Charles V, no less penetrating in his judgements than he was brave and fortunate in war, on hearing that More and Fisher had been put to death, spoke as follows to Thomas Eliot, who at the time was Henry's ambassador at his Court. "If I had had in my dominions two such lights, I would rather have lost my strongest city than have allowed myself to be deprived of them, much less permitted them to be unjustly put to death." High praise from a noble prince ! Indeed, the thing speaks for itself. The cause of his death was most unjust, the manner infamous. More's admirable patience, his piety, his learning, and his other incomparable virtues proclaim him happy in so noble a martyrdom, and Henry infamous for so unjust a sentence.

FINAL CONSIDERATIONS ON MORE'S DEATH.

Apart from its manifest injustice, there are three things which aggravate the guilt of Henry's cruel deed. First, because More was put to death by a law which he had violated neither by word nor deed. This law, moreover, concerned religion and not the policy of the State ; wherefore one who followed his conscience might well have been considered a man of honour rather than a rebel. Again, although he refused to approve it, yet he did not condemn the law nor blame others who approved it. However much he dissented from the law, yet nothing could have been more harmless, more correct, or more sincere than his attitude.

Secondly, because Henry executed a man of such learning, virtue, and integrity, so brilliant in wit, so kind and gentle, dear to all and harmful to none. Such qualities even in a guilty man would have deserved some consideration, and even perpetual imprisonment would have been a heavy penalty.

Thirdly, because the King beheaded a man who had rendered such great services to him, to the realm, and to the religion which he himself professed ; who had in so many important ways laboured for the King with great credit to himself and great contentment to the King ; who had been a member of the Royal Council for so many years, so frequently acted on embassies, and filled so many posts, including, finally, the Chancellorship.

On the other hand, there are many circumstances which heighten and increase the glory and everlasting honour of More's sacrifice. First, that although his view of the royal divorce was always diametrically opposed to the King's, yet he treated of that subject with the King so openly, candidly, and sincerely that the latter was not offended, or at least did not seem to be so.

Secondly, that when, deprived of all his goods and condemned to perpetual imprisonment, he was harassed with a new oath, he neither said nor did anything. He might certainly have spoken, and said truly and emphatically that this new law was impious to God, rebellious to the Apostolic See, sacrilegious to the whole Church, against the rights of the people, and in itself absurd. In fact, he said none of these things : he condemned it in no way : he merely kept silence for conscience' sake.

Thirdly, because he bore patiently so many heavy sacrifices, the loss of an ample fortune and of the highest honours, the companionship of his most dear family (wife, children and eleven grandchildren), liberty, and finally life itself.

Fourthly, because the only reason for his suffering all these losses was a pure love of God and a fear of offending him. No motives can be higher than these.

Fifthly, because although the cause had never before been controverted and he had hardly any guide, yet by diligent study he found the truth and established himself so firmly therein that he did not hesitate to die for it.

Sixthly, because he was the only one of the King's Council who was willing to tell the truth, and not merely to say what would please his sovereign. He would not flatter nor deceive his prince. As for honours, he would not seek them, nor, when he had them, was he willing to keep them with peril to his soul.

All these considerations are a clear proof of More's remarkable purity of heart, his deep humility, his utter freedom from guile, his heroic constancy, his admirable piety, his truly Christian patience, and his transparent sincerity.

CONCLUSION.

Gentle reader, I have now completed my task. To the best of my ability I have described all that I have been able to gather concerning the life, the character, the achievements, and the glorious martyrdom of that noble and illustrious man, Sir Thomas More.

May God, the Father of mercies, by the merits of the precious Blood of his beloved Son and through the holy intercession of so many martyrs in England, and especially of Thomas More, deign in his mercy to take pity at length upon the affliction of our nation, which now for twenty-nine years has been suffering dire schism and heretical tyranny, and lead it back from its errors to the bosom of our holy mother, the Catholic Church. To him be all honour and glory for all eternity. Amen.

DATES OF MORE'S LIFE

THIS table is reprinted, with the kind permission of the authors and of the delegates of the Oxford University Press, from *Sir Thomas More, Selections from his English Works*, etc., edited by P. S. and H. M. Allen.

1477, February 7, or 1478, February 6. Thomas More born in Milk Street, London. His father, John More, gentleman, a successful lawyer, afterwards Judge in the Court of King's Bench. His mother, Agnes, daughter of Thomas Graunger. First goes to St Anthony's School, Threadneedle Street, under N. Holt. Then enters Archbishop Morton's household ; later sent by him to Canterbury College (now part of Christ Church), Oxford.[1]

Circa 1494. Enters New Inn, London, to study law.

1496, February 12. Admitted to Lincoln's Inn.

1499. First meets Erasmus. In the autumn takes him to visit the royal children (Prince Henry aged eight) at Eltham.

Circa 1499-1503. Lives, without vow, in the Charterhouse.

1500 (not later than). Contributes verses to Holt's *Lac Puerorum*.

1501. Studies Greek. Hears Linacre lecture on Aristotle. Makes translations with Lily from Greek Anthology. Called to the Bar. Reader at Furnival's Inn. Lectures in Grocyn's church (St Lawrence Jewry) on Augustine's *De Civitate Dei*.

1503. Writes *A Rueful Lamentation of the Death of Queen Elizabeth*.

1504, Spring. Member of Parliament. Opposes Henry VII's demands for money. His father imprisoned and fined.

---

[1] Following Father Bridgett (*Life of More*, p. 2), we have adopted the later date for More's birth. See in *Proc. Soc. Antiquaries*, 1897, p. 321, an argument for the earlier date.

1505, *circa* January.   Marries Jane Colt of Netherhall in Essex ; lives in Bucklersbury, London. (?) October : His daughter Margaret born.

1505-6.   Translates *Lucian* with Erasmus.

1506.   His daughter Elizabeth born.   Translations from *Lucian* printed by Badius in Paris.

1507.   His daughter Cecily born.

1508.   Visits Paris and Louvain.

1508 or 1509.   His son, John More, born.

1509.   Composes verses for coronation of Henry VIII (June 24).   *Circa* October : Erasmus, returned from Italy, writes the *Praise of Folly* in More's house, afterwards dedicated to More.

1510 (?).   Translates *The Life of John Picus, Earl of Mirandula*.

1510, September 3.   Under-Sheriff of the City of London.

1511.   Reader at Lincoln's Inn.   Summer : Death of his first wife.   Shortly after marries Mrs. Alice Middleton.

Circa 1513.   Writes *The History of Richard III*.

1515, May to October.   On embassy in Flanders ; visits Busleyden at Malines and writes Latin verses on his house and his coins.   Writes *Utopia*, Book II.   On his return offered royal pension, but refuses it.   October 21 : Controversy with a Dutch scholar, Martin Dorp, in defence of Erasmus.

1516.   Writes *Utopia*, Book I ; *Utopia* published at Louvain *circa* December.   Wins a case for the Pope against the King.   Pressed to enter the King's service.

1517, May.   Chosen to deal with the riot on Evil May Day.   August to December : On embassy at Calais to settle disputes between English and French merchants.   December : *Lucian* printed by Froben at Basle.

1518, March.   *Utopia* and *Epigrammata* printed by Froben at Basle.   March 29 : Writes from Abingdon to reprove the University of Oxford for its opposition to Greek.   Made Master of Requests and a month later Privy Councillor.   Accepts a pension of £100 a year for life. July 29: Delivers public oration to Cardinal Campeggio, welcoming him in the name of the City of London.

1519, July. Secretary with the King at Woking. Resigns office of Under-Sheriff. (?) Summer: Visits his sister at Coventry, disputes with a friar.

1520, February. Champions Erasmus against Edward Lee. April: Controversy with a French scholar, Germanus Brixius, about the *Epigrammata*. Commissioned to negotiate commercial treaty with the Emperor. June: Attends Henry VIII to the Field of the Cloth of Gold.

1521, June. Under-Treasurer. Knighted. July: His daughter Margaret marries William Roper; both continue to live with More. July 25: To Bruges on a mission to settle disputes between the merchants; joined there by Wolsey in August and goes with him to Calais for peace negotiations; remains there until October.

Circa 1522. Writes *De Quattuor Novissimis, Remember the Last Things*.

1522. Given grants of land by the King. September: With the Court at Newhall in Essex.

1523, April. Speaker of the House of Commons. June: Appealed to for help by Oxford University. August: Grant of £100 from the King. September to October: With the Court at Woking, Guildford, Abingdon, Oxford. Under the name of Gulielmus Rosseus, writes a defence of Henry VIII against Luther.

1523-4. Owner of Crosby Hall.

1524, July. High Steward of Oxford University. Buys land at Chelsea.

1525. High Steward of Cambridge University. Chancellor of the Duchy of Lancaster. Further grants of land from the King.

1526. Controversy with the reformer Bugenhagen. Autumn: Visited by Holbein the younger, who stays in More's household, painting and drawing portraits of More and his family.

1527, July to September.   With Wolsey at Amiens to interview Francis I.   Consulted by Henry VIII about the divorce.

1528, March.   Licence granted to read Lutheran books in order to confute them.   Writes *A Dialogue* against Luther and Tyndale.

1529 (?).   His daughters dispute before the King in philosophy.

1529, Summer.   With Tunstall to negotiate the Treaty of Cambrai.   October 25 : Chancellor in succession to Wolsey ; the first commoner to hold the office. Writes *The Supplication of Souls*.

1531, May.   Visited by Grinaeus from Basle, on his way to Oxford in search of manuscripts.

1532, May 16.   Resigns Chancellorship.   Writes *The Confutation of Tyndale's Answer* and *The Confutation of Friar Barnes' Church*.   December : Writes a *Letter* on the Sacrament, against Frith.

1533.   Writes his *Apology*.   June : Declines to be present at Anne's coronation.   Autumn : Investigates Elizabeth Barton, the Holy Maid of Kent.   Writes *The Debellation of Salem and Bizance* and *The Answer to the . . . book which a nameless heretic hath named the supper of the Lord*.

1534, February.   Charged with concealment of treason in his dealings with the Holy Maid ; proves his innocence before a committee of the Privy Council. April 13 : Examined by Royal Commissioners at Lambeth ; refuses to take the oath for Act of Succession and Supremacy.   April 17 : Sent to the Tower. Writes there *A Dialogue of Comfort against Tribulation, A Treatise to receive the Blessed Body of our Lord,* and *A Treatise upon the Passion*.

1535, July 1.   Indicted for high treason, tried at Westminster Hall, and condemned.   July 6 : Executed.

1551.   *Utopia* first translated into English by Ralph Robinson.

1557.   Collected edition of his English Works.

1563, 1565, 1566.   Collected editions of his Latin Works.

INDEX TO NAMES OF PERSONS

233

Lightning Source UK Ltd.
Milton Keynes UK
UKOW06f1826240415

250319UK00006B/84/P